T0287142

DEATH OF A BOXER

DEATH
OF A
BOXER

PETE CARVILL

Biteback Publishing

First published in Great Britain in 2024 by
Biteback Publishing Ltd, London
Copyright © Pete Carvill 2024

ISBN 978-1-78590-820-0

10 9 8 7 6 5 4 3 2 1

A CIP catalogue record for this book is available from the British Library.

Set in Minion Pro and Laski Sans Stencil

Printed and bound in Great Britain by
CPI Group (UK) Ltd, Croydon CR0 4YY

FSC
www.fsc.org
MIX
Paper | Supporting
responsible forestry
FSC® C171272

CONTENTS

INTRODUCTION

THE LAST PUNCH

Berlin, Germany, 2016. The last punch I ever took voluntarily landed in the basement of a council-run gym in the centre of the city, a few months away from the cut-off date I had set for myself.

Age in boxing is different than it is anywhere else. A man of thirty-five is still relatively young on the street, but in a ring, in shorts and flat-soled boxing boots, his hands wrapped, gumshield covering his teeth, he is geriatric. He is old beneath the skin, his knees starting to creak, the unseen damage accumulated and held.

I had not wanted to spar that night, but I was still following my rule about never saying 'no'. I felt old and heavy, missing the fifth gear that had been there throughout my twenties and early thirties.

My opponent's name was Jens, and I had always struggled against him. We touched gloves and went to work. I, a southpaw, jabbed pointlessly at him with my right. He moved and jabbed back. I plodded. His punches connected, little taps to my forehead. I tried to bend my knees enough to twist and tilt my body into a shifting target.

It is dispiriting to know that you have lost so much of yourself. I moved back to the ropes and placed myself in the pocket of a corner, trying to lead him into a left-hand counter. He stopped.

I lowered my left hand, my head too far in front to slip anything coming back. Jens threw a punch. I saw his hand move from his shoulder, begin its arc, and then it was landing just above my cheekbone.

My legs shook and my hands fell. I raised them again. My brain fogged and I blinked. *Uh oh*, I thought.

It was not the biggest punch I had ever taken, but it was the biggest I had ever taken that badly. An inch lower would have put me on the ground.

Jens took a step back. I stumbled to one side and tried to straighten up. I snorted. *Keep going.* I leaned forwards and shifted my weight as if I was going to come forwards. But I did not want him to hit me again.

I waved him in. *Don't let anyone see you quit*, I thought. '*Los geht's*,' I said. I stepped forwards. '*Mir geht's gut.*'

Jens looked at me. '*Nein*,' he said. '*Du wirst nicht noch einmal geschlagen.*' No, you are not getting punched again.

I went home that evening with a headache that stretched out for days into the weekend. That Saturday, I went by myself to the Max-Schmeling-Halle to watch Arthur Abraham fight Tim-Robin Lihaug. The lights in the arena made the pain flare like a beacon in the mist.

And that was where it ended. I kept my membership going for a while and I went back a few times to hit some bags. But I was done. I drifted away from boxing until it seemed as if it were behind a glass panel, something that I looked on with a mixture of sadness, regret and awe. *That used to be me*, I would think from time to time. *I used to do that.*

I never saw Jens again. He got me out of boxing. He may have been a guardian angel.

A YOUNG MAN'S GAME

Boxing is full of lessons. Most things are, if you stay in them long enough. But I learned most of mine in the ring.

And there is one lesson that you learn at the start but which only beds itself in after a few years: boxing is hard at the beginning and increasingly merciless as you get older.

It is a lesson that all boxers eventually learn, but it takes a long time. Too long, mostly. As an old fighter once opined, the only time you have ever learned your lesson is 'too late'.

The beginning is as discernible as the end. I first walked into All Saints Boxing Club in York on Valentine's Day 2002. I was with my girlfriend at the time. My love affair with boxing lasted much longer.

I had been a tall and skinny teenager, easily intimidated. I wore glasses with a strong prescription, and I stayed away from fights. Bigger kids and grown men scared me, but when I left home at nineteen I was still an overgrown, awkward and gangly boy, and I went deep into the parts of the world where the value of a man is directly correlated with his ability to harm others.

I wanted most of all to be a man, and these were the examples set down. The path to manhood, it seemed, involved pain and the ability and willingness to inflict it. I fell hard in love with that world.

I tried to build myself. I lifted weights three times a week and boxed twice. I learned some jiu-jitsu and judo moves. I tried to make people think I was tough, even if I could never convince myself of that fact. At times, I must have been unbearable.

There was baby fat that I shed and replaced with muscle. The coach at the gym laughed at my efforts when I started and within a year had me demonstrating the basics to newcomers. But the real tough guys still viewed me with disdain.

A chance came up to compete. My eyesight kept me out of it.

I read and watched everything I could on boxing. I spent more time doing that than I did anything else. I subscribed to every boxing magazine, bought every VHS and DVD available and watched any and every fight that I could find on TV. I watched *When We Were Kings* each week, religiously. I bonded with other men in ways we never had before.

The first stories I ever wrote were about boxing. I was twenty-four and teaching in Japan, thinking that I needed to do something else with my life. I decided to write.

An insurance title in London hired me and brushed off some of the rougher edges in my reporting and writing. I started doing stories for *The Sweet Science* and *Boxing Digest*. I travelled up and down the UK at weekends to do reports. I went to Paris and met Don King briefly. I found the Fitzroy Lodge and started training there.

I became known around the office as 'the boxing guy'. I eventually got tired of the insurance title around the same time it got tired of me.

Laid off, I plotted to get out of London in 2010. I worked for a newspaper for a few months to save money while I eyed Paris. That was too expensive, so I shifted my focus to Berlin. Germany had good boxing at the time – Vitali and Wladimir Klitschko, Arthur Abraham, Marco Huck.

I came over and tried to make it work. I taught a class for a couple of years when money was tight. I became good at holding the pads for people. I was better at showing the basics than I had ever been in the ring, and I got forty to fifty students a week. I began working with the Muay Thai fighters who trained in the gym before us.

Life got in the way of the classes towards the end. Everyone got older and began to drift away. I stopped training for a year or so. I began to get old, and the wear and tear began to murmur its introductions. *The body forgets nothing you have done to it*, someone told me later.

I found the council-run gym and went there. I wanted to get back to what I had been. But the hour was too late. I still sparred a little, but I was afraid of everything that landed. I worried about serious injury. I said that I would stop when I turned thirty-five. I was running out of road, and I knew it. And then there was that final punch from Jens.

A year or so after I stopped boxing, I found myself drawn to grappling. In a gym in the north of Berlin, far from where the tourists go, I found myself, in my mid-thirties, wrestling with men nearly half my age. We were doing a derivation of Brazilian jiu-jitsu, itself derived from Japanese judo and sprinkled with techniques from English catch wrestling.

I was terrible at it. I loved it. I began to get obsessed again. All great love affairs have an element of obsession. I loved being back amongst men being made gentle by the training and wrestling they did with one another.

The second week I was there, a bull-strong Indian called Ranesh, also new to the sport, threw me to the ground and my ankle twisted when I landed. I limped home and the next day it was twice its normal size. I stayed away for a few weeks, then returned.

I injured my ribs away from the gym a few months later and had to take even more time off. Once I got back, I still got submitted by everybody. There were a lot of mornings after when I was covered in bruises.

Eventually, the teacher left to set up his own gym and tried to take along all his students. The new place was too far away, stuck deep in a suburb of Berlin. I went once and realised it was too far, that travelling there twice a week was too much of a commitment. I had run out of road again.

A VALEDICTION OF BLOOD

I am not entirely reformed. I doubt I ever could be at this late stage. There is still a switch that is triggered over the promise of watching a fight, still the anticipation of sitting in a darkened arena, sports hall or bullring to watch a succession of men enter to fight each other. And if I cannot get to the card itself, I find the darkest, smokiest sports bar that I can and sit there, with other men, to cheer and gasp and shout and say at points, 'They should be stopping this right now. He's had enough.'

It was around the time I was getting out of jiu-jitsu that I became aware of Mike Towell. This was through an editorial in the UK's

Boxing News. The piece, written by editor Matt Christie in April 2019, alluded to what were then the recent findings of the Fatal Accident Inquiry that had recently concluded. Christie wrote darkly about events that were 'shocking in the extreme'.

Towell had been from Dundee in the east of Scotland. A welterweight, he had died in September 2016 after a fight in Glasgow. Numerous warnings, said the inquiry, had not been missed but ignored, denied and obfuscated by Towell and those around him.

Here is a man, I thought, *who was looking to define himself through his physical capabilities*. He had also chosen to fly too close to the sun.

There was nothing else that connected us. It was merely a coincidence that we had both taken our exits from boxing at the same time.

Towell paid with his life for choosing boxing. The vast majority who put on gloves never do that. But prices and costs remain.

Boxing and fighting are mostly, but not exclusively, about men. Women have come more and more into its centre in recent years, but it is still – in participants and spectators – a mostly male preserve. As Joyce Carol Oates wrote, 'Boxing is for men, and is about men, and is men. A celebration of the lost art of masculinity all the more trenchant for being lost.'

Young boys and young men – two tribes not as distinct as you may think – are drawn to fighters and fighting. An attraction like that of superheroes, except the pain and damage are real.

Why do these things have such a hold on their devotees? As the late boxing coach Eddie Futch once said, 'Men just fight, that's all.' That may or may not be all that needs to be known.

Back when I was writing fiction, I often imagined an interviewer asking me about the stories I wrote and what I would say they were.

'They're love stories,' I would say to the imaginary interviewer. 'They're all love stories. Everything I write is a love story.'

I would hate to sit down and write something from a place of hate – or, even worse, contempt. You are what you put out in the world.

And that is why *Death of a Boxer* is also a love story. Or, more accurately, it is a sequence and series of love stories.

These are love stories not about fights but fighters, love songs to those who ready themselves to be tested in the ring and who grow from the experience. These are odes to the people who make little from the hard work they put in and the price extracted from them. It is for the ones who treat every kid as if that child were already a champion and for the broken ones trying to heal the cracks in others. And it is for the ones who stay on for too long, hoping to give their loved ones a chance at something better than they ever had themselves.

I hope to have written, through grace and strength, something beautiful. I hope. I tried. Apologies in advance for where and when I have failed. This is my benediction. This is for them.

This is for all of them.

PROLOGUE

THE DEATH OF A BOXER

*G*lasgow, Scotland, September 2016. It is a Thursday night and two men, somewhat friendly with one another, are ready to fight. There are just over 300 people, mostly other men, in this suite in a hotel in Glasgow, and they have enjoyed a black-tie dinner before the night's three bouts. Tonight's event will lead into the weekend, a heady evening that they can recover from on the Friday and will not affect the Saturday and Sunday with the wives and children. After all, a hotel ballroom with boxing is not a place for families.

Mike Towell, twenty-five years old, is in the blue corner. He is short and lean, his head shaved and his beard long. He wears black trunks with greenish-yellow stripes down the sides and on the waistband, and his tattoos are so thick on one arm that it looks almost black. He jogs on the spot and looks to the red corner to his opponent, a man who now stands between him and the big money.

He was tight at the weight and had to lose 3lbs in an hour, but he does not show it. It was so bad that it took a few attempts. He looks focused, maybe a little intense, but that is to be expected, because this is professional boxing, and this is a sport that you do not play.

Towell is a little nervous. This is going to be on television, and this is an eliminator for the British welterweight title. If he wins, he gets to fight for the title itself. If he loses, he goes back a few steps. Not the end of the world but a big setback, the kind that many careers do not recover from. The trick is not to lose, and it looks like he *will* win. His opponent's record is not as good – 11 wins, 3 losses and 2 draws, with 4 knockouts. Towell has won eleven of twelve, one fight even, and he has stopped eight opponents.

It is a cliché, but the fight is more than about money. It has to be; the money is not great. Towell is guaranteed 60 per cent of the total purse for winning, 40 per cent if he loses. The total purse for both fighters is a little over £8,000.

The crowd are noisy, possibly a little drunk. They cheer the two fighters.

The referee calls Towell and his opponent to the centre of the ring. The opponent, Dale Evans, wears white shorts with purple, his hair cut short. Evans's upper lip bulges from the mouthpiece wedged behind it. The respective coaches shake hands. Evans brushes his glove against his nose to wipe something away. The master of ceremonies stands behind the referee and reaches around him with the microphone, putting it beneath the referee's mouth so that the instructions can be relayed over the speakers to the crowd.

Towell is taller by a few inches. He looks down at Evans, who opens his mouth and smiles, stretching the muscles of his jaw. He rolls his shoulders.

The fight starts and Towell goes to the ground after about two minutes. Moving in, he puts his head down and a right hand from Evans loops and misses, brushing the back of his neck. But it is enough.

It is a strange knockdown. Evans's punch does not land, does not do anything significant. But Towell still goes down. Evans moves quickly away to a neutral corner. People think Towell is weakened at the weight.

Towell gets up and the referee counts and asks him if he wants to continue. Towell nods, holds up his gloves for the referee and the fight is back on.

Towell is winning on two scorecards by the fourth, ahead by single points on two scorecards and behind by the same margin on the third. His team see rounds two, three and four as the best he has ever fought.

Evans's corner see Towell pull up a little in the fourth round. They watch him go back to the corner. 'He's getting tired,' they say. 'Go out and jump on him.'

They do not know what is coming.

Towell goes down again in the fifth, but what happens after says that something is deeply wrong. He is on his knees, his arms on the third rope from the bottom. He seems to be breathing heavily, and his eyes are unfocused and filled with desperation. He rises halfway through the count, his back to the referee, and turns. The referee is at 'seven', then 'eight', and then he tells Towell to walk towards him. Towell does, but his legs look weak and robbed of their strength. His right leg shakes and his steps are tentative.

The referee waves the fight back on, and Evans comes in and he lands five punches – one, two, three, four, five – in four seconds, and the referee waves it off.

Evans celebrates.

Towell stands for a second, then goes to the ground, the referee holding him. A doctor gets into the ring. Towell gets to his knees after a minute and is helped to his feet. He is unsteady.

The doctor looks at him. 'Where are you?' he asks.

'Glasgow. The hotel.'

'What day is it?'

'Thursday.'

'OK.'

Towell is put on a stool. A paramedic asks him to breathe deeply, but Towell hangs his head. His shoulders slump. He appears unsteady. Syllables begin to fall from his mouth. Mutterings, murmurings, prayers – whatever they are, they are known only to Towell.

The doctor calls for a mask and oxygen, then he and another doctor lay Towell on the floor of the ring.

Dale Evans puts his arms in the air in celebration. His coach, Gary Lockett, walks over to him and hisses, 'Put them down, now. Not when he's on the floor. Don't celebrate.'

Evans turns and sees Towell. He sees what is happening. He sees it is serious.

Towell is no longer talking. Not because he does not want to, but because he cannot. He slips away. The doctors give him oxygen and push his head back to open his airway. His arms go rigid and tense. His jaw clenches.

The doctor calls for a stretcher. 'Get this man to a hospital, *now*.'

Nine minutes after the fight ends, Towell is placed onto a hard board, then moved to a stretcher outside the ring. He is carried downstairs to a waiting ambulance. Oxygen is given. The two doctors from the ring are in the ambulance with him, along with a third who had been in the crowd.

It takes ten minutes to reach Glasgow Royal Infirmary. On the journey, Towell's gloves are cut off so they can access his veins. They cannot place an oral airway because of the clenched jaw, so they put a smaller one into his nose.

The ambulance arrives and Towell is taken in, handed over to the medical staff. He is now in a place of healing. They give him an endotracheal tube, and an arterial line is inserted in his arm. The doctor in charge calls to ventilate and sedate him and to conduct an emergency CT scan. They suspect a severe brain injury.

The scan finds a large bleed in the brain, the organ itself shifting to the side by thirteen millimetres. Significant pressure.

An injury worse than expected.

This man needs surgery.

He needs it NOW.

Can we even do the surgery?

Will he survive it?

The doctors call another hospital. The neurosurgical registrar agrees to look over the CT scan, and he contacts the on-call consultant neurosurgeon.

They call back. They say the injury is not survivable. They say that an operation should not be performed.

The doctor at Glasgow Royal Infirmary is surprised and disappointed, but he defers to his colleagues. A decision is made to move Towell to the neurosurgical intensive care unit at the second hospital.

Towell arrives at the second hospital around three hours after his fight against Dale Evans ends. He is examined again, and his eyes are unreactive, dilated. His blood pressure is high. His eyes do not move when his head is turned.

The doctors sit down with the family, and they explain. *We cannot save him. We are going to stop ventilation, but we'll give him painkillers. He won't feel a thing.*

Towell lies in a bed for the next twelve hours. Death is coming. His family sit beside him. They wait.

Mike Towell, boxer, dies just before midnight the day after he is injured in the ring.

CHAPTER ONE

EARLY LIFE

A ROOM WITH HIS FRIENDS

Dundee, Scotland, September 1991. He was born here, in Dundee, twenty-five years before he died. His family were local. He spent his first week in the special baby care unit at Ninewells Hospital.

His father died before the son was ten. The son missed him as he grew.

It was his stepbrother who first took him to the gym. He started at St Francis's in one part of Dundee, then moved over to Lochee Boys Club. He met his partner when they were teenagers at school, and he became a father at twenty-three.

These are the facts as we know them. But facts are the branches on which we hang stories. The tenets of a person's life – who they were, and where they were born, and when, who their parents were, and what they did and whether they loved each other – are where we start. And then we move out from them as we seek to understand.

The people at the gym understood him. They still remember

him. They always will. A giant painting of him exists on the wall. It will never be removed.

They still speak of him in this place, of all his hard edges and corners, his decency. If you want to know what a man was truly like, stand in a room with his friends and just let them talk. You will arrive at the truth before long.

'He was a loveable rogue,' says amateur coach Andy Howett. 'And he was likeable. That's the right way to put it. He was full of character.'

He was just a boy when he started, not yet a man and barely on the road to becoming one. But he was drawn to the ring. Young boys are drawn to those who impress their physicality on the world – soldiers, athletes, superheroes. To be an action hero requires no introspection, no second guessing of oneself. It is about action, the ability to bend the outside world to your internal one.

The coach recognised him as soon as he walked in. He knew the family. He looked at the small boy. He knew similar faces.

'You're a Towell, aren't you?' he said.

He was intense. He liked to train. He guessed within himself that he was on this earth to fight. Some people are. There is a cache of men who, through no fault of their own, find themselves born into the wrong century. These are inherently honest men who were born to walk onto a battlefield because that is the place where the truth of a soul is revealed. They will never be politicians or doctors or academics. Their world is more straightforward than that. Put under bright lights a fighter who takes two or three punches in order to land one, and you will see an honest fighter, because what they land means more and is delivered with more truth than the one or two that sail into them.

Hit me with some of what you have, is their declaration, *and I will give you everything of mine.*

He won a championship once, they say. Then the weekend after, he walked into a McDonald's and, in his broad local accent, enquired loudly but politely whether champions ate for free. They still laugh about it.

He could be troubled at times. His friend Sean Reilly says that Towell would have been in jail if he had not gotten into boxing. It turned his life to a new route, gave him a star to follow. 'He just wanted to box, that's all. He started over at St Francis, then moved over at some point. And then, there was a time when I hadn't been in the boxing for a while, and someone told me to go up to Lochee because there was a young lad there knocking everyone down. So, I turned up, and it was Mike.'

But he was never a bully, they say. No one ever saw him take a victim. He just liked to fight.

'He was a wild one,' says Reilly, 'but here's a story I know personally. This is the type of guy he was. There was a guy we trained with once who got popped for using steroids. He was a friend of Mike's, but Mike just dropped him like that.' He snapped his fingers.

Others remember his kindness. 'He had a kind heart,' says Jamie Wilson, who would go on to be a professional boxer and one of Towell's final sparring partners. 'He had a really tough exterior, but he was kind inside.'

Wilson explains, 'He had that tough exterior because, as a fighter, he was called "Iron" Mike. He lived that style. He was not scared to mix it up. Along with me and some other guys, he was putting Dundee back on the map for boxing.'

He goes on, 'My first memory of him was playing football against his school. I got the ball in the face, and he was standing there and laughing at me. And then I saw him in the gym. He was funny. When we were sparring, I used to dread it because pride would get the best of him. I'd come out with sore ribs every time.'

Wilson remembers the jokes, the laughter, the lack of pretence. The refusal to be anything other than what he was. He did that because to not do so would be a form of lying, which is akin to cheating. And men born into the wrong century are not supposed to cheat or lie.

He says, 'The Dundee accent is pretty broad and hard to understand. When I went in front of cameras, I slowed it down, but Mikey just spoke like himself. He didn't have a care in the world.'

Wilson looks down at his hands. He misses his friend. There are some friendships that can only be made by fighting one another. 'We had a hard sparring session once, and he came out and put his arm around me. That's one of the things that no one ever saw. He did have that softer side. He looked intimidating, but he was funny. He turned up in a sauna suit to a gym in Dundee. The coach said he wasn't training in that. He said, "I've nothing else." He came out with his boxers pulled up his arse, and he said, "Hey, I had the nicest arse in my school." It was just random, random stuff.'

He still missed having a father. His memories, if he had them of him, were hazy. 'He never really knew him,' says one of his coaches. 'One time, I mentioned offhand to Mikey that I'd met his dad, and he started peppering me with questions about who he was and what he was like.'

He was loyal, too. The type of guy you could rely on. Some might say 'too loyal', but how does a man out of time know of such a thing? You are, to them, loyal or not. There is no quarter in calculating what someone's friendship is worth to you. To those men, they are simply friends.

Wilson remembers, 'I had a fight lined up with a guy who was quite mouthy. Mike said, "Don't worry about him. We'll be there as well." He was loyal. And he wasn't slow in saying his opinion on people. Once he had made up his mind on someone, that was it. There was nothing diplomatic there. Some people would stay quiet, but he'd say what he thought. That's the best thing I can say about him.'

He got smarter as he got older. He never stopped being loyal, but he knew where the wrong result could lead. 'One of his pals was being filled in one time,' says one of the guys at Lochee, 'so Mike went down and ended up fighting five guys to help him out. But once he got to his early twenties, he realised that he couldn't do that stuff. He knew he'd end up in jail and wouldn't get a professional licence. He wanted to be the next big thing in boxing.'

He remained serious in the gym. 'Mikey couldn't spar light,' says Wilson. 'Those body shots were...' He trailed off. 'I still had the bottle to fight back, but there were times when I'd think, *I don't fancy this.*'

And then he became a father. And he was, everyone says, great at that. His own son was born in 2014, and Towell doted on him.

'He was a great dad,' say his friends. 'Brilliant.'

'I've seen photos of him with the wee one,' says Wilson. 'And from that, and seeing how he spoke on the phone with Chloe, I could see that he was a great dad.'

He loved his hair, too. You can see in his early fights that he wore it almost to the shoulder, all thick and brown. But then a boxer in the gym had non-Hodgkin's Lymphoma and lost all his hair. So Towell took his off, too, just to let his friend know that he was not alone.

'You have these memories of him,' says Wilson. 'And they are so sharp. And it's a shame that he died because of a fight.'

OF BOYS AND MEN

Shamokin, Pennsylvania, US, around 1989 or 1990. He was still a boy that day when his father came to him and said it was time to go for a run. They often did this, the man jogging in front while the ten-year-old trailed behind him on two wheels.

'OK,' he said, knowing not to say 'no'. 'I'll get my bike.'

'No bike. Not today,' his father said. 'You're going to grow up and be a man.'

'What?'

'You're going to run with me.'

They set out from home and went up into one of the hills formed from coal slag that surrounded the town. The boy was small for his age, but he tried his best to keep up as they rose through the switchbacks to the top of the hill where a single path went around in a rough, undulating circle.

He began to sweat. It ran into his eyes. He continued to run. He knew not to disappoint his father.

At the top, the father slowed and, raising his hand to his son, motioned for him to stop. They breathed heavily.

'I'm OK,' the boy said, gulping down some air.

'I know you are.'

The boy leaned over and put his hands on his knees. 'OK, I'm good,' he said. 'I can keep on going.'

The father picked up a rock from the side of the trail. It was so big that he needed two hands. 'You get one,' he said.

The boy looked around and picked one. He held it in his hand.

His father looked at it and shook his head. 'No,' he said, gently but firmly. 'Get a rock.'

'Dad—'

'Get a rock.'

The boy dropped his stone and picked up a larger one. He turned it in his hands, balancing the weight and fitting its smooth sides into the flats of his fingers. 'It's heavy,' he said.

'I know. That's how it should be. You're a good boy.'

The boy's ears pricked. 'Thanks, Dad.'

The father nodded. 'OK, we're going to run now with the rocks on this path. We're going to go around and around. If you lose me, don't worry; I'll be behind you. And go at your own pace, but make sure you don't quit.'

'OK, Dad.'

'I'm proud of you, Son.'

The father took off, carrying his rock in his hands. The boy watched him go. *We usually run for hours*, he thought. *I have to do this for hours?*

He shifted the rock once more in his hands, then took off.

Shamokin, Pennsylvania, US, June 2023. Shane Manney was now forty-four years old and driving around Shamokin, talking about what it was like to grow up in the town. He had been in the Marines, but retired. Had joined the police in Virginia, but retired. He had then founded the 5 Stones Fight Club in Annville, Pennsylvania, and now worked at giving back to people. He was on a divine mission.

'That was the perfect metaphor,' he said, thinking back to that day on top of the hill near his hometown. 'It was the perfect metaphor for faith. I had to carry my own load and whenever I felt that our Father had gone on before me – well, he was just behind me, always. That's scripture.'

It was – *is* – also a good metaphor for being a human in this world.

You carry your own load, you work hard and you do not quit. These are all lessons that are valuable to learn and cannot be unlearned. There is no losing or revising of the knowledge that your experience gets better when you set a goal and work hard towards it. You can add to that knowledge, buttress it, colour it with experience and time, but knowing that life is hard and how you react to it is what actually counts is the most valuable thing that can be learned.

It is also a lesson that is taught through two ways: your experience, or someone else's.

The path from boyhood to manhood is a difficult and rocky one, and many boys fail – and are failed – when they are not guided properly along it.

THE MOST BOXING-GYM STORY
YOU WILL EVER HEAR

Berlin, Germany, around 2010 or 2011. It was a quiet, cool afternoon, and we were in the ring, finishing off a training session. We had warmed up with three rounds of skipping and followed that with ten rounds on the heavy bags. After some light pad work, we had gone into the ring to grunt through a few rounds of push-ups and sit-ups.

There was another man training in the gym. He looked Turkish, and he was nearly 6ft, athletic, his skin the colour of strong tea.

We barely paid any attention to him, other than the occasional and customary glance to see what he was doing and how well he was doing it. He did not move much, staying in one place, and his hands and feet made little but rapid and regular contact with the bag. It was the training of a man aiming to develop speed and technique.

My friend sat on the floor, then lay down and brought his knees to his chest. I pressed down on his shoes and he began his sit-ups, his hands to his temples and his elbows in front of his face, his arms shielding his eyes. I began to count the first set. 'One, two, three, four...'

At the other end of the gym was a weightlifting room in its own separate area. One of the regular bodybuilders came out from there and began to walk towards the changing rooms behind the ring. He carried a long gym bag in his hand.

The bodybuilder did not look at us, but we had seen him many times before. He was well over 6ft and wore glasses. He rarely wore a shirt. The muscles were built for show, packed onto a thin and angular frame.

The man on the bag stopped and said something to the bodybuilder. There was a shift, by meagre proportions, in the air.

Something else was said. The smaller man moved from the bag and stepped towards the bodybuilder. He said something that the bodybuilder responded to, raised his hands, shuffled forwards, and jabbed.

The bodybuilder took a hesitant and clumsy step backwards. He dropped his bag and raised his arms, but his hands were too low. He was copying what he had seen others do.

Another light jab, intent on it.

'Shit,' I said. 'I think they're about to fight.'

My friend, his arms blocking his vision, could see nothing. 'Nah, they're just moving around.'

'I'm not sure.'

'No one fights in here.'

I began to turn away and, as I did, the smaller man threw a left hook. It landed flush against the cheek of the bodybuilder. The bodybuilder's head spun.

'No, they're definitely fighting,' I said. 'Pretty sure about it.'

'Oh, shit.'

The bodybuilder stumbled and fell against the ring. He was kicked. He put his hands up. He got punched to the ground then kicked in the side.

The smaller man picked up the bodybuilder's bag and began to hit him with that. He dropped it and began to kick him again, then took him by the throat and drew back his fist.

'OK, that's enough!' I shouted. 'That's it! No more!'

They stopped and looked at me. I looked at them.

The bodybuilder scrambled to his feet, grabbed his bag and ran. No one went after him.

It was then the three of us. I looked at the smaller man stood outside the ring below me. He looked back.

There was one of those dreadful silences in which the promise of violence fills the air.

He walked to the bottom of the steps leading up to the corner and looked down for a second at the ground between his feet. He was strangely, serenely calm and his voice was gentle.

'I am so sorry for doing that in here,' he said. 'Please forgive me.'

He came up the steps and took off the light bag gloves he wore, then shook our hands. He pushed some sweat from his face back into his short and stubbly hair. 'I'm really sorry about that. My name is Hassan.'

'Are you OK?'

He nodded, exhaled. A vein pulsed rapidly in his neck. He said softly, 'Yeah, I'm OK.'

'I have to ask. What was that about?'

He looked over his shoulder to the door, past the space where he had beaten a man to the floor less than a minute before. 'That guy,' he said, 'hit two of my friends – girls – at the weekend. He broke the nose of one of them. I knew he was coming here.' He looked to the heavy bag he had been working on. It hung almost motionless, twisting and swinging gently on the four chains attaching it to the steel girder above. Hassan turned back to us. 'I was warming up. I wanted to be ready for him.'

My friend and I were in a bar a few years later and had not seen each other for a few years. He had moved to New York, then back to Berlin. It was late at night and the story of that afternoon had come up.

'Did you see Hassan again?' I asked. 'He seemed like a nice guy.'

'Yes. He is. I trained him for a while. He came to my class for a bit.'

'And?'

'As I said – nice guy. He's got daddy issues, though.'

'Haven't we all?'

'Yeah, we do. Not uncommon in our world.'

Hassan was a good man. The bodybuilder was not. The difference between the two was that Hassan's muscles had been built against the muscles of others; the bodybuilder's had been built with machinery.

Most men despise men who hurt women and children. Decades ago, I heard two men talking in Warrington about a baby they knew of who had been damaged by the mother's new boyfriend. There had been, they said, bitemarks.

'That is a man,' one of them said, 'who deserves to be taken out and beaten up by other men.'

Hassan seemed to have been taught these same things about honour and pride, about not bringing shame upon himself or those around him. He probably received guidance when he was young. He would have needed it. All boys do. A boy needs a good man to show him how to be good.

RUNCORN ABC

Runcorn, September 2018. Two boys meet on the door of a social club in Runcorn. They are arguing over a teenage girl. One of them is eighteen, the other seventeen. Threats have been made. They are guests at a birthday party at the club. When the older boy sees the younger one, he gestures for him to come outside to fight. They go into the street, but then the younger one doubles back and is given a knife with a twelve-inch blade by a fifteen-year-old friend. The two boys go back outside, where the older one takes the knife and stabs the eighteen-year-old once in the abdomen, severing a main artery and killing him. Arrested and taken to court, the seventeen-year-old pleads not guilty, as does the friend, but a jury convict them of murder and manslaughter, and they are sentenced to sixteen and seven years in prison. The seventeen-year-old sobs when the verdict is read out. It comes out later that this is the *second* time that he had stabbed the eighteen-year-old.

It was telling that the fight was to take place *outside* the club, as if they both accepted, without acknowledging it, that they were moving away from acceptable social practices. They were stepping into a space that would indulge urges that were more primal. And how much better could that story have ended if they had stayed inside, amongst others, and worked out their differences with civility? How much better would it have been if they had remained amongst older, more-mature men, who could have intervened to show them a better way? Someone might not have died that night.

Runcorn, March 2023. Runcorn Shopping City stands just over

300 yards from where the stabbing in 2018 took place. From the front door of the social club, it is a short walk across the street, past the church and down the short path towards the underpass. Once through there, you go by where the courts used to be and the police station, past the disused buildings where a big chunk of the town's social services administrative offices were housed, and you are there.

It has been over fifty years since Runcorn Shopping City was opened. It was all part of the New Towns project, in which the slum-like inner parts of major cities such as Liverpool and Manchester were razed and the populations moved to brand-new housing in the surrounding towns. The idea was to give everybody a better life.

It has not worked out that way. The latest statistics show that Runcorn is one of the nation's most deprived areas. In 2010, the local borough – which includes Runcorn and neighbouring Widnes – was ranked the twenty-seventh most deprived in the nation. Unemployment and worklessness are higher than the averages across the UK and the surrounding region.

Runcorn Shopping City, known locally as 'the City', has also suffered over the years, bouncing from owner to owner and name to name. The big-name, high-value shops went years ago, and everything is aimed at smaller budgets. It is common talk around the town that 'something' needs to be done, even if no one can articulate what that 'something' is.

The town is not a bad place, nor are its people. There is an inherent, unarticulated decency that runs through its population, and certain values that are fashionable elsewhere – kindness, decency, a refusal to discriminate – are practised easily and without fuss.

It is not unusual when out in Runcorn to see people unexpectedly come across others they knew and be happy that it had happened. Most people in the town know each other, or, at the least, everyone has a friend in common. And since a friend of theirs is also a friend of yours, that means that all are friends. Conversations start and flow easily, and common ground is found quickly.

It is easy to look down on Runcorn for all the things that it is *not*: cosmopolitan, forward-looking, cultured, affluent. But it is easy to be contemptuous of what you do not know. Runcorn is a great and good place to live if you have no other ambition than to be content and happy.

There was little productive being done at the beginning of 2023. Crowds flowed around and towards the centre of the building, known as 'City Square', then back out again in some new direction. It was the middle of the week and most people there seemed not to work, could not work, or worked in shops. The main thing they did was go out and buy things from other people who worked in shops.

Not far above the sparse crowds, on the small second floor, is Runcorn Amateur Boxing Club (ABC), which opened in 1961, has bounced around a few venues and now sits in, arguably, the heart of the town.

The gym is tucked away down some corridors and is one of the biggest in the north-west. There are two main rooms, with three rings taking up about a third of the space in one. It is in here that most of the training takes place, and there are twelve heavy bags and a large, empty area for exercises. There are portraits of fighters – Katie Taylor, Floyd Mayweather, Manny Pacquiao, Muhammad Ali, Tyson Fury, Deontay Wilder, Mike Tyson – down one wall, with flags from around the world adorning another. The third and fourth walls are filled with the club's achievements.

Darren 'Daz' O'Sullivan was running the club at the beginning of 2023. He was forty-six, had lived in the town for most of his life and looked like he craved a quiet moment or two to himself.

He was at the club six days a week and was paid for none of his time. He had two children of his own, neither of whom boxed. He was happy about that, and about them.

'I was five when I started,' he said, 'and now I'm an old man in a young man's body.'

He came to the gym that day like he did on all the others. There was paperwork to be done, and matchmaking, and he had to manage the volunteers and the amateurs who came through the door.

When he arrived, he went behind the desk and went through some of the paperwork, occasionally looking over to see what, if anything, was happening. He did not speak, but his eyes flitted from one side of the gym to the other, then back again, resting here and there on everyone for a few seconds. He approved wordlessly of everything he saw, put his head back down.

Afterwards, he came out and moved around the padded floor, watching the small kids train. He said little to them, then went to some of the other volunteer coaches. He was quiet and nodded frequently, his bearded face dipping a centimetre or two here and there to register his assent for something. His voice was gentle when he spoke.

He stopped at one point and pushed his hand through his greying hair, then gripped and pulled at his beard and inhaled. He sometimes rasped when he spoke, and it was a wet rasp from the side of his mouth, his tongue losing its way now and again.

He had been in boxing for over forty years.

'It's had a massive impact in my life,' he said. 'I've dedicated myself to it. I was born in Liverpool, then taken to London, and then back here when I was little. My father was very aggressive and there was violence at home. It was a daily thing. My brother and I were products of the same parents, but he went down a different road to me and did twenty-one years in prison. But I fell in love with this.'

The home life and the gym formed him. 'I took the brunt of it. My brother would run away, and I'd get his hidings. When you are terrified of someone like your dad, you can't be scared of anything else. I've never been afraid of anyone in a ring after him.'

He was picked to fight on behalf of England when he was younger. 'I fought until I became a dad in my early twenties. But then I had to provide financially, which amateur boxing doesn't do, so I had to get a normal job. I worked in gyms because it was all I knew and eventually I was asked to take over here.'

The early days were different. 'There was a lot of posers on steroids who liked to film themselves back then,' O'Sullivan said. 'So I sparred with all of them, and I'd be doing eight to ten rounds while they'd be doing two. And I emptied the gym, apart from one guy with the right attitude. He stayed on because I knew he could learn. That's how I started rebuilding this into a place for kids.'

He remains ambivalent about what is taught. 'I wrestle with it, and I try to make it as safe for them as I can. But they could just as easily be hit by a car or stabbed.'

He looked at the kids on the floor. 'The biggest pain they have right now is losing. There'll be a day when they can hit hard and they can hit fast, and – yes – you do become more aware of the danger. It's a hard question to answer. The doctors at the shows know and do more than they did, and I call all the parents after to make sure there's no delayed headaches. But the reality is that, win or lose, you are going to get punched in the face.'

Daz pointed to the walls of the gym. There was a poster on one about putting down knives and picking up boxing gloves.

He said flatly, 'We haven't been able to dedicate much time to it because it's hard to find volunteers, so we've made it part of our image. It's on the kits, the walls, to spread the message. The police come down here to talk about it and if we need to talk to a kid about it, we do. And we'll talk to the parents. But we're limited.'

He saw progress, even if it was tectonic. 'We'll get messages that they're focusing better in school. It's good to have a focus and a goal, somewhere to go. And they learn that fairness is not part of the game. If it was taken away, all they'd do is hang out on the streets and get into trouble.'

There were twenty-five to thirty children there, most of them boys. The trainers were all men. One, Roy Tully, was about forty and the skin of his shaved head was covered in a dark-blue tattoo. He was watching the young ones warm up.

'We get them here for all sorts of reasons,' he said. 'Some of them do come because there's been bullying going on, and we teach them how to defend themselves. We had one lad who boxed here, who was being bullied. He'd been stabbed with pencils in school by this other kid. The bully then told him that he was going to come down, and he told me. So I told him, "Be the best you can at everything." They went to spar, and the young lad landed everything he could on the bully. It sounds rough, but it's all a lesson in control, being done in a controlled environment. And he gained confidence.'

That afternoon, around six boys and their coach had come over from a different club. O'Sullivan explained that this was common, that other clubs would bring over their members to spar the boys at Runcorn ABC. He said tersely, 'The problem is that everyone becomes friends the longer that they're together and they end up pulling their punches. They get used to each other's styles as well, so you want to keep it all a bit fresh.'

The session would eventually melt into the sparring, but the children not going into the ring worked together first on pads. Supervising it was Patrick Quinn McDonagh, the loudest and most colourful voice in the room. McDonagh was from a family of Irish travellers but had lived in the neighbouring town of Frodsham for nearly two decades. He pointed to seven or so of the boys in the room and drew out his family relations to all of them. 'That's my boy there,' he said, then pointed to another at the far end of the room. 'That's my other boy. Him over there's my cousin, that's my nephew, that's my other nephew.' Another man came over. McDonagh pointed at him. 'And that's my brother.'

He walked around the room, alternately chiding and talking with the kids. It was less a conversation than a monologue of tumbling words that darted back and forth, flitting onto one subject and then off it and usually ending in some kind of punishment or light insult delivered with a smile. 'What're you doing? And to him? What're you doing that for? I can take the piss out of the fat little cunt because he's one of mine, not you. Ten push-ups. What's that? Do you know how to hit a pad? Do you even have the gloves on the right hands? I know these things, so I'm teaching you them, God help me. You can do ten push-ups as well. Steve, I didn't see you last week when you were supposed to be here. Are you well? Good. What? You're not Steven. OK, ten push-ups because I got your name wrong. What's your name? Frank. Good. Come on, Frank. One, two, three, four…'

Patrick leaned on the ropes. He was less catching his breath than looking for someone new to insult, chide or motivate. He looked paternally at the boys. 'It's all about respect,' he said, speaking sideways while looking straight ahead. 'Kids around here don't respect the elders. That's no good thing. And we're teaching kids to respect themselves, too. If you're not respecting yourself, how do you even start respecting others?'

The sparring started eventually. Patrick stood on the edge of the ring, his hands on the shoulders of one of the Runcorn ABC boxers. He was whispering gently but firmly into his ear. 'Now, remember what I told you about control,' he said. 'That's what it's all about. This – all of this – is just common sense that I'm saying to you. It's about control. You can't be a good boxer without control.'

The coach from the other club was in the opposite corner, whispering into the ear of his fighter. He looked up and called to McDonagh, 'What are we doing? Twos? One stays in, does two rounds, then gets out?'

McDonagh shrugged. 'Sure. Sounds good to me. Is that what you want to do?'

'Yeah, I mean, we're in your house, so I'll let you decide.'

'OK, let's do that. Your lad to get out first?'

'OK.'

The boys sparred for two minutes while their coaches gave them instructions. When time was called, the one from the other gym got out and one of his teammates got in. The boy from Runcorn ABC stayed, standing in the corner. 'You did good,' McDonagh said. 'But use that jab now. You're taller than him.'

Time was called again. Another two minutes of sparring, then the boy from Runcorn ABC got out.

'That was lovely,' said Patrick. 'You were looking for his counter when you were on your way out. I liked that.'

The boy nodded. There was a dribble of blood from his nose that he wiped at with his glove, smearing it across his cheek. A patch of his skin turned pink. He looked like he wanted to cry. 'OK,' he said.

'You did really well.'

The boys were still sparring an hour later. Patrick looked quizzically at one as he got in the ring. 'How many have you had?' he said.

'Six.'

'Six rounds of sparring?'

'Yeah.'

'That's greedy!' He laughed. 'OK, get in.'

This boy got in and jabbed at his sparring partner. The punches were hard. He stepped to his left, dipped his knee slightly and threw a sharp, hard hook. It landed against the other boy's head. There was the loud crack of wet leather on leather. The coaches winced. Patrick looked over to O'Sullivan. 'That's our lad,' he said, ruefully. 'He's got a problem with the world, that one.'

Daz nodded.

Afterwards, once the sparring had finished and people were packing to leave, O'Sullivan called the kids from the two clubs over to the ring at the edge of the gym. 'Alright,' he said. 'Let's get a picture together.'

It was for Instagram. The kids got in and stood at a short distance from each other. 'Get closer,' O'Sullivan said. 'They're not going to bite you.'

The kids sidled together. Each of them raised a fist to their chin. They smiled.

DEAN CRIMP

Fifteen or so children waited with their parents on the stairs to Relentless MMA. It was cold that night on the other side of Runcorn, and their breath hung in the air. One by one, they went up, and their parents paid Dean Crimp for the training session their little ones were about to undertake, shared a few words and then left.

'Alright, Dean,' said one. 'How're you? Sandy's here tonight.'

Dean looked down at the little girl in front of him. 'Hi, Sandy. How are you, champ?'

She nodded slightly. She was about eight years old and slim, with long, dark hair. She seemed nervous. 'I'm good, thanks, Dean.'

'That's good. Get inside, then, eh?'

'OK.' Sandy kicked off her shoes and skipped into the back room. Her dad watched her go in, nodded at Dean and then went down the stairs.

'Alright, Dean,' the next parent said. 'How're you? Did you get the subs last week?'

'I did, aye.' Dean looked at the small, blond boy in front of him. 'How're you, champ?'

'I'm good, Dean.'

'Good stuff. Get inside, eh?'

A father stood at the top of the stairs, watching his son play and spar with another boy. The son was tall and lean, with a shock of blond, tousled hair and pale skin. The traces of acne were just starting to appear. He looked about eleven years old.

'It's just me and him,' his father said. 'His name's Daniel.'

Daniel was paying no attention to the conversation. He carried on wrestling with the other boy. The pair of them seemed to be good friends.

The father watched the pair of them. He looked to be about fifty, and his hair and skin were grey. He had a thick, steel-coloured beard. He was shorter than Daniel and stockier.

'It's just me and him,' he said again. 'His mother—' He spat out the word with some distaste and then corrected himself. 'The woman who's *supposed* to be his mother, she gave him up to his grandmother and then fucked off. It took me two years to get him.'

The father said all of this in front of his son, who seemed not to hear a thing.

'First of all, he went to her, and she said I was unfit. So I had to fight it in court. And the woman who calls herself his mother, too. And it took two years. And then he went into care, so I had to fight to get him out. But he's out now. And it's just the pair of us.'

It was Daniel who chose to do MMA, he said. 'He can't do PE at school. He's got type-1 diabetes. I told the school and they said it's fine, but they won't monitor him. So, he can't do it. He takes insulin during the day and then he takes a slow-acting medicine at night, so he doesn't go hypoglycaemic. So, this is his PE.

'I watch him from over the road. Dean's got CCTV here, watching the mats. So, I sit in the gym across the street, and I watch what goes on and if he has a turn, I can be here in thirty seconds. I was an army medic, you see.'

He looked over at Daniel. There was love in his eyes. He waved to his son, said nothing else, and went down the stairs.

The Relentless MMA gym sits in Runcorn's Old Town on the first floor above a social care company, at the end of a street with an Indian restaurant, a taxi firm, a barber, a pharmacy and four takeaways.

There is no dedicated ring or cage in there in which to train, but the back room where all the kids went had mesh on all its walls and matting on the floor. It looked like a giant had turned an octagonal MMA cage on its side and then sat on it, bending it into some new shape so unique that it did not have a name.

Most of the kids lined up against the wall and waited for Dean. Some of them chased each other on the mats. The oldest was about eleven, but most were about seven or eight. A few looked nervous and a few looked like they struggled to sit still at school. A handful had kept their socks on because of the temperature, but the majority were barefoot. One or two ran up and jumped, launching themselves across the mat and punching the room's solitary punchbag in mid-air. They looked incredibly small in their shorts and T-shirts, their arms and legs still thin and underdeveloped; they were still all babies.

Dean came in, eventually, once he had spoken to every parent and greeted every child. He wore a pair of tracksuit bottoms, a T-shirt and socks. He rubbed his arms. 'It's never right in here,' he said, his breath hanging in the air. 'It's either too hot or too cold.'

At the beginning of 2023, Dean was closing in on forty. He lived with his partner and had two small children at home. His other three children lived in different parts of the north-west and Wales, but he saw and spoke to them all the time. He'd had short hair when he was fighting, but he now wore it a little longer and, unlike most fighters, he seemed to have gotten smaller since his days in the cage. He looked less like a wrecking ball and more like someone who ran long distances and climbed to stay in shape.

Most of the children ran onto the mats, then in circles, jumping against the walls. Some of them huddled to talk. There was some gentle pushing and shoving between them.

Lucas came onto the mats. He was about seven, too, and his hair was gelled into a spike. He was thin, not painfully, but it was the body of a boy that had still to develop, and his voice was high and gentle. His nose ran a little, and he sniffed every now and again when he talked. 'I want to be in the UFC,' he declared, as a boy in the '70s and '80s might have declared that he would be a soldier or a sailor. 'My dad brings me here, but I really want to come.'

A few of the kids did not settle when Dean came in. He admonished them lightly: 'Hey, we need to get started.' One of the boys did not look over and carried on running around. 'Callum, you're looking at a yellow card...'

The boy went and joined the other kids standing against the wall.

Dean whispered with a smile, 'The yellow cards don't mean anything, really. It's just my way of getting them to behave.'

Dean's son Romeo was in the class. He was about seven, cherubic, and loved his father. 'My dad was a fighter,' he said, pride in his voice. 'He had four fights. He won all of them. One was in about thirty seconds, and one was in fifteen.' Dean laughed when he heard about this, that this would be the first thing his own son would say.

The session started with skipping and the children took ropes and jumped clumsily over them. Afterwards, Dean showed them a sequence of techniques then allowed Matty, an amateur MMA fighter, and his protégé to take over the instruction.

He sat down against the padded wall at the far end of the training room and started to do some paperwork, ticking off names on a list in front of him. The wall was cold against his back.

'Matty's sound,' he said. 'He's really good with the kids. Nice lad, too.' He watched the class for a few seconds, then went back to the paperwork.

He began to speak about himself. His family were from Liverpool and his parents moved him and his brother Steven to Runcorn before both boys were ten. They eventually settled into an area of the town known as Halton Lodge. It was one of the poorer areas of town back then, and it is even poorer today. The homes there in 2023 are run down, often with detritus in the front yards. Around the back of the homes, in the places where even glancing tourists do not visit, wet washing hangs in the air on cold days, and the wooden fences of the homes are often rotting, the paint chipped, slats missing.

It was a difficult household and a difficult childhood. 'My parents had issues,' Dean said, 'and I love them, but it was toxic. It was poor and we were deprived as kids.'

Steven was unwell as a kid and remains so today. 'He's a paranoid schizophrenic and has been in hospital for ten years. But I always knew he was mad. He'd come at me with knives and hammers when we were kids, and I'd have to fight him off. But I still loved him because he was my brother. I love him today, too, even if he's not doing too well. But it was because of him going for me that I ended up with a reputation for defending myself.'

Dean and Steven were in trouble a lot as children. It is unclear as to whether it followed them or vice versa. 'It was a violent household,' Dean said, 'and I was always afraid. I had this fear. And the problem I had was that I took that fear and I put it in the wrong places.'

Childhood was tough for the boys, tougher than it was for most children growing up in the area. The area is one of the most deprived in the country. In 2010, seven areas within the town were listed in the top 3 per cent most deprived in the country. Life expectancy and health outcomes are amongst the lowest in the nation, and unemployment and worklessness are much higher than average. A lot happened in those years that Dean did not want to talk about, but he gave the basics: he went into the army at seventeen, but that did not last more than a couple of years. He moved to Wales at one point then back to Runcorn, when a romantic relationship broke down. There was some legal trouble from stupid bar fights that he should have avoided.

Dean hated to think of the things he had done. Hated to think that people would look at him through that lens. He still needed to be convinced that he was, indeed, a good man.

'I'm afraid,' he said. 'I'm afraid of being judged, especially after I've spent years trying to turn it around.'

He had five kids along the way, the oldest around twenty and the youngest only a few months old. He seemed to get on well with all of them. The three youngest lived in Runcorn. The oldest of those three, Romeo, lived with Dean's ex, and the other two lived with Dean and his current partner.

'One thing I'm proud of,' he says, 'is that no matter where I've fucked up, or how fucked up I've been, I've always been a dad to my kids. Always.'

He got into MMA when he was about thirty and had four amateur fights, winning them all. He was never paid for any other fights. 'It was the experience that I wanted,' he said. 'I wanted that experience that came with being in all those camps and with all those other fighters.'

He opened Relentless MMA about ten years ago, subletting it from the main tenant, but he eventually gave it back. It was too much work, he said, and he preferred what he did now: renting the mats out a few times a week so he could run his classes.

But then he injured his back. It got better and then he injured it again. The discs were degenerating, said the doctors, and his career was over. 'I walk around OK today,' Dean said. 'But I have to be careful.'

There was treatment that did not work. 'I had the operation in 2020,' he said. 'It was to do with stem cells. I went to London for that. Then Covid hit. I was told to rest for six to twelve months. While we were in lockdown, the restrictions were relaxed, so I could go do personal training back in the gym. That was six or seven weeks after the op. I was holding pads for someone, and my back went. We went into lockdown again, and I was able to rest it properly, but it's never been the same. And so I decided to let it go. I was thirty-three, thirty-four, so it was already getting time to hang them up.'

He decided to change the course of his life and began training to become an actor. 'It's something I always wanted to do,' he said. 'I'd be at school, and the teachers wouldn't let me audition for the plays because of the way I acted in the classroom. But I'm a creative person. I love art and things like that. And I always thought I'd be good at the acting, even when I wasn't being given the chance as a kid to try it.'

He stopped drinking, too. 'I wasn't an alcoholic, but I had an alcohol addiction. They're two different things. I'd be alright and then I'd go on a bender and start binge drinking. I still work on it today, and I try to help others who are in the same position I was in.'

He attends college during the week and trains kids at night. 'It was 2018 that I decided to give the acting a proper go. I was coming off my back injury and I was nine months sober, and I decided that I wanted to achieve something. I wanted to be able to look at something and say, "Yeah, I did that. That's me."'

Dean went on, 'I want to be a positive role model, and I want to be as professional as I can about the acting. The best thing I ever did was get my shit sorted. I'd love to show people how I've changed, even when I've got this fear of being judged. The one thing I'd really want is for someone to come and say to me, "Hey, Dean. You're a really good role model." That's one thing I'd love to hear, genuinely, from someone.'

He had a few plays and short films under his belt. He was pretty good, even if the writing was yet to meet his latent talent. He would always struggle to be the leading man, but he had a future as the leading man's best friend, the one who can be relied upon to do or say the right thing and cares less about the consequences than the context.

A few parents, including Daniel's father, came up the stairs and stood at the door. Dean waved to them. They had been across the road, in another gym, watching the class on CCTV. They were now coming to pick up the kids who chose to stay for only one hour.

Dean put the cameras in himself, somewhere above the mats, to keep the parents from interfering in the lessons.

'We had a reception area right where they're standing,' Dean said, pointing to a spot where a smaller MMA cage now was, 'but I took that out and put another training area in. If the parents want to watch, they can do it from the gym across the road. There's too much stress and hassle when the parents are there, and it's important for me that the kids are in a safe space.'

He looked around the kids on the mat, tumbling and wrestling with each other. All of them seemed happy. Dean seemed proud of what he was accomplishing with them. 'I'm not here to make champions,' he said. 'I like nice kids. I used to do anti-bullying talks, but it began to wear me out. I hope now that I'm teaching them by example instead.'

He hoped the acting would take off. 'When it does,' he said, 'and not *if* it does, I'm going to buy a gym here in Runcorn. Maybe this one, maybe another. And then I'm going to bring in the right people, good people, and we're going to run it all professionally.'

Dean saw a lot of himself in the kids. Some of them, undoubtedly, had started life without the wind at their back, but they were not mean in spirit. They were lost, if anything, and they needed guidance. They were not yet broken.

Most, Dean said, were not there because they were bullied. They were there because somebody in their lives wanted them to achieve.

'We do get some kids that come down because they're being bullied,' Dean said, 'but they don't last long. They usually come for a couple of months and then they drift away. We don't see them again. The ones that stay are the ones whose parents are trying to get them into something, so they can get them off the computer games and get some exercise.'

At the end of the session, a mother of two of the boys came to pick up her sons. She was called Michelle and was wiry with red hair. The two boys, Adam and Nathan, could have been mistaken for twins.

Michelle said, 'They're here because one of them has got ADHD, and the other's addicted to computer games. And they're going to grow up here in Runcorn, so I think it's important that they know how to defend themselves,' she said. 'I want that for them.'

Adam and Nathan were wrestling on the mat with each other, all smiles. 'Look at what we did tonight,' Adam said, laughing and trying to get his brother into an armbar.

'Come on, lads,' Michelle said. 'Home.'

The boys put their outdoor shoes back on, then ran and clattered down the stairs and back into the cold night. Their mother followed them. They seemed like good kids. They had *all* seemed like good kids.

Shamokin, Pennsylvania, US, June 2022. Shane Manney parked in front of a hardware store of the side of the freeway. He needed things for the 5 Stones gym.

He got out of the car and began to walk over to the doors of the store.

An old man in his seventies came out. He wore brown cargo shorts and a blue T-shirt. He wore glasses. He looked like a retired teacher. There was a young boy, about thirteen, with him.

Shane saw the old man, and he smiled. 'Hi, Dad,' he said.

The old man smiled back. His name was Norm. 'Hi, Shane.'

The young boy with Norm carried two paper bags, filled with purchases from the store. 'Shall I put these in the car?' he asked.

Norm reached into his pocket and took out his keys. He gave them to the young boy. 'Thanks,' he said. The young boy walked over to the car.

Shane and his dad spoke for a few minutes, then went their separate ways.

Later, Shane would talk about the young boy. 'He's a relative of ours,' he said, 'but his home life... Well, he needs some guidance. He lives with my dad now, and he's helping him with school, making sure he achieves something. You should have seen him a couple of years ago.'

He pulled the car out into the freeway. 'You saw my dad, right? He didn't look like you thought he would after all I told you?'

He did not wait for an answer. High-school wrestler. All those years in the Marines and as a policeman. Now, running his own martial arts gym. 'The funny thing is,' he said with a laugh, 'that even now in his later years, I still reckon my dad could take me.'

Masculinity has rightly come under criticism in recent years. It has, in many instances, been labelled as 'toxic'. But that is the wrong way to define or diagnose the problem. To be toxic is to be inherently or innately poisonous, or lethal at elevated doses. Wrong at an elemental level.

That is not a good framing. It would be much better to look at it as something with the unfortunate potential to be twisted into something awful if not channelled or directed in the right way.

It takes time and patience to build a person. It takes constant, dedicated work to show someone how to be kind and compassionate, how to have empathy. There is a lot of unseen labour that goes into showing a person not only to respect others, but to respect themselves. Most boys will learn from, and all will be influenced by, older men. Good men are needed for that.

Manney, Crimp, and O'Sullivan are good men, and they had a journey to get there. They were now helping others. And if fighting was brutal, then there was also love mixed into it. It was neither entirely one thing nor the other. As is life.

That, there, is another lesson.

CHAPTER TWO

THE FIGHT TRADE

THE SON

It seems often tragic when the children of famous boxers step into the ring. What is the point in fighting if not to prevent your children from having to follow the same path? *I fight*, said one former champion, *so that my children do not have to*.

But the rollcall of boys following their fathers into the ring is long, endless. There are a great number of former champions whose children have followed them into the trade, but it is exceedingly rare for success to be transmitted from one generation to the next. The sons with champion fathers rarely achieve the same, while the most successful offspring tend to be those whose sires were boxers of a lower level. Great leads to good, and good often to great, but rarely does greatness travel down the branches of the family tree.

For some, it is a trade passed down from one generation to the next. For others, it is emulating one's original hero. And it is innate in cases, the proverbial apple not falling far from the tree.

Cardiff, Wales, September 2023. The air shimmered above the corrugated steel sheets that covered the roof, and there was no breeze to smoothen off the heat. It was the type of temperature that made everything seem bleached in white.

This was the new gym in which Steve Robinson, former World Boxing Organization (WBO) featherweight champion, was going to work. It was his gym, which was why it was to have his name over the door, and he had opened it that week. That explained the conspicuous lack of a ring.

'It's going to go over there,' he said, pointing to one corner of the room. It was a small area that would house an equally compact ring. But that would be good in helping a boxer learn how to fight on the inside, which is how a master of this craft is truly measured.

Robinson said he was going to work out of the gym, and his declaration made one pause. He still looked, at fifty-four, like he could go back into the ring the next day. And win. He was ridiculously fit for a grandfather, with a washboard stomach and negligible body fat. It seemed that he had not received the memo about losing your shape once you have retired.

'I look alright, don't I?' he said, with a smile and a cackle.

There were rumours, too, that he was looking to get back into the ring, one final time, for an exhibition. It was said that he had reached out to Ricky Hatton about the latter coming down to Cardiff to do some rounds together. Hatton was beloved across the land; Robinson was beloved in Cardiff. It had the prospect of a feel-good event about it. It was a tempting prospect for a fan, but it seemed unlikely that Hatton would be persuaded.

But the plan in 2023 – the concrete one, anyway – was for Robinson to go about his day job, in the new space, of training fighters. He was going to train amateurs, professionals and those who just wanted to get into shape and stay there. And looking as fit as he did, he was probably the best walking advertisement for his own business.

Robinson should never have been champion. But then he became one, and a good one at that.

It was 1993, and the WBO featherweight champion was Ruben Palacio of Colombia, who had not seemed destined to be a champion, with 44 wins, 11 losses and 2 draws. His punching power was on the light side, and he had stopped only nineteen of his opponents. More tellingly, he had himself been stopped seven times. But then he went in against the UK's Colin McMillan, 23–1, and somehow beat him in 1992.

Palacio was coming back to the UK to make what was supposed to be an easy defence against John Davison. Except that he failed the medical, testing positive for HIV. And so, he went back home, and the title was declared vacant. And Davison, with 15 wins and 3 losses, needed someone to share the ring with, and quick.

The honour fell to Robinson, who had been fighting as the away opponent for years and been left with a record of 13 wins, 9 losses and 1 draw for his troubles. But it was a decent payday of £12,000 for a young father who had just quit his job in a warehouse. And, besides, when was he ever going to get the chance again?

So Robinson went to the north of England on less than two days' notice, and he won. Split decision. The world champion nobody ever expected. He rolled two sixes on what may have been his only throw of the dice.

And he carried on winning, beating fighters that should all have beaten him. He beat Sean Murphy, 22–3; Colin McMillan, 23–2; Paul Hodkinson, 22–2–1; Freddy Cruz, 44–5–5; Duke McKenzie, 36–4; Domingo Damigella, 22–2; and Pedro Ferradas, 19–1–2.

But then he lost to 'Prince' Naseem Hamed. And that should have been the end, but Robinson began to win again. He won the meaningless WBO intercontinental title three fights later. And then he won the European title.

He retired at thirty-one after a run of six losses. And more than two decades later, he was still intact, still fit. In remarkable shape after fifty-one professional fights.

Then, he began training his son Jake. 'I love it!' he said, when asked about his son boxing. 'I really do. He has all the ability. The only thing he needs to do is build his confidence up.'

The younger Robinson was twenty-nine, and he had won ten of his eleven professional fights. He was a featherweight, like his father. After stopping two of his first three opponents, he had wended his way through a litany of no-hopers, outpointing all of them. He had then lost his tenth fight, on points, against the un-defeated Nathaniel Collins. He followed that six months later with another points decision, this one over four rounds against Brett Fidoe, who was 17–73–5.

The younger Robinson was the rarest of birds, seldom seen in the wild: naturally right-handed, he chose to box as a southpaw. The assumption was that he had switched stances one day in the gym as a lark, but the wind had changed, and he had since been stuck.

He fancied himself a slick fighter and a stylist, keeping a distance that he closed now and then with his jab, and he liked to place himself in the ring centre and control his opponent from there, keeping them on the outside, where they would spend a fight moving greater, long distances than he. When he walked in, he came in a straight line, and he had picked up the old trick of keeping his jabbing hand low to draw in then deflect the mirror punch from his opponent.

Robinson's career had yet to reach the heights of his father's. But there was still time. And the elder Robinson had himself been written off much earlier along the way, before lightning had struck. There was every chance that it would strike twice.

Robinson Sr had a private client to teach away from the gym and the younger Robinson arrived as he headed out. He handed over the keys to the building.

The younger Robinson sat down at a flimsy plastic table that he carried into the centre of the gym. He sipped from a bottle of water.

There was a large splint on his wrist. He took it off and showed a long, brown scar that ran down the back of his hand and into the bottom of his arm. Then he turned his hand over and showed off a small, brown mark on his palm, about six inches apart from an identical one on the inside of his wrist.

'It's the ligaments,' he said. 'Probably from the boxing. It was a two-hour operation. It's more or less a reconstruction. I really should have had it done a few fights ago, but I've always gone into bouts with little niggles and stuff. I'm looking at about three to four months for recovery. I'm getting a bit more movement now and I'm doing physio. The splint is just for support, really.'

He put the splint back on. 'The thing is that I've got to make sure that it's going to be proper when I go back. It means I'll have to wrap it in a different way. Injuring it a second time is in the back of my head. I don't want to throw a shot and have the wrist go again.'

There was not the usual childhood story of pain or deprivation, and he was blinkered mostly to his father's profession, save for brief moments here and there. 'It was pretty good,' Jake said, smiling. 'Obviously, he was my dad to me, but other people would see us and say, "Look, it's world champion Steve Robinson."'

Jake Robinson never fought in school, either. 'No,' he said, shaking his head. 'I've always been sort of likeable, and I've always kept to myself. But it was never an issue in the playground. I've never had a fight outside. There were little scuffles here and there in school, but I've always just gotten on with people.'

He drank some more water. 'I never watched my old man fight live. I've watched the fights, with my brother, on the old tapes. But I wasn't even born when he became champion – I was still a year away. He retired in 2001, when I was about five or six. I didn't appreciate it then, but I got it when I got older. I look at his career and what he's achieved – and wow!'

He says his father did not push him. 'No, that wasn't the case with me or my brother,' he said. 'We just followed him down to the gym one day when we were kids, and it went from there.'

Robinson played rugby at first, but then drifted into boxing. 'I've always been energetic, so I channelled it into sport. I got into the boxing for the fitness for my rugby. I had my first amateur fight at fourteen, which is a bit late. And then I made the choice at fifteen to go into boxing rather than rugby.'

It was a truncated amateur career. 'I only had about eighteen or nineteen fights,' he said. 'I won a couple of Welsh titles and got to the final of a British. But I think I was more suited to the professional side.'

The tag of being Steve Robinson's son followed him around. 'I do get a little more attention because of my dad, but it does come off me when I'm fighting. A lot of people do know me through him, and it would be nice to step away from it a little if I could.'

He also found the tag followed him into the gym, where the professional fighters took note of his parentage before sparring. 'I've sparred with big names over the years. When I go in, they'll work on stuff with other guys but go straight in on me.' He smiled. 'But it's competitive!'

It may have been a tougher task than Robinson realised; his father was in the corner for all his fights. 'He's pretty hard at times,' he said, 'but he can also be laid-back. He's been there for every one of my professional fights. He did the corner for a few of my amateur fights, but he would mostly sit and watch.'

There was an element of family pride in the younger Robinson's career. When he lost for the first time, on the road in Glasgow, the first thing he did was turn to his father and apologise.

Robinson's eyes went into shadow when he remembered those moments. 'I told him I was sorry,' he said. 'And he turned to me and replied, "For what? It's just a bad night."'

Another sip of water. 'Collins is a good fighter,' he said, 'and he's won the British title now. Our fight was close, I think, and there were rounds when I didn't do enough in the champion's backyard. My dad said it was just boxing and, besides, he lost nine times before he had a world title.'

His face brightened when he thought of the future. Apart from the great physical inheritance he had received, and the name, he was also going to benefit from the experience of someone who had been through the petty and internal politics of the sanctioning bodies.

He said, 'Yeah, my dad's been there and done that. And he's always saying to me that I've the potential to go all the way. It's just about bringing the confidence out.'

A world title was on the shimmering horizon. 'If I go for the Commonwealth or the British, I'd be put up in the rankings for a world championship,' he said. 'But I do need to go back to the drawing board a little now. I'm going to have a warm-up fight, probably over six rounds, and then take it from there. I'm currently the Welsh featherweight champion, and it's the Celtic next.'

He thought he could be popular within Cardiff, too. The 7,000-seat Cardiff International Arena was a few miles down the road. Not much further along from that was the 80,000-seat Millennium Stadium. It was not hard to imagine Robinson fighting at either venue.

'Most of my fights have been in Cardiff,' he said. 'I had the one I lost in Glasgow, and I've been on at York Hall in east London. When I fight at home, ticket sales have been pretty decent. I sell about 2–300 each time.'

The family's legacy looked to be in good hands. And, besides, there was a third-generation Robinson, too – Jake's son, Steve's grandson. Jake was hesitant about his own boy boxing. He shook his head at the thought of it.

'I'll teach him,' he admitted, 'but if he came to me at ten or eleven and said he wanted to do it properly, I'd tell him that I'll look after him but he needs to give 100 per cent. If I didn't see that, I'd have to say that it's not going to work out. This is not a sport that you play. People get hurt in this.'

'To be honest,' he said, 'I wouldn't want him to box. But we do pads and that, and he's honestly pretty good. He is getting the rolling in, along with picking up everything else. I guess we'll see how it goes.'

THE FIGHTER'S JOURNEY

There are many different careers in boxing, but the one that runs through all of them like a spine is that of the accomplished kid who 'turns over' to the professional ranks, then works their way up until they become a champion. Every other role is attached to and feeds from that journey.

The best start to a great professional career is a great amateur career. Good amateurs already have the basics of being a good fighter and their natural gifts have announced themselves in unpaid competition. An Olympic medal of any sort is a golden ticket; a twenty-year-old with one of these brings with them prestige and name recognition.

Marked differences exist between the amateur and professional codes. Amateurs are not paid on principle, even if nations have extensive training programmes that often pay generous stipends to their Olympic-calibre athletes.

The most prominent gap between the two is that amateur fights are fought over much shorter distances that top out at three

three-minute rounds in the Olympic finals. On the other hand, a world title fight on the professional side lasts for twelve three-minute rounds. That jump, from a total of nine minutes to thirty-six, takes time and expertise to make. Another notable difference is that amateurs will fight a handful of times in as many days against opponents who are strangers to them, but top-flight professionals will fight a handful of times each year against selected partners who they diligently specialise their training for.

The journey from nine minutes of fighting to thirty-six is the spine that runs through professional boxing. It would be foolish to take a young man who has not developed his adult strength away from nine minutes of fighting and place them against, in a thirty-six-minute contest, a grown man. So, a young boxer will go through a few years of seasoning and increasingly longer bouts against fighters of different styles and, crucially, improving standards.

It takes around twenty fights before someone is ready to fight for a world championship and they should be undefeated at the end of them. Losses stall careers. The vast majority of promising young fighters often find their careers wash out after a single loss 'exposes' their shortcomings. There can be great danger if a fighter's record becomes 'padded', or filled with no-hopers, in that an inevitable step up in quality of opposition brings a sharp and often short reality check.

The most potent pick of such a trajectory may be that of Jeff Lacy, a Floridian super-middleweight who won a bronze medal at the 2000 Olympics in Sydney, turned professional and waded through sixteen opponents to pick up the International Boxing Federation (IBF) world title. He finished most of them in short fashion, including former World Boxing Council (WBC) champion and perennial contender Robin Reid. By early 2006, Lacy was being hailed as the division's most dangerous fighter and the sport's next big star. His own promoter referred to him as a 'miniature Mike Tyson'. All that changed, however, when Lacy went to Manchester to face World Boxing Organization (WBO) champion Joe Calzaghe, then undefeated in forty fights.

Calzaghe was old and seemingly fragile, his hands beginning to disintegrate. He was five years older too and had rarely left the UK to defend his titles. It was, the majority of pundits said, an easy fight for Lacy.

The reality was that Calzaghe schooled Lacy, winning every single round and knocking the American down in the twelfth, long past the point when the fight should have been stopped. Lacy went back to the US broken, further injuries hampering his career, and went on a run of eleven fights in which he won six times and lost five. He went swiftly from being a champion, to a contender, to a stepping stone for younger, fresher fighters. His last two losses were particularly sad. He lost against Umberto Savigne, a middling opponent with a record of 11–1, in the second round, and again the following year, to Sullivan Barrera, who was undefeated in fourteen fights. Neither went on to better things. Savigne fought twice the following year, lost both times and never fought again.

A fighter will begin as a 'prospect', meaning that they are awash with potential after an accomplished amateur career. They will be known as this until they move into contention for a title. In their first five or six fights, they will fight a succession of nobodies, opponents brought in so that the prospect can acclimatise to the longer contests, the bigger crowds and the feeling of taking professional-grade punches. The opponents at this level are not highly thought of and are usually local tough guys or 'experienced' opponents brought in from some backwater town. Most fights at this level will finish in a round or two, and a good prospect will complete this run of fights undefeated with a knockout in every bout. The losers of the bouts will go home with a decent payday for their pains but will be labelled pejoratively with names such as 'tomato can' or 'ham and egger'.

Once the prospect has been fighting regularly for the best part of a year, the people around them will put them in against a 'journeyman'. These are masterful boxers and defensive wizards who fight a few times each month, are surprised by nothing inside the ropes, have great stamina and dedication to the business and lose nearly every bout they take on, but only ever on points. Their role, for which they are paid more than the prospect at this stage, is to push and teach their opponent in the ring, providing a stiff test so that those backing the prospect can assess how their investment is doing. The best-known journeyman in the UK was Peter Buckley, who finished his career with a record of 32 wins, 256 losses and 12 draws. He was known as 'Professor', and it was not a nickname given ironically. Buckley was tough, durable and knowledgeable, and even the rock-handed 'Prince' Naseem Hamed needed two attempts to stop him.

It may be somewhat ironic that at the early stages of their career, a prospect will earn less and carry more financial risk than their journeyman opponent. At this stage, a prospect will not only be being assessed on their ability within the ring and their work ethic outside of it, but also on their ability to market themselves and sell tickets. A prospect is often not paid in cash, but in tickets that they sell to their fans. A journeyman, however, will fight for a flat fee and will worry not about who of their friends and family they can sell to, but whether there will be traffic on the road to the venue.

A few fights at this level results in the prospect moving out of the lower echelons of talent and beginning to be matched up against 'contenders' at the national or continental level. These are the fighters who are vying for a title, who may or may not succeed at winning one and who may or may not move on to the world-class stage. A few wins and a national or continental title here sets the stage for a run at global honours.

It is also at this stage that it is likely a fighter will have the most exciting, toughest fight of their career, usually when a rising young star meets a professional who is on the way out but still has some of the old fire. The best fights occur not at the top but somewhere around the middle, and an *aficionado* with enough years in the game can spot them. These may be termed in some quarters as 'trade fights'. A prime example of this would be the first fight between Arturo Gatti and Micky Ward. Neither was the best in the division, but their match showcased that they were the best for each other. Not only would their first encounter, in 2002, being labelled officially as 'Fight of the Year' and unofficially as 'Fight of the Century', but their second and third bouts were similarly lauded. Their second bout missed out on 'Fight of the Year' honours simply because it was fought in the same year as their third.

It is at this point that a 'gatekeeper' appears. These fighters can also be described as a 'journeyman to the stars'; they may have challenged unsuccessfully at the highest level, been found wanting and left to offer in their waning years a test for a contender wanting to establish their *bona fides* against someone with name recognition.

Like journeymen, gatekeepers are also masterful boxers. They bob at their own level while nearly everyone in the division is either going up or down. Beat one, and you add a name to your record and some seasoning to your skills. Lose, and the top is beyond your grasp.

One of the most prominent gatekeepers within the heavyweight division in recent years has been Kevin Johnson of Asbury Park, New Jersey. In 2009, Johnson had 22 wins and 1 draw when he got the call to fight WBC heavyweight champion Vitali Klitschko in Berne, Switzerland. Johnson lost, but he did what many had failed to do by taking the Ukrainian the full twelve rounds.

Johnson showboated and goaded Klitschko in the final rounds. 'The guy couldn't hit me,' he told me once for *Boxing News*. 'I thought I'd do what Lennox Lewis did and bust him up. His eye opened in the fourth and I tried to work it…' He trailed off, blaming an injury for the loss. 'It's not that I didn't want to. I just couldn't.'

Johnson became the guy that others went through after that. A gatekeeper. You would see him win easily against opponents that anyone would beat, and then he would take his name and standing as a former heavyweight title challenger into the ring against a prospect and do everything he could to fiddle and muddle his way to the end, not really trying to win, merely going the distance.

There were still big names, but he lost to them: Tyson Fury, Anthony Joshua. Occasionally, he would show up in some smaller location and pull a surprise, such as when I saw him in Magdeburg, Germany, in 2020, when he turned up and stopped the former cruiserweight Yoan Pablo Hernández in seven. Winning that one probably cost him some work.

He fought mostly in Germany, but then started popping up in Russia. I ran into him waiting for Felix Sturm to fight in Dortmund in 2022, when he was still hanging around on the periphery of relevance in the trade. We exchanged a few words and then he went off. I saw him lose not long after in Hamburg to a fighter called Ali Eren Demirezen, who had 15 wins and 1 loss. He lost two more fights in that city, drew one in Cologne to a body called Andre Bunga who had 6 wins, 12 losses and 1 draw, won against another body in some deep and dark village in Bavaria, then headed to Moscow. He became a Russian citizen in August 2023, after which his record dropped off, the bouts so far unrecorded. In tribute to the Russian leader, Johnson reportedly took on the new name of Kevin Vladimirovich.

After the gatekeepers are the champions. While self-explanatory, there are different types of champions. There are dominant champions running through a line of average contenders and occasionally taking on other titleholders, champions who have won a belt unexpectedly and are making the most out of it while they can, young champions at the beginning of their dominance and older champions looking to stretch their reign a little further.

The business of boxing is such that a fighter can move up from one category to another, but the movement down is near impossible to reverse once it has begun. A prospect can rise all the way to champion, but contenders do not morph into gatekeepers and then go back. It takes only a loss or two at any level for someone to go down a rung on a ladder that they will not climb again.

Every now and again, there will be the oddness of a resurgent champion, someone who seemed to have fallen in their prominence but somehow finds a last burst that extends their run at the top. However, these tend not to last long; to paraphrase Joe Louis in this regard, they can run but they cannot hide.

Jean Pascal of Canada fits this bill. A Haitian who came to live in Montreal, Pascal lost to Carl Froch in 2008 for the vacant WBC world title at 168lbs, but added 7lbs to his stout frame and won the same title in the light-heavyweight division. He defended that title four times in Montreal before becoming unstuck against all-time middleweight great Bernard Hopkins. After that, Pascal moved to the B-side of the card, with 7 wins and 4 losses. But then he defeated Marcus Browne, 23–0, for some vacant titles and ran up a few more victories over good opponents, before losing handily to a German called Michael Eifert, who outworked him, with a record of 11 wins and 1 loss. At the time of writing, Pascal has just surpassed forty years old, indicating that his career is finally, finally finished. Unless he moves into the next category.

The last, saddest category is the 'visiting attraction', which is when a great champion, usually aged in boxing, needing the money and with nothing else they can do, begins to tour, as a guest, towns and places that are as far from the bright lights as you can get. It is why Sugar Ray Robinson, the all-time best of the best, ended up losing on points in Paisley, Scotland, to a local fighter with 45 wins, 15 losses and 7 draws in 1964. It still took Robinson another twenty fights, only thirteen of them victories against poorly rated opposition, to call it a day.

THE PROFESSIONAL CAREER
OF MIKE TOWELL

It was a little after two months on from Mike Towell's debut fight that his mother, Tracey, phoned their local GP.

She did it when he was at work. It seemed best that way; he

said there was nothing wrong with him. But it had now happened twice, and she was scared. She needed help. She knew *he* needed help. One time could have been an aberration, something unexplained, the physical equivalent of dialling the wrong number. But not twice.

The first time had been a few weeks after a skinful. She had found him on the floor beside his bed, his mouth bleeding. He was looking at the blood that had dripped onto his hand, not knowing what had happened.

So she had phoned the GP. 'It happened again a few days ago,' Tracey told the person on the other end of the line on 31 May 2013. 'But he wasn't drinking this time. I'm worried that these might be seizures.'

'OK. We'll get him booked in as soon as we can, but if he has another one, then you need to take him in right away.'

She called again three days later. She had been thinking about it constantly. 'I'm a little worried over these blackouts,' she said. 'He's been having headaches, too. I don't understand; he's just had a CT scan for his boxing licence.'

'OK. He's coming in tomorrow, isn't he?'

'Yes.'

They went to Coldside Medical Practice the next day. They outlined what had happened – the sleep disturbances, the falling out of bed. He said he was confused sometimes and did not know where he was or had been, that his speech was incomprehensible.

Dr Macpherson turned to Towell. 'What do you do, Mr Towell?'

'I'm a scaffolder.'

'And you box?'

He nodded.

'Your mum says you drink?'

He nodded. 'Every now and again. Sometimes more than other times, you know.'

Dr Macpherson nodded. 'Anything else?'

'No.'

'Drugs?'

Towell looked away. 'No.'

'I'm not the police.'

'OK. Coke every now and again.'

'Cocaine?'

He nodded.

Dr Macpherson made a note. 'OK,' he said. He thought for a few seconds. 'I want to refer you to neurology.'

Towell shook his head.

'Mike...' his mother said. 'Mike...'

'No, no neurology.'

The doctor looked at him. 'You've had what sounds like two seizures. And you seem to be suffering from what we call "complex partial seizures". I recommend you go there just to be checked out.'

Another shake of the head. 'There's nothing wrong with me.'

Dr Macpherson exhaled. 'OK,' he said. 'But if this happens again, you need to go. I can't make you go, but you need to go. Do you understand?'

Towell nodded. 'I'll think about it.'

A little over three weeks later, Towell was at the Cleland Miners & Workers Society & Social Club, near Motherwell. He was to fight Martin McCord.

Before the fight, Towell went to the doctor assigned to the event for his pre-fight medical. Dr Christopher Greenhalgh took Towell to one side.

'How're you feeling, Mike?'

'Good.'

'Good?'

'Yeah. I'm ready, you know.'

Greenhalgh nodded. 'OK, this will take us about two minutes.'

'Alright.'

Greenhalgh pulled out a piece of paper. 'Just the standard questions.'

Towell nodded.

They went through the first six, then Greenhalgh asked, 'Any illness today, Mike? Anything got you under the weather?'

Towell answered. Greenhalgh ticked the wrong box, put a mark in 'yes'.

'And how are you feeling today?'

'Good.'

Greenhalgh ticked 'yes' again. Later, he would explain that he had ticked the wrong box around illnesses and that he had meant to tick 'no'.

Later that night, Towell drew against McCord over six rounds. It was the latter's first fight, and his career would peter out after four losses, punctuated in the middle by his solitary win.

To draw in your second professional bout is not a good result, but it is understandable. It takes some time for the feel of the professional side to bed in, the punches now coming wrapped in smaller and tighter gloves that augment their power. Towell may also have had at the back of his mind the knowledge that all was not well inside his own head, that he had been warned and advised not to box. Or maybe he was just nervous, or perhaps McCord was better than he had realised.

His team see it differently. 'It was a draw, but Mikey battered him,' says amateur coach Andy Howett. 'They said that if he had won, then there would have been a riot. So they called it a draw to stop the crowd from ripping the place apart.'

It was a little over two months before the next incident. He was asleep, being driven home from a site, when he began to shake and spasm. He pissed on himself and bit his tongue. It was 9 September 2013.

The seizure went on for three or four minutes. A dangerous length of time for a seizure. His colleagues called an ambulance.

The paramedics said, 'OK, Mike. We're going to take you to Aberdeen, get you looked at.'

Towell shook his head. 'No.'

The paramedics looked at each other. 'This is serious. You need to go.'

Another shake of the head. 'No.'

'Why?'

'Too far.'

The paramedics looked between themselves again. 'Would you go to Ninewells up the road?'

Towell flinched. 'Alright.'

'This is the third time, Mr Towell?' Dr Nichol said a few hours later. 'That's what your records tell me.'

'If that's what they say,' Towell said, his mother beside him. They were at Ninewells Hospital in Dundee. Towell was nervous and fidgety.

'I want to refer you to the seizure clinic. They're going to take a better look at you.'

Towell looked at him. 'What do you think it is?' he said.

The doctor shook his head. 'We can't be sure until we've done some more tests, but my guess would be something like temporal lobe epilepsy.'

'What's that?'

'It's pretty common. We can treat it.'

Nichol looked at Towell. The boxer looked down at his hands and took a deep breath.

'There are medications to help,' the doctor said, 'but until we know more, there are some things I'd advise you not to do.'

'What things?'

'You're a scaffolder, right?'

'Right.'

'You can't work at height. Not for now. And there's no boxing and no driving.'

'Are you serious?'

'Yes.'

Towell went to the seizure clinic eight days later and met with Dr Anne Coker. He took his mother with him.

Coker looked at Towell's notes on her computer. 'This wasn't the first time, was it?'

Towell looked away. 'So I'm told.'

'Three times, at least.'

Tracey Towell spoke. 'I've seen it before in my partner. He was epileptic. And after that, the being confused. It's the same thing that I used to see. That's what I remembered about his epilepsy.'

'Your partner was epileptic?'

Tracey nodded.

Coker turned to Towell. 'Is there anything else?'

Towell turned to her. 'There's other things, different to the "episodes". Sometimes, I feel as if I'm somewhere where I've been before, or I'm doing something that I've already done.'

'I've seen that,' Tracey said.

Coker turned to her. 'How many times?'

'At least three times in the past year.'

'Three times in the past year?'

'Yes.'

Coker made a note. 'And what happens?'

'We don't know,' Tracey said. 'We can't understand what he says. Sometimes, he doesn't know I'm there when they happen. And then there's a headache afterwards.'

Coker wrote more notes. 'How often?'

Towell paused and thought. 'I go weeks with nothing, then *bang, bang, bang* – there's a handful in a day.' He paused again. 'Is it the coke?'

Coker looked up from her notes. 'Sometimes that can happen. But the last time, you hadn't taken any drugs or drank any alcohol before?'

'Not for a few weeks.'

'OK.' She wrote down more notes.

Tracey cut in: 'He takes these protein shakes, though. I think it's a sugar rush from having them.'

'If that's so, then he should not take them.'

Towell was silent for a moment. 'What do you reckon is wrong?'

'There are a few things it could be, but the most appropriate idea

I can give right now would be that of temporal lobe epilepsy. I can give you something for it.'

'Medicine?'

She nodded. 'I think you need it.'

'No.'

'No?'

'I'm not epileptic. I can't be. And I've got to work.'

Coker consulted her notes. 'You're a scaffolder?'

'And a boxer,' he said with pride.

Tracey Towell looked over. 'That means you can't box, Mike.'

'A boxer, too… You'll need to go with what the boxing authority says.' Coker wrote this down. 'OK, I'm going to refer you for more tests. I want to do an EEG, an ECG, and an MRI on your brain. And I'm going to get these arranged for you today, because I think you need them urgently. I'm also going to advise you that you cannot drive and that you need to tell the DVLA about what is going on.'

'Will the MRI say I have it or not?'

'No, it doesn't do that. We'll look at it, and we'll look at the history you have, and we'll decide based on all of that.'

Two days later, a few days before he was scheduled to have the MRI, Towell was back at Coldside with his mother to see Dr Macpherson.

'Mr Towell,' the doctor said, 'with everything that's going on, I am strongly advising you that you cannot box.'

Towell shrugged his shoulders. 'Noted. But I'm still going to do it. What about work? I'll stay on the ground, and I won't drive.'

Tracey Towell leaned over. 'It's the drinks,' she said. 'The protein shakes. He takes them to build up and they make him aggressive. I'm telling you that it's the shakes.'

'Mr Towell, you cannot box.'

He decided to stay away from the sites until after the MRI. He did not work. He saw another doctor later and got signed off. He was told again not to box. Two weeks after that, he saw a fifth doctor, who became the fourth to advise him not to box. He told her that he felt fine and that he did not have epilepsy, that he was still taking the protein drinks. He had not contacted the DVLA to inform it of his seizures.

Eight days later, Towell had his third professional fight, six rounds against Billy Campbell in Motherwell. Campbell had won three and lost one.

Again, the doctor took Towell to one side for his pre-fight medical.
'How're you doing, Mike?'
'Good.'
'Yeah?'
'Yeah.'
'OK, it's the standard questions. Only take us two minutes.'
The doctor read from the paper. 'Are you suffering any illness?'
Towell shook his head. 'No.'
'You feel well today?'
'Aye.'
It took Towell fewer than four minutes to stop Campbell, finishing the fight with a technical knockout in the second round. Campbell would go on to have five more fights, losing all of them, before retiring from boxing the following year.

Towell was back at the Coldside Medical Practice six days after stopping Billy Campbell, and he was frustrated and angry; the results of the MRI were not yet back.

Dr Fiona Bullions looked up the result while he was there. 'I can see here', she said, 'that it didn't find any gross abnormalities.'

'So I can go back to work?'

'Not yet.'

Towell swore beneath his breath. 'Fuck's sake—'

The doctor looked at him. 'Mr Towell, you need a formal opinion from the neurologist before you can be cleared to do anything.'

'I'm fine.'

'You still need the all-clear from the neurologist before you can do anything.'

'That's what you say.'

'Are you still driving? You can't do that, and you need to inform the DVLA. I understand you haven't done that, either.'

'It was a sugar rush.'

The doctor shook her head. 'I can't send you back yet.'

Later on, Towell was angry. He knew the boxing was over.

'It's your fault!' he yelled at his mother. 'You did this to me! You opened your mouth about this and it's gone and ruined everything!'

'Mike...'

'You tell them these things, and they're going to stop me! I'm going to lose my boxing!'

He was back at Coldside on 21 October. The neurologist had still not signed off on his MRI. He was angry.

'Look, it's a fucking waste of time coming here,' he yelled. 'There's nothing wrong with me.'

Dr Macmillan looked at him. 'The MRI can't tell us whether you have epilepsy, but it can exclude certain things that could be causing the seizures. Lesions, for example.'

'No.'

'What do you mean "no"?'

He seethed. 'I come here, and you waste my fucking time. I guess I'll just make another appointment.'

He came back the next day. The same doctor wrote:

Aggressive personality swearing at me and general language re his dissatisfaction that I won't give him a line that says he is fit to return to work. He says that there is no situation at work that he could fill that does not require him to be up scaffolding and therefore with his undetermined diagnosis but suggestive of temporal lobe epilepsy I am not in a position to deem him fit to return to work. I suggested he could ask for occupational health assessment at work. Accompanied by his mother today. Apparently not driving.[1]

He was back with Dr Bullions at Coldside on 14 November. He had been calling Dr Coker to get the MRI results. They came on 19 November. They had no explanation for the seizures. Dr Coker wanted him to do a sleep-deprived EEG.

Coker wrote a letter to Towell. She said the sleep-deprived EEG would be 'useful' and that he should continue to avoid driving.

Towell saw a different doctor at Coldside on 27 November. This time, it was Dr Angus Oswald.

'I need a certificate to go back to work,' Towell said. 'I'm fine. Your doctors are telling me that it wasn't a seizure.'

'They've told you that?'

'Yes.' It was a lie.

'It says here that they want to do a sleep-deprived EEG.'

'Useful. They said it would be "useful".' Towell continued to lie. 'They said I could go back to work because I haven't had any more. The EEG was normal.'

'Mr Towell, I am concerned that...'

'It's fine.'

Dr Oswald hesitated. 'Can you wait outside?' he said. Once Towell had gone, Dr Oswald turned to his computer and emailed Dr Coker. He was unsure about what Towell was saying. He wrote, '[I] have to say I am not entirely confident that working on scaffolding advisable but have believed his telling of events.'

He called Towell back in.

'OK,' Oswald said. He paused. He thought. 'I'll sign off on your certificate, but I'll call you once I've heard back from Dr Coker about your results.'

Dr Coker replied the same day:

I would advise him not to work as scaffolder or at heights or to drive. He awaits a sleep deprived EEG and has contacted Ninewells asking for a cancellation for the investigation. I'm not at Ninewells today but recall he has had one witnessed generalised seizure and from my recollection additional episodes were suggestive of probable complex partial seizures but he declined anti-epileptic drug treatment as he felt the probable seizures were due to a supplement he had been taking although no good evidence to support this view.

Dr Oswald picked up the phone and tried to call Towell. He spoke to Tracey Towell and asked her to get her son to call him back.

Towell called later.

'I heard from Dr Coker,' Dr Oswald said, 'and, no, you should not be working. The certificate I've given you is invalid. And you *need* to do the sleep-deprived EEG.'

Dr Oswald wrote it all down in a letter. Towell did not reply.

The sleep-deprived EEG was set for 9 January. Towell did not show. A week later, the hospital wrote to Coldside to pass on the information. It registered another appointment.

Towell went to see Dr Brian Tansey in February 2014 for his annual medical examination for his boxing licence. He said he was in good health. He said he had had medical tests in 2013, but he gave no more information. There was no need under the rules of the British Boxing Board of Control (BBBC) at the time for them to follow up.

Afterwards, Towell went to have his eyes examined in Dundee then travelled the ninety miles to Glasgow for an MRI at Ross Hall Hospital. That MRI found no difference with the one taken at his initial licensing, so a recommendation was made for his licence to be renewed.

The sleep-deprived EEG was scheduled for 11 March. Towell did not attend. Dr Coker wrote to Coldside and confirmed that Towell had been discharged from neurophysiology. Dr Oswald heard and wrote to Dr Coker on 31 March, asking if the practice needed to do anything and whether Towell was fit to drive.

Coker replied a few weeks later. She said that she had recommended medication. She said that there was another appointment scheduled for May.

She went on, 'With regards to your question about whether he is fit to drive, I would suggest he makes contact with the DVLA. The DVLA once in receipt of all of the above information will make an assessment to determine a date when he can legally resume driving.'

During this exchange of letters between Dr Oswald and Dr Coker, Towell fought professionally for the fourth time on 12 April 2014 at the Lagoon Leisure Centre in Paisley. This time, he was facing Rhys Pagan for the Scottish Area light-middleweight championship over ten rounds.

There was a difference in the quality of the opponent. Pagan would end his career in 2017 with 14 wins and 5 losses, but he faced Towell that night with a record of 8–1.

A doctor saw him again before the fight. 'Any illness, Mike?'

'No.'

'You feeling OK today?'

'Aye.'

The fight lasted three rounds, Towell winning in the closing second by technical knockout.

He boxed once more in 2014, beating Kevin McCauley on points over ten rounds at the Radisson Blu Hotel. McCauley had 11 wins, 77 losses and 5 draws. His career would slip and slide into 2022, when he registered his 224th loss against 15 wins and 12 draws.

Towell did not attend the appointment in May, and the clinic did not schedule another. A few weeks before, Dr Oswald wrote again to tell Towell that he needed to contact the DVLA and that if he did not, Oswald would contact it on his behalf.

He was back at Coldside in January. He saw Dr Bullions.

'Did you speak to neurology, Mr Towell?' she asked him.

'I'm fine. Look, I've spoken to some sports people, and they reckon it was just a sugar rush, not a seizure. And my boxing doctor says that I'm fine to fight. Why are you doing this? Why are you and all the rest of them trying to stop me from doing my job? It's my job, you know.'

The annual medical was a few weeks later. It was Dr Tansey again. Towell indicated that he'd had some investigations the previous year, but his answer was never followed up on by the BBBC. He had his eyes tested again, underwent another MRI at Ross Hall Hospital. The MRI showed no change since the previous year. He was relicensed.

There was a slew of fights that year, and each time he told the doctor he was healthy. There was Arvydas Trizno, whom he beat by technical knockout in the first in Dundee; then the same against Lukasz Janik in Glasgow; a third-round knockout over Danny Little and sixth-round knockout over Aleksei Tsatiasvili, both in Glasgow. He finished the year with a points decision over eight rounds against William Warburton in Stirling.

None of these fights were against distinguished opponents: Trizno had 20 wins, 40 losses and 2 draws; Janik had 14 wins, 10 losses and 1 draw; Little was 3–8–1; Tsatiasvili was 8–14; and War-burton had 17 wins, 84 losses and 7 draws.

The final year of Mike Towell's life started with an examination by a new doctor. Dr Scott Henderson was a general practitioner who had been involved in amateur boxing since 2012. He was often the doctor at professional boxing events, and he carried out annual medicals for boxers from late September 2015.

Henderson carried out the examination in February 2016 at the 1314 Boxing Club in Stirling. He ran through the battery of questions.

'Any headaches, Mike?'

'No.'

The eyes were tested again. There was a new brain scan. All good. Licence renewed.

Towell went back to the Radisson Blu in Glasgow for an exhibition bout, an unscored demonstration of skills that lies on no official record.

The eleventh fight arrived: an eliminator for the British welter-weight championship, to be fought at the Lagoon Leisure Centre in Paisley. Towell told the doctor that he was fine.

This was to be ten rounds, this time against Robert Dixon, 13–1.

A tough opponent this time; no more treading water against men who came in simply to survive or fall down. Dixon came north from Gateshead. His record was padded, but so was Towll's.

Few videos exist online of Towell's bouts. He flew under the radar in that respect, his career still in the lane of smaller shows, held far from the bright lights. If he had gone on to championships and won them, there would be more. He would have left the small-er places with their hundreds of spectators and gone to the arenas with thousands, to the television stations with millions. But for the start of his career, few were watching.

The fight against Dixon is an exception. Two videos exist, posted onto YouTube in March 2016. They show only the first round of the fight and of Towell in the corner afterwards.

It is a sparse crowd, and the building has a high ceiling, making everyone seem much smaller. There are tables around the ring, and at the back of the room a large metal barrier separates most of the crowd from the inner area.

Seconds out. Round one!

Towell, in blue and white, comes out. The name 'MIKE' is stitched into the waistband of his shorts. He shifts his weight onto his back leg and then bends forwards, making himself even shorter than Dixon. His gloves are a burgundy red.

Dixon is tall and lean, almost angular. It is hard to tell in the light and from the camera perched just above the bottom rope the colour of his gloves.

Towell goes in the direction of Dixon's body, his head down. He bends his knees and throws his right hand wildly over the top. He gets in close and Dixon holds him, pushing his elbows down onto Towell's biceps, moving off when he can.

Towell is on the floor in less than a minute. It is hard to see what causes it; the bodies of Dixon and Towell are tangled, and the angle on the camera is a bad one, but it looks like a left hand puts Towell down.

A voice over the intercom begins to count. *One, two…*

Towell gets to his feet and walks to a neutral corner. *Three…*

Referee Bob Williams follows him, holding up his fingers. Towell turns. *Four, five, six, seven, eight…*

The referee rubs Towell's gloves on his shirt. 'Come to me,' he says, then walks backwards as Towell steps out, moving out of the way to let the fight go on.

Dixon throws a right hand and Towell ducks and tries to cover up, and then both of them are swinging wildly at each other.

They go back to how they were, Towell walking in and throwing right hands, Dixon moving. Towell shifts his head like a metronome, bopping side to side. He throws uppercuts, hooks, crosses over the top. But not jabs.

Dixon ties Towell up. He jabs and throws loose right hands. No power there. He leans on top of Towell, pushes down, tries to tire out his legs.

Towell pushes inside. *My strength, your strength*, he seems to be saying. *Let's see who the better man is.*

The bell rings.

The second video is only seventeen seconds long. Towell sits on a corner stool, his gloved hands in his lap. He rests his head on the soft matting behind his back. His people work on him. There are five in the corner, two or three more than is usual.

There is no more video after this point. For some reason, the match's final 1 minute 57 seconds is not online. But Towell won in those seconds, stopping Dixon on a technical knockout.

Fight twelve came and went: a first-round knockout over Miguel Aguilar in Glasgow. Mike Towell was undefeated in twelve fights. The only blemish was the draw against Martin McCord in his second fight.

She woke up to find him shaking and spasming again. It was 21 May 2016. There was blood, and Mike's girlfriend, Chloe Ross, thought, *SEIZURE*.

She jumped out of bed. 'Mike! Mike!'

He continued to shake. She took her phone and called an

ambulance. 'It's my partner,' she told the operator. 'He's having some kind of seizure.'

'OK, we're sending someone around now. Where is he?'

'In bed.'

'OK, make sure he can't hurt himself—'

The spasming stopped. Towell began to snore. Asleep again.

The ambulance turned up soon after. They wanted to take him to the hospital.

He was awake now. 'No,' he said.

Chloe looked at him. 'Mike, you need to go. Please go.'

'OK. Will you come with me?'

'I can't. The baby's here, but I'll call your mum.'

They took him to Ninewells, where Tracey Towell met them. They sat in a room with Dr Yvonne Tan.

'What happened, Mr Towell?' she said.

'I had a seizure, I guess.' He shrugged. He put a hand to his mouth. 'And I bit my tongue.'

'I understand.'

He then lied. 'This has never happened before,' he said. 'I think it's the drinking. I've been on the lash for two weeks. And I've been using coke.'

He saw another doctor, this time Dr Karen Black. He told her that he had never had a driving licence. He had, but had still not called the DVLA.

Dr Black looked at his notes. She saw he was lying. 'You've had seizures before,' she said. It was that easy to dispute.

Towell simmered.

He was discharged, and Dr Tan wrote to Dr Bullions at Coldside to ask he be referred to neurology. The referral was not made. It was apparently missed by the practice's administrative staff. And even if they had not missed it, it was unlikely that Towell would have gone.

OPENING ACTS

London, UK, September 2023. They were the first to fight that night.

Zoe Hunte-Smith arrived first, just after half-two in the afternoon. She carried her own bags through the car park, went up the stairs and entered York Hall in Bethnal Green. The opposite corner would be filled by Kerry Orton. The pair of them were to fight six two-minute rounds in the light-welterweight division in the night's opening bout.

After placing her things on one of the 700 chairs in the room, Hunte-Smith went over to the organisers and 'paid in'. This meant that she was to give them money in order to fight on their show. It was a little under £3,500, £2,000 of which was earmarked for Orton.

'Hi, Zoe,' a man called Josh said as she came in. A woman named Amy sat next to him. The pair of them were friendly but professional. 'How much is it?'

'Three-four,' Hunte-Smith replied, taking out a white envelope. She handed over a deep pile of banknotes.

Josh and Amy began to count through the money. 'How're you doing?' Josh said.

'Good.'

'Have you weighed in?'

'Not yet.'

It took about two minutes to count the money. 'We're twenty short,' said Amy.

'I'm sorry,' replied Zoe. She reached into her pocket and went to look for more.

'One second,' said Josh. 'Let's count it again first.'

The money was recounted. It was right the second time.

Hunte-Smith left the room and went back into the main hall. After all her expenses, she would earn £200 for the evening.

The economics of small-hall boxing in the UK are brutal. An A-side, home fighter makes their money by selling tickets. A promoter will give them a batch to sell on the understanding that the fighter will keep what is left after the promoter's fee, the money for their own opponent and whatever they pay their coach and cutman.

A week before the show at York Hall, I had been in Cardiff. I had met Gary Lockett, former middleweight world title contender. He was retired from boxing, but he still trained and managed fighters. He was also an accountant.

'All people see is the TV fights,' he said. 'They don't know that there's such a thing as small-hall shows.'

He laid out the economics. 'Here's how it works,' he said. 'You can't put a new pro in with a very good pro because they need to learn. So, you have to find a journeyman, and they need paying. I had a fighter recently who boxed some Russian guy on his debut. The Russian guy cost about £1,650. My guy had to sell as many tickets as he could in order to pay the guy. Let's say my guy sells three grand's worth of tickets. We've now got £1,350 left. If it's a nice promoter, he'll ask for half of that, so we're at £675. But my guy only sold £1,300 worth of tickets for that show, so I paid the £350 needed for the journeyman. So my fighter's not getting paid. I'm not getting paid, either. In fact, I'm even out of pocket.'

The hope was that a big payday in the future would balance things out. 'It would have broken the kid's heart; he'd already had a fight fall through three days before because the tickets for other boxers hadn't sold well, and the promoter was already ten grand down. If you've got eight fights on the card, the promoter needs to make a grand off each one. If he's not, he'll pull the bill. Everyone then has to give people the money back. And that happened twice with my guy. It's a hard game to sell all these tickets.'

He remembered a recent bill in London. 'This particular one is brilliant. You have to pay the opponent, then put £1,500 into the bill. Whatever's left gets split equally with the promoter. If your opponent is £1,500 and you've sold £3,000 worth of tickets, paid the opponent and then put money into the bill, you don't earn a penny.'

'It's hard,' Hunte-Smith said in the empty hall. 'And it's been a rough week. My first opponent pulled out, then we had to find another one who the Board would approve of.'

She was thirty-one and had been a professional boxer for nearly four years. She was short and lean, her hair pulled back tightly, and she had tattoos all over, most of which were related to boxing. She had won one and lost two. Her first fight had been in 2019, a loss over four rounds to Eftychia Kathopouli. She had then fought against Bojana Libiszewska and Jordan Barker-Porter in 2022, winning the first and losing the second.

It is not unusual on the female side of the code for records to be spottier. The shallow pool of talent means that the seasoning route undertaken by male professionals is often truncated, with world title fights for women often happening in fewer than ten bouts. It is also common for the same opponent to be fought multiple times, for wins and losses to be exchanged.

Hunte-Smith's fight against Orton would be her first bout in nearly fourteen months. She was going into it ranked eighth in the UK, out of ten, and fifty-fifth in the world. Orton was thirty-six years old and had had one professional fight, a 56–59 loss to Wendellin Cruz two months earlier.

She scratched her head. It had been a rough year. There had been stops and starts, but mainly stops.

'I've been scheduled to fight twice,' she said. 'But then both girls pulled out two weeks before. I would have gotten two grand for each one. So that's four grand I lost. So I ended up saying, "Sod it. I'll scrimp the money together and pay for the opponent myself."'

She liked to fight. 'It doesn't matter if it's for £20 or £200,' she said. 'I love it. I'll never turn one down. And I like to think I'm exciting to watch, too.'

The York Hall is a leisure centre mostly, a place where people and families come to spend time. It is also the home of British boxing, a place where most British fighters aim to headline at least once, and it sits within the eastern part of London, a region on the cusp of gentrification.

Opened in 1929, it first began holding boxing matches around twenty years later in a main hall that seats about 1,200 people. The time since has seen over 800 professional boxing events take place within its walls, or an average of one every thirty-three days.

The main room of the York Hall lies past the front door and up a small flight of stairs, and it is on two levels, with the majority of seating on the lower one. This is usually temporary chairs laid out in sections. The ring is set up each time, and then the whole floor is partitioned with metal fences. On the upper floor, the seats are permanent, made of wood and bolted into the floor.

That night, there was an air of neglect, if not decay, about the York Hall. The brown floors with scratched and scuffed, the dark wood pulled away in places to reveal the lighter shades beneath. And the venue looked, despite the brightness of the light, dingy.

The hall was empty, save for one of the night's referees, who was wearing a T-shirt and shorts. He sat in the cheap seats, looking at his phone. Some other boxers wandered around. The ring was empty, and one of them climbed into it quickly to have his photograph taken by his friend. They laughed as he got out, then left.

Most of the light in the main hall came from the windows at its top, which were wide and uncovered. Below that was a small rig, hung high, with bright lamps that radiated a stark whiteness. And at the end of the hall was a large stage with a stand and computer on which a DJ would later play music.

This may have been the Mecca of British boxing, but it was hard to escape the fact that if the bright lights existed anywhere, this was probably the furthest point from them. It was a place, and a show, where most boxers and the professionals around them ground out what small living they could.

Someone came over and tapped Hunte-Smith on the soldier. 'You can weigh in,' they said, and moved off.

Hunte-Smith walked over to the scales. She signalled Derek Grainger, a local boxing coach who had come in at the last minute to look after her. 'My usual coach is in Telford,' she said, referring to a large show in the north happening that night. 'He's got two of ours on that card, and two on this one, so he's asked Derek to come help out.'

Hunte-Smith wore black sweatpants, socks, sandals and a jacket with 'Team Hulky' written on the back. She had a thing for *The Incredible Hulk*. 'It started with my nephew,' she said later. 'We were playing with his Marvel toys and he yelled out, "Hulk Smash!". And it went from there. It explains all the green. And my nickname is "Hulky".'

She stepped out of her socks and sweatpants, and then took off the jacket. She wore green underwear with *Incredible Hulk* graphics and a black sports top. She walked over and got onto the scale.

An inspector from the British Boxing Board of Control looked at the display. '137.10lbs,' he said.

She had made the weight. She stepped off the scale and went back to the chairs. She got dressed again.

Kerry Orton came in. She was taller than Hunte-Smith by a couple of inches, and she had tied her long hair back. She also stripped down to her underwear and took off her socks, then stepped on the scale. She was a little over 138lbs. She had made weight, too.

Orton stepped off the scale. She went and got dressed. Neither she nor Hunte-Smith looked at each other. Orton walked away with her manager.

'That's OK,' said Hunte-Smith, sipping from a huge bottle of rose-coloured water. She shrugged her shoulders, much like anyone working in a restaurant would regard a troublesome customer. 'It's just business.'

There was some time before the fight, so she went for something to eat with her team. There was some relief that she no longer had to worry about making weight.

'I played high-level football,' she said, 'until I got a back injury that meant I couldn't do it any more. And I started to put on weight, so I began going to a boxing gym to shift that. And then I fell in love with it.'

Love is a hard bolt to dodge, and she had a good amateur career before – in the parlance of boxing – turning over. 'I started as an amateur in 2013. I boxed for London, Surrey twice. I went to Ireland. I got a silver in the Haringey Cup. But I lost a bit of love for a while. I started working, going out with mates. And I saw some bad decisions on the amateur side of it.'

She drank from her bottle. 'But this is a drug that never leaves you. You catch yourself shadowboxing at home or just walking down the street.'

There was no point fighting for money, and it was hard still as a woman to have a good boxing career in 2023. There was a dearth of women on the professional side to test and build oneself against, and this lack of meaningful opposition and talent made the nuts and bolts of bringing a fighter along even harder than usual.

'I still feel as if I get treated differently as a woman,' she said. 'Especially here on the small-hall circuit. And that's down to it being hard to match us. A woman who is a journeyman fighter

– a journeywoman – is in high demand, so they can demand more money. Some of them go up to £2,500 for four rounds. That's a lot. Male journeymen don't cost more than £1,500 for that. And I think a lot of the promoters just don't want that hassle.'

It was later in the afternoon, about forty-five minutes before the evening's first bout.

Hunte-Smith's changing room was beneath the main stage at the far end of the hall. It was a small place, around ten feet by ten feet, and there was a white wall drawn down the middle that divided them from other fighters on the card. Around thirty straps of medical tape were stuck to that wall, waiting to be applied to a fighter's hands.

It was a busy space, and somewhere between eight and ten people came in and out. Hunte-Smith was sharing it with Dean Gardner, a welterweight with 4 wins and 1 loss who was to face journeyman Fonz Alexander. As the fighters moved around and warmed up, a musky smell began to rise in the air.

Hunte-Smith was to walk to the ring at six o'clock. Her hands were wrapped. She wore black shorts with green and gold patches. 'I've had the same shorts for all my fights,' she said. 'The tassels and stuff are OK for some people, but not for me. I keep these shorts because I want the colours to be a recognisable look.'

She walked around, stretching and flexing her arms, and jogged a little on the spot. She pushed her feet down into her boots, making sure that everything was in the right place. Then she took a blue yoga mat, put it on the floor and lay down. She stretched her arms above her head and flexed her legs and ankles.

Loud music rolled down into the changing room from the main

hall. It was a constant and flowing thing, one dance track segueing seamlessly into another, and the walls shook with their rhythm.

Hunte-Smith got up and took out a snack from her bag. She opened the packet, squeezed the food into her mouth and then dropped the waste into a large bin.

She began to move, her hands cutting through the air. She kept her fingers loose, as a professional does, only snapping them shut at the end of their arc, and she stepped from side to side. She rolled her head.

Her legs were like those of a footballer, and she was slight in the upper body. A good boxing physique. She stopped and drank some water. Heat came off her. She leaned against the wall and closed her eyes.

A few silent moments, then she went back into her bag and pulled out a black tub that she handed to Grainger. 'These are my shields,' she said. 'The green one's my main one.'

Grainger motioned to Gardner. 'See that, Dean? That's organisation.' He looked over. 'What time we got?'

'It's five thirty-three.'

'OK.'

There was a hard, smacking sound from the next room as someone worked the pads. The team ignored it.

The gloves were taken twenty minutes before the fight, opened up and pushed down onto Hunte-Smith's hands. Then she went over to Ian Burbedge, her cutman for the night. He took some grease and began to rub it across her face.

She sniffed. 'Have you been eating peanuts?' she said.

Burbedge's face dropped. 'Are you allergic?'

'No.'

He relaxed. 'Jesus, I thought you were allergic then for a second. That would be a new one for a fight not going on.'

Everybody in the room laughed.

When the grease was on, Hunte-Smith took some more water then spat it into the bin. Cold water cramps the stomach.

Grainger picked up some pads and began moving around with Hunte-Smith. 'One-two...' he said, then caught the jab and cross that came back. He arced his left hand over her head, and she stepped to one side. 'Then the right. OK?'

She nodded, did as he asked.

'Mind her jab. The moment she starts catching you with it, that's when you're not moving your head.'

'I know, I know.'

A member of the promotion came in to say that it was time for the fight. Hunte-Smith, Grainger and Burbedge left the room, went through part of the drawn wall that had been opened, stepped through the other dressing room, went up behind the stage and stood behind a wooden door. Its wood vibrated from the music.

It was a few seconds of waiting, but then the door was opened, and Hunte-Smith walked out into the near-empty main hall. About thirty people were there.

The fighters were announced to the crowd then called over to the referee. He had changed into trousers, a shirt and tie. Orton wore a black-and-yellow gladiator skirt above black shorts.

There was the sound of the bell, and Hunte-Smith bent her knees to stay low, and she looped her shots around Orton's arms. Orton threw her punches long and would reset every few seconds, as if her internal coach was telling her, *Get back to basics, don't try to be a star.*

Hunte-Smith pushed Orton into a corner. 'Settle down, Zoe!' someone yelled from ringside.

The fight moved into the centre of the ring. Orton landed a right hand. Hunte-Smith bent her knees a little more. Orton jabbed, tied up when Hunte-Smith came close.

'Counter the jab, Zoe!'

Hunte-Smith moved her head when Orton's jabs came in, letting them sail past her down the sides. The old-timers used to like cauliflower ears for this reason; it meant that a fighter could slip punches.

The second round began. Hunte-Smith countered from the outside. Orton threw jabs and moved and clinched when the fight went to close quarters. Hunte-Smith shifted her head and returned with jabs. She was landing more.

Orton tried to become tighter in her defence, her palms held facing down to punch for speed, not power.

Hunte-Smith let Orton punch at her arms in the third, and she bulled her way in and started to bring uppercuts up into the space between them. She went to the ropes now and then, leaned her weight against them and rolled away from Orton's punches. And then when she brought the fight back to the centre, Orton was no longer clinching.

It shifted to the ropes and then away from them, and it became the fight that Hunte-Smith wanted.

She shifted her strategy a little in the fourth, coming in close to

Orton but then moving away when she could. She ducked under some punches and came back up with hooks. One landed against Orton's head, then another. And one after that.

Orton tried to move back and put the fight at a distance. Hunte-Smith threw punches over Orton's arms, dropping them onto her head.

In the fifth, Hunte-Smith went back to the ropes more; she covered and shifted when she needed to, and she went inside every now and again. Orton began to look a little flummoxed.

'It's a good one,' said someone in the moments before the sixth round.

Hunte-Smith chose to stay close in the last round. It may have been exhaustion. She moved off when she could but would be drawn in every few seconds. She crossed the hot air with uppercuts and hooks.

The final bell rang, and Hunte-Smith and Orton embraced. They went to their corners, where their coaches rubbed them down with towels, handed them water.

They were called back to the centre of the ring. Hunte-Smith won, 58–56. She held her arms in the air and embraced Orton one more time.

She left her team behind and went out into the crowd after the verdict. She walked down into the stands where she saw her partner, who put her arm around her. Hunte-Smith laid her head on her shoulder. Some friends came up here and there to congratulate her and have their picture taken together.

Eventually, she made her way to the dressing room. The team were already beginning to have Gardner ready when she got back. The game was starting again. She went to Burbedge, who slid a pair of scissors beneath the gauze around her fists, and cut it away from each hand.

'How're you doing?' he said.

'Good. I'm still coming down, but I'll be tired soon.'

He nodded. 'Good fight.'

'Thanks. I might take a day or two off now, before starting again.'

He nodded. 'That's good.'

'Give me a second, and I'll pay you.'

Hunte-Smith paid Burbedge, then got changed. She put on a pair of dark-grey jeans, a black T-shirt and some green-and-white trainers. There were no showers in the room, so she pulled and plucked at her shirt as it stuck to her skin.

'That was a good one,' she said, thinking back on the fight. 'A good battle to open the show with. Promoters like that. And I've been off for so long that it was good to get back in the ring.'

Her mood darkened as she thought ahead. 'I've got good sponsors. Before they came on board, it was looking like I might have to do something else. It's hard to try and find three-to-four grand every eight weeks. But I believe in myself. I know that if you keep at it, you eventually come out on top.'

She took out her bottle of rose-coloured water and drank from it. There were still some beads of sweat around her eyes. She did not notice them. Her hands trembled, the adrenaline beginning to drain out of her veins.

'I'll be back, hopefully, before the end of the year,' she said, the word 'hopefully' deep and vast. 'I've just gotten engaged, so I've that to celebrate. And there'll be a wedding, too. And, obviously, I need to get back to work.'

It was time to go. She wanted to be in a good seat for when

Gardner, her friend, walked to the ring. She drank once more, then took a breath.

Then she stood up, said goodbye to everybody in the room and went back out amongst the crowd.

THE RICHEST PRIZE IN SPORTS

One time, I was most of the way up – or some of the way down, depending on the direction of travel – the Zugspitze, Germany's tallest mountain. We were in a small valley, a low-slung scrabbly hillside about 300 metres from the top, the clouds had just opened over the Alps, and we could see hundreds of miles away.

We stood and took in the view, the landscape millions of years old, my companion and I ultimately insignificant to its existence, then and ever.

'It's things like this', I said, 'that you could spend your life just sitting here and watching.'

That is the way with nature's miracles and excesses. Sometimes, the only right and proper thing they deserve is awe.

All Saints Boxing Club, York, UK, around 2002 or 2003. The taller of the two was the first to get into the ring. He was young, then – we all were – and he knew a thing or two about what to do in the ring. And he was big.

So was the shorter one, the 6ft 2in. Swede who was all brawn and muscle, like a Nordic Frans Botha. And he also knew a thing or two about what to do in the ring.

They were the only two heavyweights in the gym, and they were sparring.

We sparred every night, to the body only, especially for those of us who did not have cards or who were doing it merely to prove a point to someone or to themselves. And the sparring was mostly ignored when it was the lighter ones, the middleweights and the welterweights and the lightweights with their speed and their athleticism and their movement.

But it was different when those two were in the ring. Their names were Billy and Tor. Billy went to his left, jabbing at Tor's head. And Tor, so much shorter, spread his feet a little wider and bent his knees a little further, and he dipped his head side to side, and he pushed his weight down onto his front leg and sought Billy's body.

Everyone stopped, the punches dropping away from the bags and pads. And then everybody moved closer to the ring and watched, keeping a respectful distance from the ropes, their gloves on their hips.

There is something special about watching two heavyweights fight, more so if the bout itself is for the heavyweight championship of the world. The air vibrates in a different frequency.

Wrocław, Poland, August 2023. It was two days after the Ukrainian Day of Independence, and the path to Wrocław Stadium was garlanded in yellow and blue.

Draw a line from the border Poland shares with Germany to the one it shares with Ukraine. Wrocław is about two-thirds of the way along that. The city was the third-largest in Poland after Warsaw and Krakow, but its population had risen from 673,000 to over 900,000 after Russia began its war against Ukraine. A quarter of a million Ukrainians were making their home there in 2023.

It had been a hot day, and the incoming night had done little to lessen the heat. The temperature had dipped weeks before and when everyone felt that the season was over and autumn was beginning, it crept back up.

The heat, miraculously, did not remain beneath parapets and a cool and temperate night was going to follow the hot afternoon.

The Ukrainian themes running through the event were anything but subtle. Beams of blue and yellow light swept over the 40,000 crowd, the A-side of the event was stacked with Ukrainian fighters, and the colour scheme – the decorations, the graphics on the large TV screens – was taken directly from the flag of Ukraine.

It was an open stadium and the weather had held well that day, and so on the pitch, where football is usually played, the crowd walked back and forth and stood and huddled in small groups as the night's undercard began to sputter into life. It is one thing to fight in front of a full stadium, but another when that stadium is still a shell, a skeleton with little flesh on its bones.

The two fighters were not far apart. They were the Ukrainian Oleksandr Usyk, who was the WBO, WBA (World Boxing Association), IBO (International Boxing Organization) and IBF champion, and the British Daniel Dubois. Usyk was undefeated and a national hero. Dubois had recently lost and shakily rebuilt, and there were questions about his foundations.

A couple of hundred yards separated the dressing rooms, and the two men would each walk out along the same narrow corridor. Dubois would go first.

Many had begun to write the British fighter off. He had started in the right way, been tested correctly and had beaten his first fifteen opponents.

But he had begun to struggle. He slipped into a sloppy fight against the Ghanaian Richard Lartey, who did more than was expected. It was an ugly and boring fight for the first two rounds, and it turned sloppy and ugly in the two rounds after that. Dubois stopped boxing and slugged with Lartey, who slugged back, and it looked for seconds at a time that one or the other would fall. In the end, it was Lartey who lost in the fourth round. Afterwards, he, who had lost once before, would lose his next four.

Dubois lost his sixteenth fight, which was against Joe Joyce in London, when he went to the floor in the tenth round and stayed there, resting on his knee as the referee counted him out. He seemed no longer willing to fight, and his eye was grossly swollen and closed from a broken socket. There were questions about Dubois's tenacity afterwards, and more were raised after uninspiring wins over third- and fourth-rated fighters. There was a bright spot when he won the vacant WBA (Regular) title against Trevor Bryan in Florida – Usyk being the WBA's Super champion – but then he was knocked down three times in the first round against Kevin Lerena in London, a situation he managed to right in the third by technical knockout.

Fighting against Usyk was a good match for Dubois, who had won nineteen and lost one. It may have seemed early, but the loss against Joyce and the bumpy road since indicated that his career was not set to reach the highs it once promised. And if that were the case, he was either going to make a lot of money for one night, more than he had ever made before, or he was going to walk away with his hands on most of the heavyweight belts.

Oleksandr Usyk may have been the greatest cruiserweight in history, but there was debate over whether he was the best or second-best heavyweight in the world. Such is the nature of boxing.

Usyk was thirty-six years old and came from Ukraine. He had won an Olympic gold in the 200lb division at the 2012 Olympics, then turned professional the following year in Kyiv. But after 2015, his matches had been held solely on foreign soil. He won the WBO cruiserweight title in a decision over Krzysztof Glowacki in Gdańsk, Poland, and defended it against Thabiso Mchunu and Michael Hunter in the US and Marco Huck in Germany. He then unified against WBC cruiserweight champion Mairis Briedis in Latvia and picked up more belts against Murat Gassiev in Moscow and Tony Bellew in Manchester. He then moved to heavyweight with wins over fringe contenders Chazz Witherspoon and Derek Chisora in Chicago and London before fighting Anthony Joshua twice for a set of championships.

But while Usyk was a modern great, there was little light as to who the best heavyweight on the planet was. The consensus champion in 2015 had been the Ukrainian Wladimir Klitschko. He lost to Tyson Fury on points in Düsseldorf, but then Fury had gone into retirement for three years, and a host of other fighters had won, lost or been stripped of the belts. By some quirky default, the best two during that run were Anthony Joshua and Deontay Wilder, but then Fury had come back. Joshua then lost to Andy Ruiz and Usyk. Wilder drew against Fury, who had somehow become an underdog. Fury then beat Wilder decisively, twice.

It was confusing, although it did not need to be. By 2023, there were four to six heavyweights at the top of the division, with a plethora of good second-tier fighters, all of whom promised great matches.

But those matches were not being made. When Usyk and Dubois met, Fury was set to match a former UFC fighter called Francis Ngannou in Saudi Arabia, Joshua had just knocked out fringe contender Robert Helenius after a last-minute abortion of a second fight against contender Dillian Whyte, and Deontay Wilder – well, no one knew what he was doing after knocking out Helenius in one round the previous October.

Usyk–Dubois was made against this background. And it made sense. Professional boxing is less a sport than showbusiness with blood, and the event was essentially a homecoming fight for Usyk. And, despite his popularity, 40,000 people would not pay to watch him shadowbox, so the call had gone to Dubois.

The phrase 'heavyweight championship of the world' still has weight and significance. It is a phrase that sits in the veins, passed from one generation to the next. In the '20s and '30s, it was a yardstick against which all other men were measured – and judged to be inferior. It was an unspoken and commonly held belief that the heavyweight champion of the world could beat any other man in the room, no matter where that room was.

Its lustre had been stripped in recent decades as other combat sports rose in prominence and its titles became fragmented. It also hid itself away from crowds, stuck on pay-per-view, and the seat of the heavyweight champion receded from the bright lights and big audiences of the US to Germany and the rest of Europe.

But it still held something special. People still remembered. And it is true that every band eventually becomes its own tribute act. The Rolling Stones may not be the Stones of the '60s, but they are still the Stones. An audience would still pack an auditorium to hear a croaky Sinatra sing a lullaby or two.

The rain had begun to fall an hour earlier, and it soaked everything and everyone. It fell in long, straight lines onto the heads of those not under the parapets. But it was not cold, and when you got wet, you were not uncomfortable. And you did not care, because you were ringside for the heavyweight championship of the world.

Everyone tried their best to get beneath the shelter erected above the ring, but most gave up and stood in the rain, so the seats out where the football pitch usually was were largely empty.

Ring announcer Michael Buffer stepped out into the centre of the ring. There are many ring announcers, but Buffer sits on a level by himself. He had, by 2023, seemed to have been part of boxing – and, in particular, big-time boxing – since the first ape thousands of years before men walked the earth had put on gloves to punch another ape.

'Ladies and gentlemen,' he said, and this was the true start of the heavyweight championship of the world, 'at this time, we have a very special message. We are moments away from our main event. At this time, your attention please, as the message comes from the President of Ukraine – Volodmyr Zelensky.'

And then Zelensky was on screens around the arena. He stood in his office, bearded and wearing his now-iconic army-green T-shirt. A Ukrainian flag hung behind him. He addressed the world in accented English, and he stumbled over some stilted words and phrases.

'Hello, Poland,' he said. 'Hello, everyone who are with us now. Tonight, Wrocław will witness something very special. Ukrainians, Brits, Poles and the whole world, tonight on the eve of the 550th day since the full-scale Russian invasion has started. And we keep standing, and Ukraine is fighting because of the strengths of our people, as mighty as Oleksandr Usyk, the strengths of our friends, as solid as Daniel Dubois, the strengths of our will for victory as powerful as all the help we received from the people of the world. The world which always supports fair battle and not unjustified aggression. I thank each and every one who are with us tonight. And until that victory, Ukraine's victory, my warmest thanks to you, people of Wrocław and Poland for standing with us. Glory to Ukraine. *Slava Ukraini*.'

There is no other contest in the world between two men in which the leader of a war-plagued nation would take time beforehand to address.

Slava Ukraini.

A video package played for Daniel Dubois, and then he came to the ring. He wore purple-and-black robes, and he smiled when he walked through the crowd to 'So Much Things to Say' by Bob Marley and the Wailers, and the words of the song played on his lips as he sang them.

Dubois went into the ring and moved around it, hopping and skipping to test the feel of the floor beneath his feet. He raised one hand as he walked around.

Buffer stepped forward and introduced the champion. 'Now, making his way to the ring, from Ukraine – Oleksandr Usyk!'

Another package, and then Usyk left his dressing room, went down the corridor and walked towards the stadium. 'We are fighting for our freedom and our country,' he said on the video package. 'This victory will be for my people, the heroes of Ukraine.'

The song 'Brothers' began, and its singer, the Ukrainian star Vasyl Ivanovych Zhadan, sang (or mimed) to the crowd. Blue and yellow lights began to bathe the stadium.

Usyk walked out along the same path that Dubois had taken minutes before. His head had been shaved for previous fights, and his moustache had given him the appearance of a pirate. But he wore his hair longer now, and he had lost the flamboyance of his earlier ring attire, sacrificing helmets and robes for a simple white T-shirt with a graphic on the front and his name on the back. He wore one blue boot and one yellow boot.

A crashing noise came over the speakers, the music stopped, and Buffer introduced the national anthems of the United Kingdom and Ukraine. The first was played over a speaker, the second was performed live.

The crowd began to sing. Some flashed peace signs. There was no music, just a choir of tens of thousands of displaced refugees, singing for home.

There was a moment of silence, then Buffer stepped forward again. 'Ladies and gentlemen, this is the moment we've been waiting for,' he said. He went through the long list of promotional companies. 'Champion versus champion. Twelve rounds of boxing for the unified heavyweight championship of the world.'

Buffer ran through some sponsors, along with the referees and judges. The rain continued to fall.

'The man in charge of the action,' said Buffer, 'world champion veteran referee from Puerto Rico – Luis Pabon. And now the officials are ready. The fighters are in the ring, and they are ready. So, for the thousands in attendance and the millions watching around the world, ladies and gentlemen… LET'S GET READY TO RUMBLE!'

Dubois's trainer began to unzip his robe. 'Introducing first, fighting out of the red corner,' said Buffer, 'wearing purple and black. Official weight 105.8kg, or 223.2lbs. His professional record, an outstanding one – 20 fights, 19 victories, including 18 of those 19 wins by knockout, with only 1 defeat. He's the former Commonwealth champion, former WBC silver belt champion, former WBO international champion. From London, United Kingdom, the reigning and defending WBA champion of the world – "Dynamite" Daniel Dubois!'

Dubois was shirtless, now, and he hopped and jumped around the ring. He pumped his arms, banged his gloves together then raised his hands into the air.

'And across the ring,' continued Buffer, 'fighting out of the blue corner, wearing white and officially weighing in at 100.2kg or 220.9lbs. His professional record – a perfect one – 20 fights, 20 victories, 13 big wins by knockout. He is the former undisputed, undefeated, cruiserweight world champion, fighting out of and fighting for the people of Ukraine. Presenting the reigning defending, undefeated, unified IBF, IBO, WBA, WBO heavyweight champion of the world – Oleksandr Usyk!'

Water continued to swirl down through the air. Usyk and Dubois came together in the centre of the ring to hear the final instructions from the referee. They were relatively small amongst the heavy-weights, the bigger ones like Joshua, Fury and Wilder all weighing 245lbs or more, but they remained near-giants amongst normal men.

They went back to their corners, and then the bell rang, and they went to fight.

Usyk was a southpaw; Dubois, orthodox. The gameplan in such a match would be to own the lateral space – the left side for the orthodox, the right side for the southpaw. Usyk was looking to move to the outside of Dubois's leading foot, his jab in Dubois's face, looking to throw his left hand straight into the gap occupied by his opponent's middle. Dubois would also be seeking to put his lead left foot on the outside, taking away Usyk's jab and throwing his right hand into the space Usyk's middle occupied.

There was not much to differentiate them in the first round, which on home soil meant it would go for Usyk. The occasional jab from Usyk had flicked back the head of Dubois.

Usyk moved backwards a little more in the second, and he began to signal to the referee that Dubois's punches were straying low. Dubois threw an uppercut near the end of the round that landed, but he was stiff and moved in straight lines towards Usyk.

The crowd were wet now, but few cared as their clothes became damp and heavy, and the rain continued to hit the shelter above the ring and run from it in torrents.

Usyk threw more jabs in the third, and they caught Dubois at the end of their orbit, more of an irritant than a blow. He moved and slipped what came back, and put his own punches into the gaps.

He complained again when Dubois hit him to the body, and the referee gave an informal warning but let them fight on.

Dubois seemed troubled at the end of the round as Usyk's punches whipped and lashed at him. He was not being hurt, but he was frustrated. He seemed a man growing increasingly irritated and disappointed that he was not able to offer anything that could change things.

Usyk began to dominate in the fourth round, happy that Dubois had nothing to trouble him with. A right hand from Dubois threatened a little but meant nothing, and Usyk jabbed and moved. He was behaving like a man about to slip from a second gear into a third, and from there, whenever he wanted, into a fourth gear, then a fifth, then a sixth. He began to throw his left hand, too, crossing it into the short distance between them, announcing its arrival, letting Dubois know if it was not quite there, then it was coming.

The low blow came in the fifth. Dubois threw a right hand to Usyk's body, and it landed on the beltline, and the Ukrainian was down. It looked from ringside as if his ankle had twisted in the fall, and that this would become a championship fight that would end with a victory for a champion still on the floor. Usyk's hands shook, and he gulped at air. He moved his head from side to side.

Pabon said the blow was low, and that he would give Usyk time to recover. 'You've got five minutes, OK?' he said, then turned to the judges. 'It was a non-intentional foul,' he said.

Usyk got to his feet and placed one hand on the rope. The crowd roared, but for some minutes the fight looked over.

Dubois stood in a neutral corner, and he moved and flexed his shoulders.

'Come on, let's go. Let's go!' Pabon said. The crowd began to yell. Chants of *Usyk* began to roll around the stadium. The crowd waited.

The referee gave Usyk another minute, but then the Ukrainian crossed himself and stepped forward into the middle of the ring, and he had won the crowd and his championship.

Pabon asked the fighters for a clean fight, and they went back to it. Usyk moved backwards, and he stumbled once, and he moved, and he slipped while Dubois pushed and pushed at him.

And then he was back, the heavyweight champion of the world, and he put his jab once more into the face of Dubois, and he started to light up the ring with his punches.

A right hook made Dubois go backwards, and then the punches from Usyk began to cross over, tracing lines across the tense air. The bell went and they fought after it, punches still going, and the referee stopped it.

Dubois's shoulders began to sag. It was not going to be his night.

The rest of the fight became a channel to the end. Usyk hit Dubois when he wanted to. And Dubois slipped down his own gears and became a man who knew his best was no match for the man in front of him.

Dubois's hands dropped in the seventh, and he rolled around the ring as each punch landed against him. He bled psychically from Usyk's scalpel, and he went into the eighth throwing his most-powerful punches. It was a sign of being defeated.

The combinations began. One, two, three, four. Usyk landed them and, with the contempt of a matador in the final *tercio*, he barely moved after they landed.

Dubois went to one knee at the end of the eighth round, and he seemed to want to escape the three or four punches that whipped around his head. He got back up, and the bell went, and he was back in his corner, and the end was coming.

The rain had stopped. Or, at least, no one felt it. Loud rock music rolled out around the stadium, but few paid it attention.

It was over in the ninth. Usyk landed punches against Dubois with the finesse of a painter applying the last strokes to a masterpiece. It was a hook and a jab. Jab, jab, jab. Then a final jab.

Dubois went to his knee, and he watched the referee count in front of him, and he got up when it was over and he had lost, and he walked defeated to his corner.

The cheers began, and the hands of the crowd went into the air. Usyk walked around the ring, and Dubois sat shrunken on his stool. A towel was pushed against his nose. Bodies began to mass on the canvas.

It was a few minutes later and Usyk stood in the ring with his gloves off. His friends came and embraced him. He looked like a man who had just gone for a light run and encountered a steeper hill than he had expected.

The crowd had already begun to disperse, feeding out from the stadium into the early morning.

Michael Buffer took the microphone. 'Ladies and gentlemen,' he said, 'here in Wrocław, Polska, referee Luis Pabon reaches the count of ten at forty-eight seconds of round nine. The winner, by KO victory, still undefeated, still the unified heavyweight champion of the world, fighting for the people and nation of Ukraine – Oleksandr Usyk!'

It took some time for anyone to appear at the press conference, but the first to arrive was Dubois's promoter, Frank Warren. Warren, who ran Queensberry Promotions, was angry. They were lodging an appeal, he said, with the authorities to have the bout ruled a no-contest or, at the least, have an immediate rematch ordered.

The ruling of a low blow in the fifth, he said, was wrong. Dubois should have won by knockout for a shot to the body.

'No cry-baby stuff,' said Warren. 'Fine. We're here, and all we want is a fair shake. And we didn't get it. We didn't get it at all. But, look, we could go on about it all night long. What is going to happen is I've said, and I'm confident that once all the evidence is reviewed and so forth, they will either declare it a no-contest or order an immediate rematch.'

Dubois did not appear. He was, his team said, so distraught that he had left the building.

Dubois spoke to the BBC a day later. His face and head were bruised, and his voice was soft and gentle. He raised a hand to his head when he spoke.

He said, 'I've seen it. I looked at it and you know I was there. I threw the shot and I felt it land perfectly, smack, into his stomach. They just cheated out of it … He weren't gonna make it in time. He was out. That should have been a knockout. And I think you know that this needs to go further. It needs to be pushed, and this wrong needs to be corrected because I should be a world champion right now.'[2]

It seemed that Dubois was a frontrunner, the type of fighter who can only win when they are ahead. Once they trail into the slip-stream of their opponent, they lose their bearings. They may fear to lose, but the process of losing is a foreign country to them.

The blow in the fifth *was* below the belt. The blow in the fifth *was not* below the belt. Both views were right. Both were true. And both were unimportant. What *was* important was that the referee had ruled it to be below the belt, and it was incumbent upon Dubois at that point, fighting for the heavyweight championship of the world, to find an alternative route to victory.

That he did not is what divided him from a championship that night.

There was no easing of the rain afterwards. It continued to fall on the stadium for hours, and it drenched the spectators on their way home. It ran down the roofs and onto the streets and into the gutters of Wrocław, and it washed everything away, and it made everything clean. The air returned to vibrate at its normal frequency.

It had not been a memorable fight. Apart from the low blow, few would speak in the following years of Usyk–Dubois. Amongst the stories of the heavyweights in the 2020s, it will be little more than a footnote, a punctuation mark at the end of a sentence. A champion fought dominantly against an inferior opponent brought too quickly into a title fight. And the champion won.

But it was still the heavyweight championship of the world. And it still meant something.

THE GATEKEEPER

Wrocław, Poland, August 2023. Anthony Yigit may have been the opponent that evening, but he was happy because he liked to fight.

There was history between him and Denys Berinchyk. They had fought a close fight in the Olympics in 2012 and then gone their separate ways professionally. It was, Yigit insisted, a fight he always wanted to have on the professional side. He was now going to have it in front of more than 35,000 people.

And he was aware he was fighting an undefeated Ukrainian two days after the Ukrainian Day of Independence, in a stadium in a city that had just recently seen an influx of Ukrainians fleeing Russian aggression. And he, being a Swede, was aware that he was supposed to lose and make the hometown guy look good.

But he was still happy; he liked to fight.

He liked Berinchyk as well, as much as one person could like another who they barely knew. He liked him despite the loss in the Olympics. And he liked him even though he was being brought in to fight and be competitive but, ultimately, lose.

'He was tough, very tough in the Olympics,' he said, looking over the crowd. 'It was a case of two hard heads clashing. But this time around, I think it's going to be one hard head against a smart head. The smart head is me.'

Berinchyk had the credentials to be a tough guy. He had fought a Russian, a former UFC fighter named Artem Lobov, the year before in a bareknuckle bout.

Yigit pointed at himself. 'I know what to expect,' he said, 'but I don't think he does.'

He arrived, left the tools of his trade in the dressing room and went out with his family, friends and coach into the crowd. It was seven o'clock and he would be fighting in a few hours.

Yigit's mother, sister, brother and fiancée were with him, along with coach Redouane Kaya, his friend Bryan Shacklady and his manager Conor Slater. They walked almost unseen through the crowd and into his dressing room, deep in the stadium.

He had the room to himself. It was about ten metres long by three metres wide, with lockers and a bench down one wall. A bathroom adjoined the room. The team picked up a table by the door and moved it to the back.

His shorts lay on the bench, clean and ironed, the words 'LEGACY' and 'DIG IT' stitched onto them. His shoes, standing on the floor, were worn, having moved miles across canvas.

It was nearly eight o'clock. Fight time was in ninety minutes.

He had been an Olympian, drifting into boxing from kickboxing. Then he had turned professional. The fight in Poland marked over ten years on the professional side. He had been the European champion, defending twice.

The honest assessment of his career was that he had been good-but-not-great, much better than the man on the street or the libidinous amateur who has hit a few bags and thinks he knows a thing or two. But Yigit had come up short in the thinner air of the professional ranks.

He had 27 wins, 3 losses and 1 draw. And he was not a big puncher, having stopped only ten men. The twenty-seven victories told one part of the story. The other side of his ledger told the rest of it. His sixth professional fight had ended in a draw against Tony Pace, who had won four and lost five, would lose two more and then retire. Then Yigit had won steadily after that until he was invited to take part in a fight for the vacant IBF light-welterweight title in New Orleans, as part of the World Boxing Super Series. He lost that one on an injury, his left eye bulging grossly and he unable to see.

Then he won three more and was asked to go to San Antonio to face Rolando Romero, who had knocked out eleven of his twelve opponents and never lost. Romero kept dropping that right hand in, and Yigit took it, and then he was down in the fifth and the seventh. That was a loss that hurt on multiple frequencies.

But then he won another two, against foes who were OK, before going back to the US to fight for some vacant titles that might have meant something to someone, but he lost that fight too, when Keyshawn Davis stopped him in nine.

So, he bided his time for a few months and took on a body called Jacob Quinn, in a hotel in Malmo, and he won that on points. Now, he was in Poland.

Shacklady was a commercial litigation lawyer from London. He and Yigit had met in a UK gym, where the latter was teaching boxing. They had become friends, and Shacklady had helped extricate Yigit from a contract.

'I don't understand these contracts,' Yigit said, 'so I sent it to Bryan. And he told me, "OK, if you win your next fight, then it means that these other promoters own you for some fights." The promoter asked me if I wanted to fight, and I said I would if the contract was right. So the promoter signed it for me, and said he could do that. I sent it to Bryan, and he said he couldn't.'

Shacklady said, 'Then they sent us a letter from some lawyers in London that was trying to scare us off.' He smiled. 'It was a good letter, definitely the type of letter that I would have written.'

Shacklady liked Yigit immensely and genuinely. 'It would be good to bring out how intelligent Anthony is, how people think that boxing's a stupid person's sport, but actually it demands very high-level thinking and so sometimes you find boxers who are very interesting people. On the day of the fight, Anthony and I were walking around talking about whether the UK should maintain a nuclear deterrent, the history of Wrocław, Lebanese food, Indian food and God knows what else. He soaks up everything and he teaches me stuff all the time.'

Yigit was a professional fighter. He was scheduled to fight again six weeks later in Denmark, against someone called David Rajulli, who had 13 wins, 11 losses and 1 draw.

'Here's the thing with Scandinavian boxing,' he said. 'It's very small. So I've made a promise to most of the promoters in Scandinavia that I'll fight on their shows. Even if it barely pays anything, I'll fight on the shows. Just to keep the boxing going.'

He still thought he could be a world champion. 'I'd like to go for a title again,' he said. 'I've done it twice. I'm still out there, still having good fights. I put on a good show. I've had some bad luck with management problems and Covid, which meant I wasn't fighting. And then when I did get fights, I wasn't prepared for them. I had to take them for the money. But it feels like it is all behind me now. I can focus on training.'

He was to be paid €28,000 for the fight. No Polish fighter, he said, had wanted it, so the call had come to him. 'They offered me less, but I wanted more,' he said. 'We met somewhere in the middle.'

'I've been doing nothing but training for this fight,' he said. 'I've been training, I was fit, but I wasn't fighting fit. You need to polish your art in the ring, and I wasn't doing that. But I've done it this time. We have a great plan and I'm very confident. Everyone says there's a different aura around me. I can feel it, too. I think it's going to be an upset because people see him beating me, but I don't see that happening.'

Some members of Berinchyk's team came in just after eight o'clock. They had come to watch the cutman tape Yigit's hands. The smaller, more vocal of the two knew Yigit.

'You remember me?'

Yigit looked at him for a few seconds, then clicked his fingers and pointed. He smiled. 'Crimea? We were in the training camp together?'

'Yeah, that's it.' They hugged.

'It's been a long time, man. You good?'

'Yeah, I'm good.'

The wrist wrapped, the cutman laid a pad of gauze on top of Yigit's knuckles, then began to tape it in place. He began to lay the strips between Yigit's fingers, then took a pair of scissors and trimmed at the loose, fat edges.

An inspector from the WBO entered the room. He wore a bright blue suit with running shoes and spoke in accented English.

Yigit picked up the scissors and laid them between the knuckles in the middle of his hand. The sharp, lethal end of the scissors pointed out. 'This is OK, yeah?'

The inspector smiled. 'Sure. As long as it's just the one.'

'Where are you from?' said Yigit.

'Hamburg.'

'Hamburg? I lived in Germany for a bit. I can speak German.'

'You can?'

'Yeah, man.' He spoke with the inspector in German for a few minutes. Then, turning to the room, he said, 'How many professional boxers do you know who can speak six languages? Can't be many.'

The first Ukrainian smiled at him. 'Is one of them bullshit?'

Everyone, including Yigit, laughed. For the record, he spoke at length in four languages that night – Swedish, English, German and Turkish – so the benefit of the doubt would put that at six.

Yigit picked up his phone. 'You like music?' he asked the Ukrainian.

'Yeah.'

'You stick with me, I got the best tunes.' He put on a song. 'You like it?' he asked, nodding his head.

'It's cool, man,' said the Ukrainian.

The first hand was finished. Yigit flexed it. 'Hey,' he said to the cutman. 'You want some Instagram love?'

He took a picture. 'I'll do something with that later,' he said. 'How're you guys doing?' he said to the Ukrainians. 'It must be difficult to leave.'

The Ukrainian nodded. 'Yeah. It's hard to get out.'

'I'm sorry, man.'

The Ukrainian shrugged. 'Fuck Russia.'

'Yeah, fuck Russia.'

The Ukrainian shook his head. 'We are completely different nations. We are Ukrainian, not Russian. But it's OK, because we will win. We are not Russian. We will fight and will win.'

'Lots of Russians hate Putin,' said Yigit.

'They do. And they're against this war.'

Both hands were wrapped by eight-thirty, and the wraps were signed. The inspector looked over his shoulder as he left the room. 'And no scissors!' he said.

Yigit called after him. 'We don't need them!'

A member of the promotional team came in soon after with some gloves. He handed a pair to Yigit. He unwrapped the plastic from them and tried them on. 'These will do,' he said.

'You want to try the others?'

'No, I'm good.'

The team merrily went about destroying and breaking down the leather on the new gloves. They put them on their hands and punched the walls, they crushed and bent the knuckle part as much as they could, they twisted and turned the main heft of the glove. At one point, Shacklady put the gloves down on one of the benches, laid his knee upon them and pressed down with all his weight.

'Is there a rule against this?' asked Shacklady.

Yigit looked at him, smiled. 'There's no rule that says we *can't* do it,' he said.

The inspector came in and saw the gloves being flattened on the bench. He smiled. 'I didn't see anything,' he said, then left.

Yigit put the gloves on. They were tight when being drawn over his hands. 'It's the friction,' he said. The laces were tied.

Kaya held up his hands. Yigit hit them to check the gloves. He nodded. 'They'll do,' he said. He took the gloves off again.

The referee entered the room to give his instructions. 'This is for twelve rounds,' he said. 'I want a good, clean fight. Protect yourself at all times. Always face your opponent. Anything below the belly button is a low blow. If I say "break", you take one step back. If there's an eight-count, I want you to walk over to the neutral corner.'

Yigit nodded.

'OK,' the referee said. 'Then I wish you all the best, and good luck!'

Yigit turned to Shacklady. 'You've got the water?' he said.

Shacklady nodded. He held up about ten bottles of water, wrapped in plastic. 'Yes.'

'OK, I don't want too much in the fight. I don't like to get drenched. I'll put my head back, you put in a little bit, and when I begin to move my head back down, you stop. OK?'

'OK.'

Yigit went into the small bathroom next to the main room. He took some Vaseline and rubbed it around his ears and over his eyes, down the sides of his face. Kaya took some and rubbed it on Yigit's chest and back.

Yigit and Kaya began to move together in the narrow room. They moved quickly, and Yigit threw fast punches that tapped lightly against Kaya's shoulders. Kaya slapped back, his fingers touching Yigit lightly in the body and arms.

They sped up. Yigit bumped his leg off the bench. It was a glancing blow.

'Don't get injured now,' said Kaya, laughing.

The referee came back into the room, along with an inspector from the Polish Boxing Union. They watched Yigit put on the gloves for the final time then signed the tape around the wrists.

'You've got about twenty minutes,' someone from the promotion said.

Yigit turned and began to punch the wall, the air hissing from his gloves with every impact. Some smears of yellow ink from the gloves began to appear on the plaster.

There was a knock on the door a little after nine-thirty, and a muffled voice said, 'It's fight time!'

The team went out into the corridor and turned right. They passed through the media centre and went into a holding area. 'Hey Jude' by The Beatles could be heard rumbling over the speakers.

The sound cut out and someone from the production yelled, 'Gents!'

Yigit and his team stepped out into the stadium and stopped. There was a wide walkway to the ring.

The master of ceremonies began to introduce a video package. Yigit walked to his left and touched gloves with some in the crowd. He went back to the middle, waited a second during the video, then went to his right and bumped gloves with more fans. The TV production crew ushered him back into the centre.

Then, we were walking. Yigit put one arm around his brother. They waved to the crowd. There were some boos and some cheers. As they got closer, the walkway thinned and there was no barrier between the crowd and the team, and Yigit stopped a few yards before the ring to kiss his partner, Elin.

The fight was for the World Boxing Organization's international lightweight title. It meant something to someone, but mostly it meant some more money for the WBO.

Berinchyk looked bigger, and he seemed more compact in the chest and shoulders. He came forwards in the first round, standing as a southpaw against Yigit, and he slipped once halfway through on the wet canvas.

Yigit moved, staying on the edges of the ring. He shifted and tried to draw Berinchyk into hitting him, and it turned ugly at the end of the round when they clinched and grabbed at each other.

Berinchyk switched to an orthodox stance in the opening seconds of the next round, and he pushed and bundled Yigit back. The referee separated them, told them to step away from each other. Yigit jabbed to distract then threw quick punches.

Berinchyk settled into a rhythm in the third, and Yigit began to just hold his opponent off in the fourth. He threw in flurries, and he seemed to be settling himself into becoming reactive to the moves of his opponent. He countered and seemed to be winning the round.

A cut appeared over Yigit's eye in the fifth from a clash of heads. He had been cut before, and this was not as bad. It began to trickle and pour down his face, circling the socket. He went to his right, and he dashed in and out, throwing quickly on the inside. It was a risky plan. He could get hurt in those seconds when he was close, and he could lose the favour of the judges for being on the back foot so much.

Blood began to appear from his nose in the sixth. Yigit was not getting beaten up, but he was getting beaten.

Cries of 'Berinchyk' began to be blown up into the air as if by bellows.

Yigit's face began to shift in the eight, and it looked like something had been lost from it. Did he know that he was losing? His white shorts began to stain with blood in the ninth, and his jabs became weak, were countered.

The rain began to fall in the tenth, drops falling onto the crowd. A combination shook Yigit in the round.

They began to trade in the last few minutes, punching wildly the way a gambler speeds up on his bets when he is desperate. Yigit began to throw from a place beyond caution, and he gave all of himself. Most men were reminded of their cowardice and had to look away.

Yigit and Berinchyk came to the centre of the ring after the bell, and the referee held them by the wrists. Yigit held one hand in the air. Berinchyk did the same. The scores were 117–111, 115–113, and 116–112, all for Berinchyk.

Yigit was already swelling when he got back to the changing room, and the blood dripped from above his left eye. His arms and his chest were bruised, his shorts soaked in sweat and stained pink with blood. He was limping.

He took off his shoes, left them on the floor. His cutman came over and cut the wraps from his hands. His family applauded.

Slater came into the room. 'Hell of a fight,' he said. 'I would have given it to you. You won, but you were never going to get the decision.'

Yigit smiled. His leg jittered. 'Can you get me another fight?'

'Sure.'

'I had five weeks for this,' Yigit said. 'You get me another five, I can put more effort into the training.' He looked around the room. 'Now, *that* was the main event,' he said.

Shacklady nodded. 'I think it was a good fight.'

'It was a *very* good fight.'

'You looked great… compared to last time.'

Yigit's mother came and sat next to him. He picked up her hand and kissed it.

'I'm alright, mama,' he said. He looked at the room, nodded at her. 'She doesn't want me to fight.'

His mother shook her head. 'No, no…' she said.

'It's OK. I'm where I should be. I'm happy and healthy.' He smiled at her.

Representatives from the Voluntary Anti-Doping Association (VADA), which is generally considered to be the best agency for testing fighters for substances, came into the room for a urine sample. 'I need to shower quickly,' Yigit said. 'That'll help.'

'We'll have to watch you.'

'OK.'

He showered quickly, then tried to urinate. There was not much there.

'How much do you need?' he asked.

'About half a cup.'

That was difficult. He reached for a bottle. 'OK, I'll drink more,' he said.

'No, not that one,' a VADA worker said. 'I don't know if it's yours, but the cap is broken.' She pointed to another, unopened, bottle. 'Take that one instead.'

'OK.'

Slater stood in the corridor outside, where it was cooler. Fighters and members of the media passed by. 'This was a good fight for Anthony,' he said. 'Big show, and he did a good twelve rounds. I'll get him more fights. He's always up for it, always training, and he's the guy who's been at the fringes of world class, so he's going to get a lot of offers from people wanting to test their guys.'

Yigit had still not been able to urinate enough. There was gauze on top of the cut above his eye and some more gauze to the side of his head. There was a white, webbed net that he wore to keep it all in place. Some blood from above his left eye had begun to seep through the gauze.

His right eye was engorged, and the skin beneath it and the left eye was pink and swollen. He had changed into a burgundy tracksuit.

An hour went by, and one of the medical staff came in. 'You need stitches,' they said.

'Can you do them here?'

'No, we don't have the stuff here. You need to go to hospital.'

'When I've been cut in Germany and Denmark, they could just stitch me at the arena.'

'Not here. We don't have the stuff.'

'This is a boxing event, and you don't have the stuff to stitch me with?'

'No. You need to go to hospital for that.'

'OK. Where is the ambulance?'

'No ambulance. You need to get yourself there. Take a cab.'

'You don't have an ambulance?'

'We have one, but it's for life-threatening injuries.'

'I have to take a cab?'

The news went out to Slater. He was angry and came back in. 'What do you mean you can't take him to hospital? If he was in the street looking like this, you wouldn't hesitate.'

'It's for life-threatening injuries only.'

'He's just been punched repeatedly for thirty-six minutes. That is life-threatening.'

'I'm sorry. We can't. We only have one ambulance.'

'This is ridiculous. Why are you here? What is the point of you?'

'This is all we can do.'

'OK, we're going to need to speak to your boss.'

The medical staff left. They came back a few minutes later. It had now been three hours since Yigit's fight had finished. 'OK,' the paramedic said. 'The main fight's over. No one's hurt. We can take you now in the ambulance.'

Yigit pushed himself off the bench. 'What about the VADA stuff?'

'We'll come with you. One of us will go in the ambulance, and I'll follow in my car.'

The ambulance took him to the hospital and left him there. It was nine o'clock in the morning before he got home. Nobody from the promoters went with or checked on him.

THINGS LEARNED IN TIME

There comes a time when you realise that your heroes are not superheroes. Empathy is difficult when the subject is under the bright lights. There is no connection between you and them. And everything begins to turn in you when you realise how human they are.

There is a point when you realise that fighters get bruised, they get cut, they *hurt*.

It was 2005 and I was at the George Carnall Leisure Centre in Manchester to watch Jamie Moore defend his British light-middleweight championship against London's David Walker. The match took place in a cramped sports hall, under bright lights, and was being broadcast on Sky Sports.

Moore remains the best fighter never to have gotten a world-title fight. Throughout his career, he seemed to consistently get within an arm's grasp of a world-title challenge then lose.

He was fast and fluid and exciting, a British Arturo Gatti. And he could punch as well, winning twenty-four by knockout. He got all the way to the European title, which is a good stepping stone, but lost in the seventh round of a defence to Ryan Rhodes. Rhodes, meanwhile, fought two fights to make up the time then went to Mexico to fight Saul 'Canelo' Alvarez.

Moore might not have won a fight against Canelo. But he should have had it.

I was there to watch Jamie Moore that night, but my attention was drawn to someone else. There was a young lad in front of me, in his early twenties, and he did not cheer or clap, but he shook and cried at times. One of his friends put his arm around him.

'Is he OK?' I asked the friend.

He pointed at David Walker, who had just entered the ring. 'That's his brother in there.'

The fight was never competitive, although Walker tried his best. Moore knocked him down in the third at the end of the round and again at the beginning of the fourth. The towel came in then.

Walker's younger brother put his head down between his knees and began to sob. A few hundred people around him were cheering.

Afterwards, I walked past the brother near the entrance to the building. He was leaning against a table, and he looked pale, nauseous. A kind, older man went over to him and touched him on his arm. 'Your brother's going to be OK,' he said. 'He did well in there.'

Another thing you learn is that fighters are also gentle. It seems like an oxymoron, but they are. When you spend your life getting hit, any meanness gets beaten out of you. You invite comfort. You look for kindness in others.

One time, I was at the Fitzroy Lodge in London when one of the people I was training with brought in his little boy. The boy was about three or four years old and had come to watch his dad train. So the fighters put gloves on the kid, got into the ring with him and promptly all got 'knocked out' by the little one.

They were kind and they were gentle. They hugged that little boy and tried to make him feel special. They made him part of the joke and they made him laugh. And then they got back to the business of hurting each other.

And fighters give. A few years ago, I wanted to write about fighters and fighting, and I reached out to the boxer Erik Skoglund. Erik invited me up to Sweden to visit him and see him train, and then he sat for a few hours so we could talk, and then we hugged afterwards.

I went away and wrote the story in two parts and when it was published, Erik reached out and told me how much he had enjoyed it and how he appreciated so much that I had written with grace about him. He said he would do anything to help in the future.

So when I was writing this book, I reached out to follow up on the piece and we spoke again. And then he asked me what the rest of the book was about.

'They're all love stories,' I told him.

'Seriously, what's it really about?'

'OK, I'm just spending my time doing cool things in boxing and then persuading some fools to publish my writing about it.'

'Yeah, that sounds more like you,' he said. 'What's next?'

'I'm off to Poland in a few weeks to watch Usyk–Dubois.'

'Really?'

'Yeah.'

'Oh, man, if I'd known... My friend Anthony Yigit is going to be there. I was supposed to be in the corner, but I can't make it.'

'That's a shame.'

'Shall I put you guys in touch? It'll be good for your book.'

'Yeah, if that's OK.'

'No problem, man. No problem.'

Erik gave me Anthony's number and I reached out a few days later. I explained the book and what I wanted to do, and that I appreciated it was a huge ask, especially when he was arguably going to be on the biggest stage of his life.

'Yeah,' he wrote back in a message. 'I'm definitely up for helping you however you want!'

Months later, I sent him the artwork for *Death of a Boxer* and its release date.

'When your book comes out and I get a fight in the UK,' he wrote back, 'we're gonna promote the shit out of it. On my shorts and everything!'

Neither Erik nor Anthony had to help me. They drew nothing

from it. There was no profit or bonus for them, no quarter in their aiding me in writing this book.

It was the same with all the fighters who appear in this book. They all helped when they did not need to.

And they often help each other.

Weeks after I wrote my first stories on Erik, I spoke again with Joe Mesi. He had undergone a similar journey.

'I spoke with Erik this morning,' I told Joe, 'and he said that he may like to talk with you at some point. Would it be OK to pass on your contact details?'

Mesi replied. 'It would be my pleasure,' he wrote, 'and an honour to speak to Erik.'

Mesi had wanted to give. Not because there was something to be gained, but because there was something that he could do.

FIGHTING FROM THE AWAY CORNER

Madrid, Spain, September 2021. The bullring in Valdemoro, a small town of rust-and-yellow-coloured buildings on the outskirts of the city that lies past the industrial zone, is a working bullring. The changing room for the fighters that night was the place where, after each fight, dead cattle are dragged in and hung from a pulley on the ceiling. It was not hard to imagine the clean floor often slicked with blood.

When Brian Rose entered the room that night, there was no blood on the floor, just old strips of grey tape and gauze that had been pulled and ripped from the hands of those on the undercard.

He sat down on a cheap plastic chair, his hands on the back of another in front of him, a small towel taped to its slats. His trainer

Bobby Rimmer was wrapping his hands. They had their own corner by themselves, their equipment piled on a table next to them.

Rose was nervous. His leg shuddered and tapped against the grey, speckled tile of the floor.

'This is going to be your night,' said Rimmer. 'I really believe in you. Martinez has seen you. He's seen that you're in great shape. Everything we've done. Everything. It's all fitting together like a jigsaw.'

Rimmer was working on the second hand now, layering gauze upon gauze. He turned occasionally and pulled pre-cut strips of tape from the wall, pinched them so they came up in a 'v', and laid them between Rose's fingers and on the back of his hand. 'We're going to make history tonight,' he said. 'You're going to go in there and you're going to be fearless and sharp. That's why they call you "The Lion".'

Rose thanked Rimmer each time he finished one part of his hand. 'It's been me and you, Bri,' said Rimmer. 'We've done it together, haven't we? And we're fucking good at our jobs.'

Sergio Martinez, the Argentinian former middleweight champion of the world, was a few feet away, preparing for the third fight of his comeback. He was trying, at forty-six, to put himself back in the title picture. After victories over the unheralded Jose Miguel Fandino and Jussi Koivula, the Martinez camp had selected Rose as the next opponent.

This was the biggest fight of Rose's career. Winning would open new roads for him. Losing would close them. He had arrived in Madrid on the Thursday. Fifty people had flown over from Blackpool to be in the crowd.

A camera crew wandered in to film Rose having his hands taped.

Rose and Rimmer said nothing until they began to leave, and then Rose thanked them for coming in.

Someone from the promotion came in with gloves, still in the plastic bag. A member of the Board asked if Martinez was wearing the same gloves. 'Yes, but in a different colour,' he was told. Rose thanked them as they left.

The wrapping was finished. 'How does it feel?' asked Rimmer.

'Good.'

Rose left the room briefly, then came back in. There was no toilet other than the one in Martinez's room. 'I'm not going in there,' he said. He went outside again.

At ten o'clock, someone came in and confirmed that everything would start at half-past eleven. 'He's not going out until then,' someone said of Martinez. 'That's when it's going on Argentinian TV. There's no way he's going out before then.'

Rose sat down. His leg shook with nervous energy. 'I feel good,' he said. 'I've put so much work in. I've been training for fourteen weeks. I feel as fit as I'll ever be. If I'd been half-hearted about it, if I hadn't put the work in...' He looked at Rimmer. 'I'm only 12 stone, you know,' he said, pleased with himself. '168lbs this morning.'

'That's good. That extra half-stone is what we want,' said Rimmer. One of the undercard fighters walked in and, in broken English, wished Rose luck. As he left, Rimmer said, 'See that lad over there? Trains in the street, he does. Took all the weight off in a single day.'

Someone asked when Joshua–Usyk, taking place that night in London, began and someone else looked it up on their phone. The room leaned heavily towards Usyk. 'He's British,' said Rose of Joshua, 'so I want him to win it, but there's something about the other guy.'

A TV crew came in again to do an interview. Rose went off with them to the other side of the room. 'I've been in front of bigger crowds before,' he told them. 'I'm used to them. I feel great, ready to go.' When the interview was done, he thanked them as they left.

Rose sat down again. This was his second fight in Spain in 2021, after beating Jose Manuel Lopez Clavero by majority decision in March. The calls to come over had begun at the beginning of the year.

'I suffered a bit with my mental health,' he said. 'I was drinking too much at the beginning of the year until Kieran Farrell got hold of me and got me some fights over here. It was the best thing that could have happened, getting back in shape. I took the first fight, which ended up being a war with some Spanish kid. I was a stone-and-a-half overweight for that.'

He began talking about the Martinez fight. 'I've got a plan,' he said, 'and it's to win systematically. I don't want to fall behind, but the plan is get him into the late rounds.' He reflected on what it might take to win. 'Sometimes,' he said, 'the only way is to stop and have a fight. I can do that. I know I'm not a concussive puncher; I can't rely on my power. But I'm strong. If it comes, it comes.'

Rimmer came back and took out the pads. Rose hit them lightly at first. He tapped his left shoulder with his glove. It was the shoulder that would deflect and turn jabs from a southpaw. 'I'm prepared,' he said.

They did more pads. 'You've got to push him back,' said Rimmer. 'But he's smart. Don't run into him. Remember that we've got ten rounds. Be confident.'

Rose sat down again. He started talking about his podcast. 'It's called "The Lion's Den". I've got Dave Allen and Natasha Jonas,' he said. 'Ricky Hatton's on, too. We're doing a live one in Blackpool as well, where people can buy tickets and come and watch. I've got my first dinner talk coming up in a few weeks, too – only 100 or so people, to get me used to it.'

Someone wandered in to take a photo. Rose posed with them then thanked them on the way out. He then needed the bathroom again. He looked at the sink in the changing room, debated it in his mind for a second then went out the door.

When he came back, Rimmer picked up the protector and walked over to him. 'Shall we start?' he said. Rose nodded, took another sip of water and tried on the protector. 'Does it feel OK or is it a bit tight?' asked Rimmer.

'Bit tight.'

The protector was adjusted. 'Do you want to put your T-shirt on?' said Rimmer.

Rose shook his head. 'No, it's warm enough out there.'

Someone from the promotion came in to check that everything was alright. As he left, Rose asked him if it was his company that made the gloves. 'Are these yours?' he asked, waving his hand. 'They're very good. Brilliant.'

Rose put on his shorts then hit the pads again. Someone came in and asked the team to start taping up the laces on the gloves. Rose stopped them. 'I'm going to go toilet again before I put gloves on,' he said.

Robert Rimmer, Bobby's son, was in the room when Rose came back. The pad work started again. The younger Rimmer spoke as Rose moved around, his voice low but intense. 'Work the feet, in and out. Move, that's the key. Move in and out. Move the feet. Move around.'

The older Rimmer smeared Vaseline over Rose's face and neck. They hit the pads again. 'Sharp, sharp,' he said.

At eleven twenty-five, the man who had brought the gloves came in, clapped his hands twice and said, 'Let's go.'

Rose went out of the dressing room, circled through the edge of the bullring, came out onto the platform and went down a runway to the ring. Martinez followed a few moments later.

There were about 3,000 people crammed tight in the bullring. They gave Martinez a rapturous reception. The Argentine, who had been living in Spain since 2002, seemed to be considered a national, if transplanted, hero, and he walked to the ring bedecked in silver shorts and a black waistcoat.

Rose fought better that night than anyone had expected, and it seemed he would rewrite the story already put down for him. He moved from the first round on, gloves high, and centred everything around his jab. It seemed to be Martinez, though, who won the first round.

In truth, it was a night of shifting tides – Rose trying to walk down Martinez, who showed flashes of his old brilliance even if his punches no longer landed with the same accuracy. Rose seemed to take the second, third and fourth rounds. In the second, Rose caught the Argentine with a right hand that made him stumble and, a few seconds later, bundle to the ground. A cut from a head-butt opened up on Rose's left eye in the third.

Martinez seemed to win the fifth, catching Rose with jabs. There was little to separate them in the sixth and seventh. Rose went down from a slip in the eighth, got up and hit Martinez with a jab. Martinez grinned, and the crowd began to chant his name as he dropped his hands and darted his head back and forth to miss everything that was coming back. Rose slipped again in the ninth and pointed to the wet floor; someone asked for it to be dried.

After the tenth, they embraced briefly, then separately walked around the ring with their arms in the air. The referee brought them together, facemasks on, and the crowd waited for the result.

Martinez won. Unanimous decision.

When the result was announced, Rose turned to his corner. His face dropped. He had been betrayed. He walked away, ducked quickly between the ropes and jumped down to the ground. Security stopped and guided him back onto the runway. He climbed back up, walked down it, away from the ring, and went back to the changing room.

He paced the room. 'It's fucking bollocks,' he said. 'I worked hard. I worked *fucking* hard. I thought I'd won it. I fucking won it. I know I did.'

The corner came back now. Rose was angry. 'I need to get out of here,' he said.

Everyone agreed that he had not lost the fight. Bobby Rimmer looked at him and said, 'Brian, I thought you had it by four rounds. We all did.'

It had been a close fight and four rounds was maybe a bit generous. But it was hard to escape the sense of injustice in the room. There were many close rounds, but you do not win those when you fight abroad. Still, Rose had done more than he had been expected to. He had trained hard and now his big chance was gone.

Rose sat down in a chair. His face crumpled. The road to those bigger fights had been closed to him. It all – his career, the victory over a big name, the sense of validation – seemed to be gone. He began to cry.

Bobby Rimmer kneeled in front of the chair and put his arms around Rose. 'It's his promotion, his show. He lives in this town and it's a massive event for them. They don't get fights like this. You were never going to get the decision.' Rimmer put a hand on his shoulder. 'Brian, that's the business you're in.'

'I won't come back from that. I had to win tonight.'

The younger Rimmer came over. 'Look,' he said. 'We were up against it. He's a national treasure over here. We weren't going to win on points. You'd have to knock him out three days in a row to get the decision. You were much better tonight than you were against Fowler.'

Rose took off his boxing gear and put on a dark grey tracksuit with white trainers. He and his team went over to Martinez's dressing room to offer congratulations, but the Argentine was giving an interview for television. They turned and came back.

Back inside the changing room, Rose took a bottle of water and drank from it. He was calmer. 'It's shit, isn't it?' he said to no one in particular. 'I absolutely outboxed the boxer tonight.'

His face began to relax. The tension dropped from his shoulders. It was not his fault that the decision had gone the other way. The judges had taken it away. He had lost, but he had not been defeated. The deciding factor had been out of his control. 'I've never been that up for a fight,' he said, ruefully. 'It was nothing to do with fitness.'

Some medics came in and looked at his eye. It had been cut from a headbutt early in the fight. They decided to stitch him there and then; they came back a few minutes later, cleared off two of the tables beneath the photographer's lamp, laid him down and used the light to guide their work.

Robert Rimmer stood to one side, reading messages on his phone. Some others took photographs with theirs. 'This isn't the first time,' said Rimmer of the cut.

The medics laid a small sheet of gauze with a hole in it on Rose's shoulder and face and began to work on the eye. 'Thank you,' said Rose, gently and softly, beneath the blue gauze. 'Thank you.'

Ilsenburg, Germany, December 2021. The fight was in an empty hall, in the centre of Germany, that usually held 2,000 people, but there was no crowd because of the Covid pandemic. It had been three months since Madrid. Rose was facing Denis Radovan.

It felt different this time. Flatter.

Rose looked nervous and unsure from the first bell. He moved backwards and to the side. His hands shook, counter punches coiled and ready in his arms.

Radovan was not special, but he was younger; he walked in, threw heavy shots and hoped for the best. Rose jabbed when he could and covered up when Radovan hit, but he looked different, as if the contested loss to Martinez had irreparably and permanently taken something from him. His jabs missed and went over the crouching Radovan's head, and his crosses went awry, and what he did land lacked grace or fluidity.

There is getting beaten, and then there is getting beaten up. Radovan did the second to Rose. Rimmer was in the corner again and he asked how Rose felt after six rounds, in a tone that did not sound good.

Radovan fell in the seventh from an errant punch that strayed too low. But then he got up, carried on and punched at Rose; he moved out of the way of or dodged everything that came back at him. Rose began to yell when he punched. It was the desperate sound of someone with nothing left but the fear of quitting.

It was over at the beginning of the eighth. Rimmer turned as the bell went and waved to the referee that it was over. The referee called it, then Rose got up from his stool and walked, dejected, to his opponent and embraced him.

The referee brought them together and held each man by the wrist, then he raised Radovan's hand. Rose stepped over, took Radovan's other wrist and held his arm aloft, then he stopped and looked, a little lost, for a way out of the ring. He found it a time later and that was it.

He was gone.

CHAPTER THREE

NINETY MILES
TO GLASGOW

NINETY MILES

Dundee–Stirling–Edinburgh–Glasgow, Scotland, July to September 2016. The road from Dundee to Glasgow is roughly ninety miles. If you leave from the centre of the former and cross over the windswept Tay Road Bridge, you will follow the A92 down past the Bow of Fife and go through the villages of Moonzie, Ladybank, and Strathmiglo. The route skirts and bends about thirty miles in around Kinross and then goes almost directly south past Dunfermline and through Inverkeithing to North Queensferry where the M90 rolls over the Firth of Forth. It then misses Edinburgh and cuts a sharp right onto the M8, goes through the towns of Whitburn, Harthill and Kirk o' Shotts, before winding through the eastern side of Glasgow.

It is impossible now to know the route that Mike Towell took to be at the Radisson Blu Hotel at the end of September 2016, but it started with a call for purse bids for a final eliminator for the

British welterweight championship, a match to be held between him and Dale Evans.

A purse bid in boxing is when whoever oversees a title – a world title or, in this case, the British championship – has to affix a contest between the champion or the highest-available contender. In the case of the fight between Mike Towell and Dale Evans, the match was to decide on who would be next in line for a championship fight.

The process was overseen by the British Boxing Board of Control, which opened the process on 14 July. The winning bid was made by Iain Wilson of the St Andrew's Sporting Club in Glasgow, with an offer of £8,226. From there, it was agreed between Towell, Evans and St Andrew's that the winner of the bout would receive 60 per cent of the purse, with the loser picking up 40 per cent. A draw would see an equal split. At most, for twelve rounds of boxing, Towell or Evans would be paid £4,935.60.

The smart money would have been on Towell. He had 11 wins, 0 losses and 1 draw, with 8 knockouts, and he was fighting as the 'home' boxer. Evans, meanwhile, had a more-potted record: 11 wins, 3 losses and 2 draws, with only 4 knockouts, which was not suggestive of inordinate punching power.

The blemishes were more telling. Evans drew against Leon Findlay, who had a single victory and nothing else, in his second fight. Findlay would go on to win four more and lose five, his last bout taking place in 2014. Evans lost his eighth fight on points over three rounds in the one-night Prizefighter tournament against Glenn Foot, who had been undefeated in seven. He then had a technical draw against Mark Douglas after a second-round knockdown, followed by a cut eye. The light-punching Larry Ekundayo then stopped him in five rounds, before the 16–2 Sam Eggington beat him on a large margin on points over twelve.

Gary Lockett was the coach for Dale Evans. He had fought, eight years before the fight between Towell and Evans, for the middle-weight championship of the world.

He knew what Evans was facing. 'I thought it was an uphill battle,' he says. 'We looked at Mike Towell, and we knew he was a terror. He was aggressive and he'd stopped most of his opponents.'

Evans had had an up-and-down career, but Lockett had managed him towards a British title eliminator. 'We got him in this position for that fight,' Lockett said. 'And no promoter really wanted it, apart from Iain Wilson. And he's a nice guy. I think the purse bids were around seven grand.'

The scaffolding company Towell worked for gave him twelve weeks of unpaid leave to train. The plan, his coach later said, was for four weeks of light training with some sparring, then four more weeks of intense sparring alongside training, and a tapering-off period of another four weeks of light training.

Towell went down to Edinburgh to spar. He was there at the end of July. He worked against two boxers. It was rough. He looked slow and lethargic.

They toyed with him, moved around, made him look foolish. Towell threw, missed. They stepped back, got out of his way. His punches missed by postcodes. He was not sharp. He did a few rounds with the first partner, a few with the second, and then the first one again.

He was embarrassed and angry at the end.

'You OK, Mike?' his coach asked.

He shook his head. 'Fuck no. I lost everything in there. I took a fucking hiding.'

The coach shrugged. 'It's just something to learn from. You're just not sharp, yet. That's all.'

Towell shook his head. 'Fuck that. I'm not coming back here.'

The coach nodded.

The headaches started just after, and he took as much paracetamol as he could. Sometimes more. *It was nothing major*, his partner thought, *just a sore head*.

He was sparring every week, sometimes in Stirling and sometimes in Edinburgh.

Marion Docherty was the secretary of the 1314 Boxing Club in Stirling. She had known Towell for four or five years. He phoned her at the beginning of September.

'I've got this pain in my side,' he said. 'Like a stitch.'

'How bad is it?'

He sounded worried. 'Pretty bad. I went down while running the other day. And I've been sick.'

'You still have it?'

'Yeah. I've got pain in my neck, too.'

'That doesn't sound good, Mike.'

The phone rustled. 'No, I need to get it rubbed. Do you know anywhere?'

'Like a massage?'

'Aye.'

'Look, shall I get hold of Scott Henderson for you?'

'If it's no bother. I sent him a message, but I've not heard back.'

'Leave it with me.'

Dr Henderson had been the doctor for Towell's annual medical earlier that year, and he hung around the gym in Stirling. He was also licensed by the British Boxing Board of Control to work with the gym. He saw Towell there that week. They were alone in the locker room.

Henderson wrote in an email that October:

Around 4-5 weeks ago, I was asked to talk to Mike by the team in his gym. They were concerned that he was having bouts of abdominal pain in the upper right quadrant. On talking to Mike, I felt this may be in keeping with either gallstones or gastritis. I suggested he attend his GP for investigation. At the end of our chat, he asked if some discomfort in his neck and the back of his head was related. This was mild and made worse on moving his neck and I felt was in keeping with a muscular injury. I felt the two were not connected but advised sharing this with his GP.

I contacted Mike around a week or so later to check he had been to his GP. He advised he had and [sic] a scan [ultrasound] and blood tests were normal. He said he was feeling good and had no on going symptoms at this time.

Dr Henderson found no numbness, weakness or tingling. 'Are you taking anything?' he asked. 'Any painkillers?'

'No.'

'Is it stopping you from doing anything?'

Towell shook his head. 'No.'

'How's everything else? You've got the fight coming up, haven't you?'

'Aye, I'm looking forward to it.'

Towell called his local medical practice on 9 September. He spoke with Dr Joanna Boileau. She noted,

Telephone encounter 3 days ago felt pain in R front of abdomen when running (trains as a boxer). Pain eased off once rested. Today same again but more severe and had to stop running. Doesn't feel like a stitch. No nausea, vomiting, diarrhoea, constipation, urinary symptoms, fever. Sounds calm and undistressed on the phone – lots background noise sound like in a busy shopping centre or similar. Imp – ? Muscular Plan [*sic*] – routine appt booked for Monday. Cut back on exercise until then if required.

He sparred again two days later. There was something wrong.

He drove up to Stirling with his friend Jamie Wilson. Wilson was also a boxer, also once with Lochee ABC. He had won ten and lost one. They went together in the car with Wilson's father.

Towell was his normal self on the drive up. He said nothing about the headaches. He laughed, he joked.

They trained, then Towell got into the ring for sparring.

He looked bad. Slow and lethargic. He went to his corner between rounds.

'What's going on, Mikey?' his coach said.

'I'll be alright.'

He went in for a second round. It looked just as bad.

Towell went back to the corner. He winced. 'I can't do it,' he said. 'The pain. My head's banging.'

Towell's coach looked over to Stewart Burt, his opponent, who was stood in the opposite corner, his gloves resting on the ropes. 'That's it,' they said. 'He's hurting.'

'Hurting?'

Someone shrugged. 'Headache,' they said.

Towell got out of the ring. He sat to one side and put a towel over his head, drank some water. The other coach came over. 'Mikey,' he said. 'Shall I take you home?'

'Nah, it's alright. It's not that sore.'

'Get it looked at by a doctor, yeah?'

'I will.'

'And call me if it goes on.'

'Will do.'

Towell got into the car forty minutes later and left with Jamie Wilson and Wilson's father. He lay down on the back seat. 'My head,' he said. 'It's banging.'

The Wilsons were concerned. 'Mikey, we're going to take you in. Hospital's around the corner.'

'No, take us home.'

'Mikey...'

'Take us home.'

'We'll take you to Ninewells.'

Towell squeezed his eyes shut. 'OK, take us there.'

His mother was waiting for him at Ninewells Hospital in Dundee. They went inside. Towell began to text his partner to tell her he was at the hospital.

They sat in the chairs. There were tears in his eyes. They waited.

A nurse took him in. 'It's really, really bad,' he said. 'There's whooshing in my head. Something's wrong.'

'Is it just today?'

'A few weeks. We were sparring today, and now it's worse.'

'OK, we'll get someone to come and see you.'

Dr Elizabeth Skelly came to see him. She dimmed the lights. 'How long have you been having the headaches?'

'A week and a half.'

'Any headache this morning?'

'No.'

'Where is the pain?'

He rubbed his head. 'On the left.'

'Have you been unconscious? Any vomiting?'

He shook his head. 'No.'

'OK, has this ever happened to someone in your family?'

'No.'

'Do you take any regular medication?'

'No. Some paracetamol every now and again.'

They went to an empty room at the end of the hall. She took his history. He said he had no past problems.

'I've got pain here, too,' he said, pointing to his stomach. 'It's grumbly.'

'Grumbly?'

He nodded. 'I spoke to my boxing doctor about it.'

'Did you speak to them about the headaches?'

He shook his head. 'No. I didn't think I had to.'

Dr Skelly thought he looked well. She shined a light in his eyes. His pupils were equal and reactive to light. He knew where he was.

His cranial nerves were intact. There was no bruising behind his ears, no blood in them. Everything was normal.

She asked him to stand up and to touch his nose, then her finger. She made him walk heel to toe. It all looked good.

'OK.' She thought it was stress, gave him painkillers. 'It's a migraine. A really bad one.'

'Can you scan me?'

'No. I don't think you need one. But you have a doctor's appointment tomorrow?'

'Aye.'

'OK. Make sure you attend that. Go home, rest, take painkillers, come back if you vomit. And stay around someone.'

He went back to his mother's house and slept for a few hours, then got up and went back home to his partner. He said he felt better and went back to bed.

There was no CT scan; he did not fall within the guidelines then to have one done. This would be examined in the official report. Dr Martin McKechnie, a consultant in emergency medicine, was asked by the local health authority to look into the care given to Towell on 11 September.

The official report reads,

Agreeing that clinical presentation was absolutely a matter for the consultant, Dr McKechnie did, however, disagree with Dr Skelly's assessment of Mr Towell. He did so on the basis that not all clinical examinations which are normal mean that everything is normal. The subtlety of head injury presentation caused him to conclude that there should have been a CT scan. A normal examination does not exclude the possibility of something going on in the brain. His opinion was that a CT scan that day would have been appropriate and reasonable in Mr Towell's circumstances.

Even so, Dr McKechnie 'conceded' under cross examination that the decision to not perform a CT scan that day was 'a reasonable one'. The fact that it was a 'new and different' headache had not been written into the contemporaneous notes, only coming out later. Another consultant said he would have done the same, assuming the local GP would have made a referral for a CT scan.

The later inquiry found no fault with the work of Dr Skelly on 11 September, but Towell had spent at least six minutes that day taking blows to the head. Given his history and everything that came after, it is not unreasonable that he may have been suffering minor bleeding in his brain that day, symptomatic of an underlying condition. Untreated, any minor bleeding on 11 September could have become catastrophically bad during his fight against Dale Evans less than three weeks later.

In 2004, the American heavyweight Joe Mesi faced former cruiserweight champion Vassiliy Jirov of Kazakhstan. Mesi was seen as the next in line to a heavyweight title shot, undefeated in twenty-eight fights and rated as the top contender.

The Associated Press reported the day after the fight, 'For eight rounds, Joe Mesi lived up to his billing as a heavyweight star of the future. In two furious final rounds, Vassiliy Jirov may have exposed

him as something far less. When it was over, Mesi remained undefeated – but just barely.'

Mesi was down three times – once in the ninth, twice in the tenth.
A unanimous decision that was as narrow as it could possibly be.

There was worse to come. He says now that he knew immediately that something was wrong. He felt different in a way that he had
never felt before.

'I went home from Las Vegas and a week, ten days, after the fight,
I still hadn't quite come around,' he says. 'There was forgetfulness,
my balance was off. I wasn't detrimentally engaged, but I knew I
had to be checked out.'

An MRI scan revealed one bleed. Another eight days later was
inconclusive. Two bleeds were found on the next one. Found again
later in the month. Gone a few weeks later.

In Mesi's case, the blood was reabsorbed back into his brain.
But it seems possible that Towell suffered a small bleed that day.
It might have been weeks later that the small bleed, or bleeds, was
reopened during his match against Dale Evans.

This is known as 'Second Impact Syndrome', and it was covered
in the Fatal Accident Inquiry, held in 2018.

Towell's autopsy found a small chronic subdural haematoma, but
it was difficult to ascertain when it had first appeared. The evidence,
said consultant neuropathologist Professor Colin Smith, was that
the haematoma was between seven days and a few months old.

C. D. Turnbull, the sheriff principal, overseeing the FAI in Glasgow, wrote,

If one proceeds on the assumption that the chronic subdural

haematoma was present on 11 September 2016, the question then arises as to whether it would have been visible on a CT scan, had one been carried out. The starting point in addressing this question is the size of the cells in question. Professor Smith spoke to this. He described the cells as quite flat, being in the region of 50 to 60 microns in depth and 150 to 200 microns in length. It is worthy of note that 200 microns is 0.2 mm. Put another way, utilising the greatest length of cell indicated by Professor Smith (200 microns) and assuming five such cells laid end to end would give a length of 1 mm.

Turnbull would conclude that, if the haematoma had been present on 11 September, then it would have been too small for the hospital staff to have detected.

Towell woke up early on 12 September. It was his birthday. He sat up in the bed. He retched. He vomited. Chloe Ross googled the symptoms and thought it was migraines.

Towell rubbed his neck. He said nothing about the advice Dr Skelly had given him. He did not go back to the hospital.

He went to see Dr Oswald at Coldside Medical Practice. He did not mention being sick. He told him of the headaches and said he had been to hospital. Dr Oswald looked at his eyes, got him to look from one side to another, asked if he felt any soreness. Towell pointed to the back left part of his head.

Dr Oswald did not recommend a CT scan, but he checked Towell's abdomen. He took blood, but he did not think it was gallstones.

The doctor thought the headaches were related to the pain in the neck, and he prescribed aspirin. He ruled out meningitis, bleeding to the brain and a tumour.

He did not advise Towell to not box.

Towell went home and phoned his coach. 'I'm good,' he said. 'Doctor says it's just stress.'

The prescription of aspirin underlines how a brain bleed was not suspected. In 1983, the amateur boxer Tony Bruno was grievously injured during a sparring match. It became apparent later that he suffered a minor bleed one day in the gym. He sparred again the following day, from which the injury was worsened. Someone gave him an aspirin.

As Bruno's friend, who later became a paramedic, later reflected in a documentary called *After the Last Round*, 'It was a very bad thing, as it turns out. He had actually developed a brain bleed that night, and the aspirin was just going to make him bleed harder.'

Towell did not spar again. He went back into training on 13 September. He ran up hills. He hit pads, bags and bodybelts. But he neither hit another person nor was hit in return, until the fight.

'It's just stress,' Towell told Jamie Wilson. 'That's what the doctors said. Nothing to worry about.'

'Are you going to spar?'

Towell shook his head. 'I can't be doing with the pain,' he said. 'I'll just get through it on the night.'

He spoke to Dr Henderson again. 'How're you doing, Mikey?' Henderson asked.

'Just fine.'

'Fine?'

'Aye. The doctor said it's stress. They did some bloods and an ultrasound, and it's all fine.'

'How's everything else?'

'All good. All good. I'm looking forward to the fight.'

No one saw if he was sick. He was, they all said afterwards, his normal self. He did not mention headaches. He said he was comfortable with the weight. His coach and his training partners accepted it. They knew he had been at the hospital.

He told them the doctors there had said he was fine.

They knew he had been to his own doctor, and he had said it was fine.

They knew he had seen Dr Henderson, and Towell had said Dr Henderson told him it was fine.

And it was fine.

But he still got headaches, and he still took paracetamol to shift the pain.

He went to the Radisson Blu the day before the fight. He was nervous. People saw it. They thought it was because of the fight, because he was going to be on television. He was going to fight for the British title if he won. That meant a lot to him. It meant a lot to everyone else.

All he had to do was beat Dale Evans, and then he would be in a match for the British welterweight title.

All he had to do was beat Dale Evans.

The weight limit for a welterweight fight is 147lbs, or 10.5st. Making the weight is the hardest part of boxing for many fighters as they push and grind their dehydrated bodies down even further, sweating out the last few pounds and ounces. The imperative is to go as low as one can, and to do it in a safe way. But it is a hard line to judge.

It was reported in 2023 that the Liverpool fighter Liam Smith had forced himself to lose 42lbs in thirty days in the run up to his rematch against Chris Eubank Jr.

Such measures are neither exceptional nor uncommon.

A fighter may reduce their food intake to almost nothing in the last week before a fight, dehydrate themselves, drag their bodies into saunas, run and exercise to lose the last few pounds. A fighter can often take a scalding bath, getting out every ten minutes or so, to scrape a credit card down their arms and legs in order to carve away sweat.

And making weight can be dangerous. As the US fight physician, author and artist Ferdie Pacheco once observed, your brains float in a bed of water.

The perils and dangers of fighters cutting weight led directly to the weigh-ins before the fights being moved from the day of the event to the one before. The idea was to allow more time for weakened and dehydrated fighters to replenish their bodies.

In truth, all it did was give leeway for some to push even further, taking off, and then putting back on within a day, 15–20lbs.

Towell told everyone that he was good at the weight. He told sparring partner Stewart Burt he was good at the weight. His coaches thought he was good at the weight.

But he missed. Not by much, but he missed it. It was more an oversight than anything else. He got on the scales, and they registered just over 149lbs.

The rules said he had an hour, so he went into the sauna for a bit, then ran on a treadmill. No one was really bothered. It was one of those things that happened all the time in boxing.

He went back fifteen minutes or so later. He had lost 2.5lbs. He had made the weight.

The day of the fight came. He went for dinner with his coach and his friend Marion Docherty. She said he was nervous. 'I just want to get it over and done with,' he said.

Towell went back to the hotel. He saw the doctor. He said he was fine. He gave the same answers he always did.

The doctor looked at his eyes, his ears. He said later that he thought he had asked about headaches, but he could not be sure.

It was time to fight. He was at the thinnest end of the wedge. Every decision, every action, every move had brought him to this place. He stood in a spot he had defined for himself, a spot that defined him.

Son, father, partner, friend – all left to one side. It was the moment for him to be seen for something else, as someone else, as the thing that more than anything made him into *him*.

He was a boxer and a fighter. He was about to walk out and go to work.

He believed he was ready for whatever might happen.

ERIK

Nyköping, Sweden, August 2023. Erik Skoglund was walking on similar ground.

He would not admit it, of course, and there were things that he probably could not admit to himself, but he remained determined. He had a goal and he was going to achieve it, no matter the cost. Even if it meant dying.

That was why he was still training in 2023, still sparring, still looking for answers, still looking for validation. Even if he was still fighting a war to which everyone else had signed the truce.

But that was OK, because he believed things. He believed it only took hard work, dedication and knowing the alleyways, the snickels and the gunnels. These were good things to believe. And he believed in himself. And he also believed that there was no call to develop a Plan B until Plan A was entirely spent.

He had never believed in a Plan B, because to do so would be a tacit admission that his destiny might never entirely work out.

But that is why Plan Bs exist; they are an escape route for when Plan A is no longer possible.

He had had a fine career until the injury. European champion at light-heavyweight, with three defences, and then in the mix at world title level. Sure, he had lost one, but there was no shame in dropping a decision to Callum Smith, particularly when he had nearly done the impossible and gone down a weight division for that fight. But his career was still looking good, and there was another fight on the horizon.

But then came the injury.

He was training at home in Nyköping, getting ready to fight Rocky Fielding in London. It was a few months after the loss, and it was a decent make-or-break fight that would either place him back at the top as a viable contender or throw him towards gatekeeper status.

What happened had to be pieced together later, assembled from the words of others. They all agreed on a basic narrative, a basic story, and it was another reason that Erik was lucky they were there.

He remembered nothing of that day, everything malfunctioning before the fleeting, short-term memories could be seared into permanence.

The plan had been to do six rounds, three minutes each. He had gone from two sparring sessions a week to three, and he had changed his style. He no longer wanted to stick and move, everything in his arsenal predicated on the jab. He figured that was not how he was going to win on the road. 'I was going to start taking one to give one,' he said.

His brother Marcus was there, helping him get ready. His girlfriend Angelica, too.

Things started going wrong around the third round. Something unclear, the springing of a gear inside him that he had never been aware of. He ignored it, carried on. It was just a bit of dizziness.

At the end, he went over to the sagging ropes, to the corner where his brother was standing.

'Good session. Now let's get some rest.'

Skoglund blinked, trying to clear the fog in his head. 'I don't feel good,' he said.

'That's OK. We'll go again on Monday.'

'No, this is different. I feel bad.'

Marcus pulled the gloves away from Erik's hands. There was a shudder, and Skoglund began to tilt, his stomach lurching. His girlfriend pulled out her phone and began to dial an ambulance as he fell, shaking and screaming, to the ground.

It took thirty minutes for help to come. Brother sat with brother, one convinced the other was dead.

They took him to hospital and, from there, to Stockholm. He needed surgery right away; waiting two hours would kill him. There was another surgery a few days after that. A second bleed. An induced coma. The doctors tried to wake him a few days later. He stayed beneath the noise of the world. His parents flew back from Spain to sit by his bedside. The doctors left him to wake up when he was ready.

When he did come back, the thing he remembered was the white coat. His confused brain, signals firing everywhere, began to put everything in the context of boxing.

'Every time I'm in hospital,' he said, 'it's always been after a fight for the medical check or something like that. So I was looking at the guy, thinking that he's there to check out my knuckles, my eyes and my throat, then he'll sign a piece of paper saying that I'm fit to fight.'

The cells and synapses were firing away. He could laugh about it years later. 'This competent guy', he said, 'with his white coat is asking me to put my arms out in front of me. I'm thinking, *What is this? What does he want me to do?* So, I decide to play his game. So, I'm trying and then it's as if I can see myself from above. There's this poor bastard who can't move his left hand higher than his shoulder and his right's completely lost. The whole right side. And I'm thinking, *Wow, this guy has some problems.*'

The mental fog took time to lift. He would look around. 'What's going on?' he would ask those in the room. They would tell him and he would nod, then thirty seconds later he would ask the same question again, his brain either still protecting him from the trauma or rebuilding its pathways.

He moved eventually from a bed to a wheelchair. Then rehab. Having to rebuild everything he had lost. Eighty-seven kilograms, down to seventy-two in a couple of weeks. He said to his father that he could now fight at a lower weight. His father lowered his head.

From the bed to the wheelchair, then back to walking. One side of his body lagging behind the other. Parts of his brain now dead. He did rehab, but cannot remember all of it. Memories slowly re-emerged. 'It came back step by step,' he said.

Not all of him came back, nor will it. He knew he was different. 'I have two careers. There's the one that ended with my injury, and then I had to start a new chapter in my life. That's my life in general. I had one that ended in 2017. Now, I kind of have a new one.'

The depression haunted him, too. 'There have been times when I've been really down because of this,' he said. 'And there have been times when I've *not* been down or depressed, but I haven't been happy since the injury.'

It was now nearly six years later, and he had still not given up on the dream. And he thought he could still do it, that if he bent his shoulder deep enough and pushed as hard as he could, then time could go backwards, and the water would run back up the hill.

He had struggled with the idea of enforced retirement, but he concluded that there was no struggle if he refused to accept that he was finished. Or, at least, it would be a different struggle. Not to cope with retirement, but to circumvent and prove wrong those whose best interests laid in him stopping.

'It's not that I want to be disabled or anything like that,' he said, 'but that might have made this easier, because I'd know for sure that it wasn't going to happen if I was in a wheelchair. You can't fight without your legs.'

He was training again, although he was guarded about what he was doing. He had no trainer, but there were people he worked with who helped him, and he knew enough after all these years to train himself.

'I really feel that it's something I can do,' he said. 'My body is working fine. I'm training and my reactions are coming back. I can feel the rhythm of it. And I've been sparring.'

There were many who did not want him to fight again. They did not even want him to put on a glove. He had a good life in Nyköping with Angelica and their son, and he felt well and moved well and sounded good.

The problem was that he could not get fighting out of his system. Most likely, he never would.

'Going without boxing,' he said, 'is not something that I'm interested in. I've been doing this for my entire life, and I need to try again and have another run at it.'

He had, he felt, solutions to his problem. There were ways, he said, that he could fight again. There was just the problem of the people with power telling him that he should not.

But you do not become a champion without hope. He knew that. Had always known that.

'Hope,' he said, 'is the last thing to go.'

CHAPTER FOUR

THE BRAIN GAME

DAMAGES

It is impossible to escape. Watch people fight for long enough and it gets you. These people are damaging themselves.

Stick with it for enough years and you begin to see the erosion happen in real time. The fighters who can no longer walk properly, listing as they move from place to place, their balance shot and their floors forever moving. And it is in their voices, too, their words dripping with misplaced vowels, the strain evident as they focus and try – because they know, *know* they can if they just try hard enough – to not sound like they took too many.

But it is always there. And the longer you watch, the worse you feel because you are not damaged, because you have paid for and enjoyed the sight of these people damaging themselves and one another.

Put simply – boxing is not good for the brain.

Thomas Hauser, one of the great boxing writers, once wrote that boxing is a 'marvellous showcase' for the brain, being that 'skilled

fighting requires balance, coordination, speed, reflexes, power, in-
stinct, discipline, memory, and creative thought'.

It is all a delicate balance, though. Hauser wrote in the following
sentence that 'these assets enable a professional fighter to deliver
blows that smash an opponent's head backward and twist it violent-
ly from side to side'.

There are two separate tracks of damage in professional fighting:
the acute and the chronic. Or, those received immediately within
a bout and those that develop in later life, usually decades after the
gloves have been taken off for the final time.

As Harry L. Parker wrote in the *Journal of Neurology and
Psychopathology*,

> For purposes of description, the injuries received by pugilists in
> activities of their profession may be divided into those received
> during an actual bout, serious enough to cause death immediate-
> ly or a few hours later, and those which more by their repetition
> than by their severity lead to slower development of disability
> during the fighter's career.[3]

Acute brain damage announces its presence in the arena or the stadium. A fight finishes – and it did not have to be a torrid, high-oc-
tane bout – and the fighters stand, waiting in the ring.

One blinks. He puts a hand to his eyes as if there is something
there. He blinks again, but these are strange movements, heavy and
slow, as if he is trying to clear his mind of some great thought. He
squeezes his eyes tightly and then reopens them. *Did that do it?* he

asks himself, in an internal voice that is about to be drowned into silence. *Did that clear it?*

No.

Shit.

He blinks again, and maybe he begins to shake this time. He puts his head down, and it is now that he feels that something is deeply and seriously wrong, that whatever it is that is going on is not in the normal course of things.

There are always aches and pains, and you are never 100 per cent.

Headaches happen, of course.

But not like this.

He sinks, down to his knees, but then he carries on, falling until he is lying down. And the bright lights above him, the feet of others by his ears, may be comforting.

That is if he is without pain.

But he will scream if the precious, liminal, limited space between the hard bone of his skull and the softness of his brains fills with blood. Something, hit too hard or too often, has given way and between the soft place and the hard place, it is the former rather than the latter that begins to be squeezed and die under the pressure.

The other way is attritional, a gradual wearing down over time. These are the shots that land in the ring and in the gym that sound little bells, bells that will continue to ring for decades.

These are insidious. A debt taken out, the total of which is never clear but which announces its presence a decade or two after the fighter thinks they are finished with it.

It is the 'punch drunk' thing, a term that people in the past used frequently, but it has been made academic in this century, made not respectable, but recognised, put in its place, made clinical, like the gentrification of an old neighbourhood.

The old-timers knew it went on, though. That is the thing with boxing people. They know more in some ways than the doctors, even if they cannot articulate them. In 1980, Muhammad Ali underwent all the medical tests in the world, and those tests cleared him to be fed to Larry Holmes. But the old hands knew. They could look at him and see he was gone, that he had no hope, that he should not have been in that ring. That the balance was gone, and the speech, and the speed. He had that name, though.

They knew. They have always known. They had terms like 'punch drunk' and 'slug nutty'. It was a truth acknowledged at some gut level and spoken about in hushed whispers laden with empathy.

See him over there? He's gone too far. He's walking on his heels now. Yeah, he could have been someone. He could have been a contender.

They knew. They always knew. It was common sense. Getting punched in the head never did anyone any good.

At least not medically.

DEATH IN THE RING

Rave Eagles Club, Milwaukee, US, March 2014. Something is wrong with Dennis Munson Jr.

He is about to begin the second round against Michael Vang. It is Munson's first fight, and he has lumbered and been amateurish in the opening minutes. But a debutant following his opponent around the ring, his footwork sliding into unorganised pieces and his punches being thrown with inexperienced abandon, is not unusual.

The video will become evidence and, shot from above, angled down, it makes Munson, 5ft 10in. and 148lbs, look like a child. He stands barefoot in red shorts, black gloves taped with more red. He has seven tattoos – 'Trust No One' on his upper chest and neck, 'Only God Can Judge Me' below that, 'God', 'FEAR', 'See Evil', 'Speak Evil'. The longest, but not the largest, reads, 'Loyalty, it's what we live by. Respect, it's what we die for.'

Now, the second round begins and Munson staggers as he walks to the centre of the ring, falling into a half step to his left.

Narrating the video later is Sherry Wulkan, medical chair for the Association of Boxing Commissions.

She says,

He looks fatigued coming out already. He takes a jab, he takes a leg kick, and then there's a time out for a groin kick. You see, the ref breaks it from what I presume he felt was a groin kick. And then the ref turns away. But the African American kid stumbles, he doesn't have his feet under him at that point. That's not ex-haustion, that's lack of coordination. He takes a weird step there. That's the first thing I would notice where I'd be watching really careful.

Munson looks shaky, almost frail. He walks rather than steps, and he looks like he has been breathing carbon monoxide. His move-ments are sluggish. He begins to throw his punches in the direction of his opponent, rather than at him. Forty seconds before the end of the round, he teeters backwards.

The bell goes. *Ding*. Munson lists to his corner like a man stepping across a rocking ship. He sits, his head begins to slump. His coach takes him by the chin and pushes his head back. He does it a second time, then a third.

Ding. Munson stands and slips to one side. His coach takes his arm and pulls him up, back into balance.

Vang begins to hit Munson, who stumbles backwards. He ends up in the ropes and takes more loose punches then staggers to the other side of the ring. Not many of these long and looping punches that glance, at the end of their arc, against the corners of his head are landing. But they are still landing.

The fight ends, and Munson goes to his corner. He stands for a while, but then he tips to the side. His coach taps him in the face. *Come on, dude*, he seems to be saying. *Can you straighten up?* He keeps his hand on Munson's shoulder, holding him against the ropes, and he signals to the doctor.

Munson collapses like a detonated chimneystack. He lands in a sitting position, his chin resting on the chest, legs splayed beneath him. He tips again. He lies on the canvas.

After a few seconds, he is rolled out of the ring and made to sit on the ring's edge. The doctor comes to him.

It takes some time to get him to the hospital and when he does arrive, he is comatose. He dies a few hours later from a swollen brain.

Imagine the completeness of the skull. The roundness of it from the temples and eyes, up and around the ears and to the back of the neck. A completely enclosed system.

Evolution made it a helmet to protect the most vulnerable and important part of the human body: the brain. The thing that makes a person who they are and allows them to function as a sentient, automotive human being.

But now something happens. A blow lands and the head turns sharply, too sharply. There is a rip, a tear. Something gives way. The human body is so good at protecting itself, but it takes little for something to go wrong.

The head is hit again and the neck twists, the brain sent careening and rotating in the skull, and it rotates and scrapes along the inside, across all the ridges and crenulations that make up the inner surface. And something is stretched too far, or something scrapes in a way it was never supposed to. Something rips.

Blood leaks. Maybe a little, maybe a lot. The head begins to hurt.

And this is where the body works against itself. The hardness of the skull, the protection that it gives the brain, is now that same organ's liability. Because the blood that is coming from that tear has nowhere to go in this completely enclosed system and now it is doing the only thing it can – squeezing the soft and vulnerable brain.

There is confusion, drowsiness. Nausea. Vomiting. Speech slides into a soft noise. Vision doubles. Thoughts tumble away.

Time is ticking. Time is ticking.

Caesars Palace, Las Vegas, Nevada, US, November 1982. It is hot, and Deuk-Koo Kim is about to fight Ray 'Boom Boom' Mancini for the World Boxing Association's lightweight championship. Kim has 17 wins, 1 loss and 1 draw. He has won eight inside the distance. He is 5ft 6in., handsome and perfectly proportioned to fight on the inside, all squat and broad muscle.

Mancini is a star. From Youngstown, Ohio, he is the face of the aspiring working-class American. He is young and white, the boy next door with a great smile who seems like he would be a good neighbour. The type of guy who would come and help you move house for the price of a couple of beers.

He can fight, too. He has 24 wins and 1 loss, with 20 knockouts. His loss was a fourteenth-round knockout against Alexis Arguello for the World Boxing Council's lightweight title. But to have lasted that long against *El Flaco Explosivo* is an impressive feat.

The television loves Mancini. Why wouldn't it? He is handsome, and he is an honest fighter, meaning that there is no smoke and mirrors about his work. He does not cheat his fans or his audience, and he is warm and funny, kind.

But he needs a co-star.

There has been no great call for a Mancini–Kim fight. It is Mancini's show. Kim is the 'opponent', someone good enough to last a few rounds against a telegenic star. But he is not listening to popular wisdom. He takes a piece of paper and writes on it, *Kill or be killed*, and he puts it by his bed and looks at it each day on the approach to the fight.

The fight is to take place in an outdoor arena, put up in the space where cars are usually parked. Despite the late month of the year, the temperatures are still blistering, and there is little shade. This is, after all, a desert.

The fight begins, and Kim comes out and throws his best punch at Mancini. The fight is on.

The men fight in the hot Nevada sun for thirteen rounds. Kim wears yellow shorts, Mancini brown. They grind at each other in the heat. Mancini begins to edge in front, winning closely but decisively.

The thirteenth round ends, and Kim sits in his corner. The sun burns across his bare shoulders. His eyes are swollen as he waits to come out for the fourteenth. He is tired and spent.

The commentator says, 'You may not have heard of him before, but you will remember him today. Win or lose.'

Once more unto the breach...

The bell rings, and there is a short exchange. Kim's legs sag and Mancini sees the opening in the following millisecond and puts his right hand on him, and Kim falls backwards.

His head lands outside of the ropes, his hands landing above his shoulders. Kim rolls over and pushes himself up. He reaches and takes hold of the ring's lowest rope and then he grabs the next one up, and he tries to pull himself to his feet like a man climbing a ladder. He stumbles and falls backwards, but he keeps his grip and pulls himself forwards. He is on his feet, but the referee waves it off.

Families, friends and hangers-on gush into the ring. A swollen, bleeding, sweating Mancini is given his belt. He waves to the crowd.

Somewhere in all of this, the Korean falls limp to the floor. He is put on a stretcher and taken out of the ring. An unaware Mancini gives an interview.

At the hospital, Kim deteriorates. The doctors drill into his skull to relieve the pressure. They put ice around his head to reduce the swelling.

Mancini hears the news, waits. He is a decent man. He speaks highly of Kim, but the dread begins to rise. It is the fear of the accidental killer.

The days go by. Mancini waits. His world implodes and collapses around him.

It takes five days for Kim to die. Mancini wins four times in the years to come, but his fortunes shift, and he finishes his career on a four-fight losing streak.

Many years ago, I knew a former policeman who ended up near-blind after a tug-of-war game. Pulling on the rope, he said later that he felt something pop in his head. 'A part of me just went,' he said later. That night, he lifted something heavy and his memory after that is blank.

But he found out later. His wife said he screamed an ungodly noise and she found him on the floor, and the screaming would not stop.

There was bleeding in his brain. He was rushed to the hospital and, because the pressure was so high, his blood hit the ceiling when the surgeons drilled into his skull.

When I knew him, he told me this with his guide dog by his side. The problem was that in the doctors' rush to relieve the pressure, they had damaged the parts of his brain that processed vision. So it was not the injury that had robbed him of his sight, but the cure.

This is what happens when the blood is trapped between the skull and the brain. If there is only a little blood, the doctors do nothing;

it will be reabsorbed into the body in the next few days, the tear or the rip healing itself.

But if it is large, the treatment will be drastic. A surgeon will drill into the skull and drain the blood through the holes. They may also perform a craniotomy, removing a whole section of bone so that they can go in and access the haematoma.

If luck is there and on the side of the angels, that can be the end of it. A few days' recovery for a small bleed, months of rehab for a large one. But at this point, a boxing career tends to end.

The Theater at Madison Square Garden, New York, US, November 2013. Sometimes, they survive.

Magomed 'Mago' Abdusalamov is a thirty-two-year-old heavy-weight from Makhachkala in the Russian state of Dagestan. He has a record that looks good on paper: 18 wins, 18 knockouts, 0 losses. A southpaw, he is 6ft 3in. and weighed in the day before at 231.5lbs. But he still looks thin, even with this frame, as if he has squeezed and tightened himself down as much as he can. He is doing all this for $30,000.

He is facing Mike Perez, a Cuban who lives in Ireland but is fighting tonight in the US. Perez is a little shorter, a little heavier, and the chances of who is going to win tonight inch a little further in his direction. He has 19 wins, 12 knockouts and 0 losses, and he was one of Cuba's top amateurs.

Both men are southpaws and heavyweights, but that is where the similarities pretty much begin and end. The Russian's legs and upper-body movement are stiff. He comes at his opponent in straight lines. He is what could be known as an 'honest' fighter with a not-bad, slightly padded record. A good B-side for the casual fan who does not know what they are looking at.

Perez, meanwhile, is short and neat, and he bends at the waist as much as he can, shifting and dipping his body to zip in single counter punches, and he moves his head away and back from the blows that come back at him.

The commentators love the fight. They praise the good punches and the rapid and frequent action. It is rare to see a good heavyweight fight like this one, they say. They harken back to Ibeabuchi–Tua, the gold standard of recent heavyweight fights.

Abdusalamov is what people would call 'game' and, while he is getting beaten, he is not getting beaten up.

The ten rounds end, and Perez wins clearly, if not easily: 97–92 on two scorecards, a too-close 95–94 on the last.

Afterwards, Abdusalamov goes back to his dressing room. He curses lightly beneath his breath. 'My face,' he says. 'It hurts.'

Someone fetches ice. A doctor looks at him, gives him the all-clear.

John David Jackson, a former world champion who is now a trainer of champions, does not like what is going on. He insists Mago goes to the hospital.

Someone asks Abdusalamov again. 'Where is the hurt?'

'My face.'

'Any headache?'

Yes/No/Yes/No. No one is sure what Abdusalamov says next. There are too many things getting lost in translation.

Someone stitches a cut.

Abdusalamov gets up later to piss in a cup. He is feeling worse. Progressively worse.

He gets taken outside. No one calls an ambulance. An inspector tells his team to put him in a cab and take him to the hospital. He stumbles against a wall on the way out.

Outside, in the middle of Manhattan, Abdusalamov goes down on one knee. He begins to vomit.

They get him into a cab. They race to St Luke's–Roosevelt Hospital near Central Park. It is about a twenty-minute drive. Valuable time lost.

Abdusalamov gets to the hospital and is told to wait. He is put into a line of people. His team go outside and call an ambulance to take him to another hospital. He vomits again and the hospital staff notice.

They cut open his skull and drain the blood. They put him into a coma. He has a stroke the next day.

He survives, somehow. Sometimes, they do. Somehow. But he is broken.

He is still alive, still with his family, but he needs 24-hour care. Lots of therapies, given consistently over time, have given him some level of communication. His family understand the grumblings and mumblings.

Financially, he is fine. His family sues the State, which was supposed to be looking after him that night. They get $22 million in compensation. It is the largest payment ever made by the State of New York to a single personal-injury victim.

It is a brotherhood that no one wants to join, made up of those who find a line drawn for them, through injury, between who they were going to be and who they were forced to become.

There was Maria Lindberg and there was Frida Wallberg and there was Armand Krajnc in Sweden. And there is also Jermain

Taylor, a brain bleed in Berlin in 2009 making him turn the corner into the end of his career, ending up haunted by his own mind. There was Lamar 'Kidfire' Parks and Tommy Morrison, their careers punctuated by flunked HIV tests. There was Sugar Ray Seales, whose eyesight faded as he danced and ducked his way through the medicals until the walls closed in.

And then there was 'Baby' Joe Mesi, heavyweight contender. He was selling out over 19,000 seats in Buffalo, New York. Hometown hero. The next great franchise. *Can't miss* written all over.

But a sure bet is still a bet.

Everything changed in March 2004, when he fought against Vassily Jirov in Las Vegas.

The story: Mesi to be solidified as the next in line. He was undefeated in twenty-eight fights, ranked first amongst the contenders. Jirov was a former IBF cruiserweight champion, seen on the downside, his name making up space on the right-hand side of the poster. He was to be a pitstop.

Mesi dominated most of the fight but was knocked down three times in the final rounds. He scraped the win but forgot things over the next few days. He lost his balance. There were bleeds on his brain that were small enough to be reabsorbed. But it still came at a cost.

The Nevada authorities, when the news broke, acted quick and said he could no longer fight. The other US states followed suit. Two years slipped by, then a loophole.

'My licence expired,' says Mesi. 'That was how we won the case. It wasn't on clinical evidence, but on whether anyone could suspend a fighter whose licence had expired. It meant I was free to go and apply anywhere I wanted.'

The first fight back was in Puerto Rico in April 2006, an uninspiring eight rounds. To Canada, a fight in Montreal. The last five were in the US, in places like Russellville, Arkansas; Manistee, Michigan; Chester, West Virginia – about as far from the bright lights as you can get.

'The thought at the time,' he says, 'was that I'd fight in these smaller shows and lesser-known states so that I could prove myself physically and show that I was healthy. I'd climb the ladder and get back into contention.'

But the momentum was gone. Not dissipated, blocked. He became yesterday's man. The one people looked at politely with a mixture of pity and awe. *Didn't he get the message? Doesn't he know it's over?*

Controversy followed. No one wanted him to fight. But he wanted to. Mesi knew he was smart, felt he was making the right decisions. His own doctors said, *OK*. Even now, he sounds, when he talks about it, as if he cannot believe what he was up against.

'It was very challenging and very depressing,' he says. 'And very political.'

It takes time, but life eventually teaches us that there are some fights you are not meant to win. 'I thought that if I proved myself,' says Mesi, 'maybe HBO and New York would invite me back. And I got in shape around the fifth or sixth fight back. I was in tip-top shape.'

Things were not the same, though. 'Two years went by, with the smaller fights and training and travelling and then there was a point when I heard, through the grapevine, that no one was going to let me fight in California or Las Vegas.'

The end came on a plane going into the air above Connecticut in

2007 after the last fight, against Shannon Miller in Rhode Island. 'I turned to my then-fiancée,' says Mesi, 'and I said, "I think it's over. I don't want to fight this political battle any more. I'm on a treadmill." And the truth is that I didn't want to fight physically, if I didn't have the potential to reach my goal.'

He is in a better place now. Marriage, children, a job he enjoys. But he understands the feeling. He was thirty-one when he was injured. 'I know what it's like to have someone tell you that you cannot do what you do,' he says. 'You're being told that you can't earn a living. It was difficult at the time, especially after all the hard work and effort. I was one fight away from a title shot, so the timing was also very bad. But I'm in a different place now. I have a different life and lifestyle today. I'm happy, so I guess it all worked out.'

It does not take much to die from a subdural haematoma. The American university UCLA puts the mortality rate at between 50 and 90 per cent for an acute injury. Other researchers, looking at these injuries overall, put the mortality rate at just under 40 per cent. In 1991, the *Journal of Neurosurgery* said that the most critical factor was the speed of treatment, with mortality rates falling to 30 per cent for those undergoing surgery in fewer than four hours, with functional survival rates as high as 65 per cent.

Any bleeding in the brain used to signal the end of a career, but that stance has shifted. In 2023, you can still be licensed to fight in many places – parts of the US, the UK, some other European countries – if the bleeding has been minor. And in more-distant lands, where the licensing consists of a basic medical and not much else, such questions are rarely asked.

But these are the ones for whom medical treatment is sought. How many fighters must go home from the gym with a splitting headache that lasts for a day or two but do not seek a doctor? How many small, microscopic bleeds resolve themselves without intervention?

A great and unanswered question is how many fighters go into a match while hurt. The pains are mostly minor – a sore hand; teeth still loose after an errant, too-hard punch; a cut that has only just closed; a hip that does not feel quite right.

It is not unusual, nor even uncommon, for this to happen. And when it goes wrong, when it goes *really* wrong, it seems always that the signs were there. In 1995, Gerald McClellan was injured gravely when fighting against Nigel Benn in London. It came out afterwards that McClellan had been having strange neurological symptoms in the ring during sparring, often stopping and blinking his eyes, shaken in ways that should not have happened by the lightest of punches. But he carried on, anyway, as that was his business.

Kyiv, Ukraine, March 1998. It is a low-rent affair, but that could just be the graininess of the videotape. You can hear the low voices of an unseen crowd at the Palace of Sports, but the film is so bad, so poor, that the figures on it look like a badly done child's picture, the paint dragged over a cheap canvas with a thick brush.

The American Douglas Dedge stands on the mat in his black *gi* pants, bandages wrapped and taped around his hands, going up into his wrists. He is barefoot.

The opponent, Yevgeni Zolotarev, does not look much better.

He wears wrestling boots and blue shorts, and his hands are unwrapped.

It is two minutes into the fight and Dedge has fended off a takedown by sprawling on the mat. He has also removed one of his wristbands and tried to use it to choke Zolotarev, a bizarre move that Dedge has tried once before in a fight against Sean Brockmole in the small US town of Griffin, Georgia. It took Brockmole fewer than two minutes in a non-standard ring with sagging ropes and a rucked-up canvas to submit Dedge with an armbar.

But now Dedge is in Kyiv, and the stakes are higher because everything about the event, from the promoters to the managers to the staff, feels looser and more amateur, with a greater number than usual of corners cut.

Dedge is a father of five, Ned Flanders in a martial arts outfit, and he moves like an amateur. He walks in behind one weak kick, and he falls forwards and attempts, badly, to take Zolotarev's legs. He fails and Zolotarev lands on top of him, takes his back, flips Dedge over, and mounts him.

Zolotarev begins to punch, his back to the camera. Something like sixteen punches go in, and it seems that most of them land. Dedge squirms and struggles, with little idea of how to defend or escape.

Somehow, the pair rotate so that they are in profile towards the camera, and Dedge has given up trying to do something, do anything, and he slaps his hand against the mat to signify that he is quitting.

It has lasted fewer than five minutes.

Dedge gets up and puts his hand to his eye. Something is wrong.

Something is deeply wrong. He stumbles and falls backwards. Some medics rush in and lift him onto a stretcher, and they run with him to the side, where they begin to work on him. He is rushed to the Kyiv Institute of Surgery, where he dies. Head injuries.

It becomes clear that Dedge should not have been in any type of fight. A reporter examines what happened and talks to the other fighters, all of whom had misgivings about the professionalism of the show, and he discovers that Dedge was just a warm body to the promoters, who did not check his few credentials or his overstated experience.

Dedge had clearly been unwell.

'He would lose his vision and get extremely lightheaded,' says one of his Florida training partners. 'We would have to stop grappling with him, as he would be staring off into space, and his face would be white as a sheet.'[4]

Dedge was fighting for $2,000 and travel expenses. Neither his wife nor his family receive any money from the promoters.

DEATH IN THE BRAIN

It is something that you notice as you get older and your perception of risk changes. As your own body ages, as you become aware of all the ways in which it can break or be damaged, when the echoes of youth begin to sound on your bones, you wince more at the sight of the blows to the head, those shots running up a bill that gets paid later, with interest.

And it was easy to assume that the people you saw being hurt in their youth would be OK when they got older. But the folly of youth, always, is to think that it is somehow different from previous generations, that the current way of thinking and being is markedly different and remarkably better than everything that came before.

But the truth is that while history never truly repeats itself, it *does* have a longstanding habit of rhyming.

West Concord, Massachusetts, US, June 2023. It was a peaceful place, nestled up in the woods about half an hour from Boston, not far from where Thoreau took himself off into the trees to write *Walden*. A big, steel train goes once an hour from the centre of the city, then north, gradually curving west to beyond the commuter belt, into the small-town part of itself that America loves to mythologise.

It was a short walk from the station, made a little longer and more pleasant by a brief dally in the New England woods, to the Dr Robert C. Cantu Concussion Center.

It was less a medical facility than a suite of offices at the Emerson Health Center and looked to provide what it called 'traditional as well as integrative, individualised treatment for those suffering from concussive brain injury'.

Dr Cantu may well have been the most prominent voice in sports concussion medicine in the United States. By 2023, he had written more than thirty-four books on neurology and sports medicine, authored more than 400 publications, was a clinical professor of neurology and neurosurgery and a co-founder of the CTE Center at the Boston University School of Medicine.

He was writing emails at his desk that morning, dressed in a pink, checked shirt with his initials, 'RCC', stitched onto the pocket. When he spoke, he often put his hands together in front of him, his fingers raised into a steeple, and he deliberated carefully over each word.

'Here,' he said, patiently, 'is a place where we treat people with concussions, who have post-concussion syndrome and present with persistent post-concussion syndrome. We also evaluate and treat people with symptoms consistent to CTE [Chronic Traumatic Encephalopathy]. Unfortunately, it's not yet one of those things that we can diagnose with 100 per cent accuracy in any living individual.'

Newark, New Jersey, US, 1928. These were things already known, things that were never told in order to be polite. But it was always there in the older fighters who shuffled along with cloudy thoughts, lost in the decaying landscape of their own minds. If you took a guy too far, long past the point when looking at them started being painful, and you abandoned them on the other side, far too broken to do anything else, it was called 'cutting paper dolls'.

But it took a pathologist to medicalise it, to give it a polite and scientific name even if much of what he assumed was wrong and he could offer no real solution or treatment.

Dr Harrison Martland was in his mid-forties and worked at the Newark Medical Center. He was also the chief medical examiner in New Jersey. He had been in that post for a year when he sat down and wrote a paper called 'Punch Drunk' for the *Journal of the American Medical Association.*

Martland was heavyset, his hair parted to one side, and he wore thin, steel-frame glasses. There is a picture extant of him performing an autopsy, a half-smoked cigarette hanging from his mouth and pressed gently between two lips. His skin in those pictures looks sallow and loose, beginning to sag with age, the outer layer of a man who seems to not spend enough time in the daylight. Someone whose skin has been soaked for too long in darkness.

He had been born in 1883 in Newark, graduated with his first degree in 1901 and attended a medical school until 1905, becoming a pathologist with the Newark City Hospital in 1909. He went to France during World War One and then returned to Newark.

In 1925, he became an expert on radiation after examining the rotting of jaws from watch dial painters inadvertently digesting radium paint by licking their paintbrushes to reshape them.

And in 1928, he turned to boxing.

As the authors Abhinav R. Changa, Robert A. Vietrogoski and Peter W. Carmel described in the journal *Brain*,

> To understand Martland's role in the story of punch drunk, we must first look at his scientific predecessors. Dr Wilfred Trotter, an accomplished British surgeon, noted in a talk entitled *On Certain Minor Injuries of the Brain* delivered in 1924, that concussion is an 'essentially transient state' that 'does not as such comprise any evidence of structural cerebral injury, and is always followed by amnesia for the actual onset of the accident'. This understanding of concussion would be contested in the years ahead. Dr C. B. Cassasa, one of these contesters, published a report in 1924 that documented perivascular haemorrhages after the incidence of head trauma.[5]

Cassasa believed that trauma to the head caused cerebral spinal fluid, which flows over the surface of the brain and down the spinal cord, to be disrupted in its movement, leading to lacerations in the muscle fibres between the blood vessel walls and the dura, ultimately resulting in bleeding on the brain. This was followed three years later, in 1927, by the work of Dr Michael Osnato and Dr Vincent Gilberti, who published a case series lending further credence to Cassasa's work.

Martland looked at the case studies of twenty-three boxers, five of whom he personally examined. Those five, he wrote, had been deemed 'punch drunk' by a promoter.

It was determined later that one of them had been the light-weight Nathan Ehrlich, about whom little can be determined with finality. The nature of record keeping in the early half of the twen-tieth century is more whispering, fluttering myth than cold and hard, verifiable, fact. Even the year in which Ehrlich was born is up for debate.

Modern records, gleaned from multiple sources, indicate that Ehrlich had around fifty-five fights between 1905 and 1911. Howev-er, the actual numbers will vary by a great degree as many will not have been documented and the ones listed may not be accurate. There is also no indication as to how much training Ehrlich did or whether his career carried on after 1911, with him adopting the common practice of fighting under different names and in towns and states where the results were not recorded. It is highly likely that Ehrlich's career was lengthier and comprised more fights than will ever be definitively known.

But what can be determined from current records is that Ehr-lich fought many six-round fights, often only a few weeks apart. He appears to have fought six times in 1905, four times in 1908, twenty-seven times in 1909, twelve times in 1910, and six times in 1911. That is fifty-five fights in 2,497 days, or on average a fight around every six weeks. His busiest year – 1909 – saw Ehrlich fight around every twelve days.

Martland determined that Ehrlich had been 'punch drunk'. Ehrlich became the first boxer in history to ever be diagnosed this way.

Much of what Martland termed to be symptomatic of being 'punch drunk' remains unchallenged today. Mood swings, forgetfulness, a loss of balance and an ongoing deterioration were all symptoms set out in the original 'Punch Drunk' paper.

Or, as Harry L. Parker neatly surmised, 'The point that Martland urged … was that the high frequency with which professional pugilists [boxers] develop crippling disease of the central nervous system of one sort or another suggests a result of the repeated injuries to the brain that they received while carrying on the activities of their profession.' [6]

There are some mistakes and assumptions in Martland's work. He determined erroneously that the type of fighter picking up damage was not the boxer, the one who glided around the ring practising what A. J. Liebling would later call 'the sweet science', but the swinging and wild brawler who employed the philosophy of taking three to give one.

Others would follow Martland in his work. Over twenty years later, the British neurologist Macdonald Critchley would publish his own, similarly titled paper, this one called 'Punch Drunk Syndrome: The Chronic Traumatic Encephalopathy of Boxers'.

What is notable about Critchley's work is that it is the first time that the determination of chronic traumatic encephalopathy (CTE) is used. He also noted that the onset of behavioural and neurological change began six years after retirement, with an average of sixteen years passing before symptoms appeared.

More work followed in 1989 when Professor John Arthur Nicholas Corsellis and his team looked at the brains of fifteen boxers, producing their paper 'Boxing and the Brain' for the *British Medical Journal.*

Wrote *Kinesiology Review* in 2012,

> Corsellis and his colleagues autopsied the brains of 15 boxers who died decades after quitting the ring. Over half of the boxers investigated had participated in more than 300 fights and many had careers spanning longer than 15 years. In their examination of the brains of these former boxers, they saw consistent neurological changes that were atypical for men of their age. To confirm that the changes were consistent with chronic traumatic encephalopathy, Corsellis also interviewed the men's wives and other family members about the physical presentation of the condition. The symptoms described during the interviews were similar to those mentioned by previous authors describing dementia pugilistica or CTE.[7]

This may have been neurology, but it was not rocket science. The evidence had been clear for years, even if the lines of causality remained murky.

In 1983, *Sports Illustrated* ran a long piece called 'Too Many Punches, Too Little Concern'. Robert H. Boyle, the writer of that piece, asked three boxers – Jerry Quarry, who was retired but looking to make a comeback, heavyweight contender Randall 'Tex'

Cobb and bantamweight journeyman Mark Pacheco to undergo brain testing.

Quarry had been retired for just over five years after sixty-three professional fights. He was thirty-seven. Cobb was twenty-eight and had a record of 20–3. Pacheco had 11 wins, 11 losses and 1 draw.

It was no surprise that Quarry performed the worst of the three. Wrote Boyle, 'Like the others, his neurological exam was normal. But his CAT scan was slightly worse than Pacheco's – it showed a cavum, enlarged lateral and third ventricles and a suggestion of cortical atrophy. And his neuropsychological results were poor.'

The doctor examining Quarry said,

He did poorly on the test of visual motor perception. He did poorly on [the] test of connecting the dots. The only one he did well on was the digit symbol test. The psychologist and I are not saying that Quarry is punch-drunk where he can't walk straight, that kind of thing. What we're saying is that he has problems with certain cognitive functions – short-term memory and perceptual motor ability.[8]

Quarry would remain sanguine, acknowledging that he fought fights with a broken hand, a broken back, hepatitis.

But, he said, 'You step into the ring, and you know there's a chance of getting knocked out, of getting hurt, but you figure your abilities are good enough that you can handle yourself appropriately.'

Yet he came back three more times – twice in 1983, and once in

1992. And he would become the poster boy for brain damage in boxing.

Still, there were deniers, a position that would come to look ridiculous over the years. A. J. Liebling, a *New Yorker* writer who would doubtlessly appear on a Mt Rushmore of boxing writers, produced two of the definitive books of boxing literature – *The Sweet Science* and *A Neutral Corner*. In the former, he wrote of the chronic brain damage found in fighters: 'If a boxer ever went as crazy as Nijinsky [a Russian ballet dancer who was committed to a mental asylum], all the wowzers in the world would be screaming "punch-drunk." Well, who hit Nijinsky? And why isn't there a campaign against ballet? It gives girls thick legs.'

Denial is the price we pay for our love.

West Concord, Massachusetts, US, June 2023. They know why they are there when they come, burdened with that feeling that they are at the top of the rollercoaster, tilting and coasting, about to come down. They can see, *feel*, what is ahead of them.

It is a short road to get here, the body beginning to creak and fail. Words lost, thoughts beginning to scramble. The knowledge rising that they were not the ones to outrun the inevitable and that something – *that thing* – is coming, and they need help to, if not stop it, hold it back.

'Some of them have very mild problems,' said Cantu of the men and women that come through his door. 'They might have trouble remembering what somebody told them an hour or two before. They might have some mild memory problems or executive dysfunction issues, so their insight and judgement aren't perfect. They may score as having "mild cognitive impairment" on the tests we give them.'

He went on, 'Mentally, they are deteriorating. And there are behavioural dysregulation issues, such as flying off the handle and getting into fights, or being severely depressed. Those are the three main buckets.'

But they are still functioning, Cantu said. 'They're still independent. In terms of daily activities, they're still driving, still feeding themselves, still dressing themselves. That's probably the majority.'

And they know what is coming: 'Very few of them are already worried about CTE. They've learned enough from talking to people. Most don't do reading, but they talk with other people, so they know CTE is out there and they're at risk of it. And they know that it's a progressive problem without a cure, so they are apprehensive.'

This is what CTE is at its most basic definition and understanding: each blow to the head has the potential to release a protein called 'tau' into the brain. Once this tau latches onto parts of the brain, it starves them until they die. And the rest of the brain falls like a line of standing dominoes.

'CTE,' wrote lead author Dr Ann McKee,

is a distinctive pathology characterized by neuronal p-tau aggregates that are focal, perivascular, and cortical in mild disease in young individuals and widespread and diffuse in severe disease and in older individuals. CTE tau consists of a distinctive molecular structural configuration of p-tau fibrils that is unlike the changes observed with aging, Alzheimer's disease, or any other tauopathy.[9]

It generally takes over a decade after the end of a career before the symptoms start to show, but there are plenty of fighters still getting into the ring in their late twenties and early thirties whose speech has already begun to slur, their minds beginning to scramble.

The symptoms are insidious, a battery of things that seem random but whose design becomes apparent over time. It begins with the odd incident – the forgotten name, the item that cannot be found, a mood swinging into anger over the smallest, most insignificant provocation. But then these incidents persist, until it seems a darkening pattern is forming to an unheard tune.

There will be disorientation and confusion, sometimes dizziness and headaches. The body pains all over. Lack of insight and poor judgement come eventually. Depression, panic attacks, anxiety. And then the overt dementia kicks in, the final cans being kicked over in the mind.

'Severe cases,' wrote McKee in 2009, 'are accompanied by a progressive slowing of muscular movements; a staggered, propulsive gait; masked facies; impeded speech; tremors; vertigo; and deafness.'

She went on:

Corsellis, Bruton, and Freeman-Browne described three stages of clinical deterioration as follows: The first stage is characterized by affective disturbances and psychotic symptoms. Social instability, erratic behavior, memory loss, and initial symptoms of Parkinson disease appear during the second stage. The third stage consists of general cognitive dysfunction progressing to dementia and is often accompanied by full-blown Parkinsonism, as well as speech and gait abnormalities. Other symptoms include dysarthria [slurred speech], dysphagia [difficulty swallowing], and ocular abnormalities, such as ptosis [drooping eyelids].[10]

And it is mostly, almost entirely, due to head trauma. McKee, Stein, Huber et al. (2023) found that 97 per cent of CTE cases were related to individuals with a history of repetitive head impacts (RHI). Other studies amongst the general population have found CTE usually in fewer than 3 per cent of those studied.

Of those affected, it said, the evidence highly suggested a causal relationship. There were, they summarised, no alternative explanations.

Even though it was well known amongst the boxing trade a century ago that fighters would become 'punch drunk' after too many fights, the dangers of concussions were not well known. Or, indeed, they were not considered to be dangerous, more a temporary blip in consciousness, the human body restarting itself.

But a concussion is much more. It is a change in consciousness brought about by head trauma. But the damage does not end when a normal state of mind returns. Its after-effects can lurk for years and decades.

West Concord, Massachusetts, US, June 2023. Cantu had seen many patients over the decades. It was for him that many came across the country. He looked at them, examined them, sometimes referred them to other doctors in their local areas.

He was a doctor at his core. 'My role is to help everybody who comes through the door,' he said, with a touch of sombreness. 'They come to seek my opinion on a neurological condition that they may or may not have. I'm not here to condemn what they do they, or even to tell them that they cannot do it. I'm here to point out the risk that they're at and how to modify it if they are still early in their careers. And I will tell them, if they are still active and have neurological symptoms, whether I think they should stop.'

He could not condemn boxing, though.

'I feel the same way about it that I did when I watched Evel Knievel jump canyons in the 1970s,' he said. 'People do risky things for money because society wants them to. I won't say it shouldn't go on and people shouldn't make money if they understand the risks. But at the same time, I wouldn't ever recommend someone box for health reasons.'

It is a diagnosis in valediction, impossible to confirm until after death. And much of what comes before, of whether someone has it and how badly, is guesswork. Educated guesswork, but still guesswork.

The most commonly used barometer is the McKee staging scheme, which ranges from the mildest at Stage 1 to the most severe at Stage 4. But even this is applied only after death.

And the conversation has shifted into CTE being experienced in two stages: a 'low' stage, equivalent to Stages 1 and 2 in the McKee system, and a 'high' stage, equivalent to Stages 3 and 4 in the same.

But it is still, for all that educated guesswork, like a painter squinting one eye and looking at their work around the focal point of their thumb.

Even Dr Cantu admitted it. 'Depending on how abnormal and severe the symptoms are,' he said, 'and on how high their exposure is, we can think in terms of the probabilities of them having CTE as being suggestive, possible, or probable. But we can never be definite without doing an autopsy of their brain.'

It is sometimes said that the toughest opponent for any athlete is retirement. The crowds chanting their name disappear, the arena lights fade, the body begins its decline. The fighter can no longer do what they once did, and in so many ways. And yet they are still young, still strong, formidable.

But being old in the boxing ring and being a young man still come at the same age. Two trains at the same station on different tracks.

And then the forgetting begins. The mood swings come, too, and take with them the feeling the fighter had that they were truly special, that everything they did to abate and stem the damage taken may not have been enough.

There are often no pensions, no pots of money to fall back on. There is a former world champion, a nerve injury impeding the muscles in one arm, the limb now withered and useless, who went to his former promoter and asked for $30,000 to help save his arm. The promoter told him to go fuck himself.

'Boxers are kind of a disenfranchised group,' said Cantu, 'and they don't have people looking out for them unless they are very successful. They don't have unions and there are no lawyers, and it's especially true with the fighters who never made a lot of money or didn't do much after their careers ended. And when they start to go downhill, there's often pretty scanty medical coverage for them.'

All sports are businesses, but boxing is more of a business than any other sport. It is also entirely focused on the next big fight and the next cash grab.

The UFC, which has trampled boxing in recent years and is the backbone of the mixed martial arts (MMA) economy, has a long-term plan.

Dana White, its president, once said, 'Boxing doesn't run a real business. What these guys do is every event is a going-out-of-business sale. They're trying to get as much money as they can in the door. The two guys at the top of the card make all the money. And how many fights a year are they doing? One? Three? Five?'

He went on, 'One of the other things we do and why we run a real business is we reinvest in the sport. Not just the business of the UFC, but we reinvest in the sport, and we've built a global business over the last twenty years. We have infrastructure. We have 450 employees.'

The US has no national commission that oversees boxing like the NFL oversees football. Each state has its own commission, if it has one, and even then there are outliers, in the same way that some Native American casinos run on their own rules. At best, there is cooperation across borders.

'There is no oversight,' said Cantu. 'And there is no national boxing commission. There are fifty states in the US, each of whom has their own rules and regulations. They're all different and there's no uniformity. And there's no fund for boxers who have suffered brain damage or other injury to collect welfare from. They're independent contractors and on their own. Yes, there are some who can make and keep incredible amounts of money, but very few do.'

Hemet, California, US, 1995. Jerry Quarry rattles around his brother's home, four years from death, his thoughts thick and curdled. He would live by himself if he could. But he cannot, even if he could afford it. And he cannot do that, either – his money gone, the only thing he has left is the $614 a month he receives in disability payments.

His brother James looks after him though, the pair living with James's partner. And there is Mike, one of his other brothers, but he is not doing too well these days either. The pair of them beyond merely damaged, irreparably broken, going to get worse.

Quarry was one of the great contenders, the guy who would have been champion if the four or five guys above him had picked up a basketball instead of boxing gloves. But that is what happens when you are a little on the small side not only in a land of giants but in the deepest and richest seam of heavyweight talent in history.

He fought them all: Muhammad Ali, Joe Frazier, and Floyd Patterson, twice; Ken Norton; Jimmy Ellis; Earnie Shavers; Ron Lyle. George Foreman was afraid of him. All diamond names in a golden age. He won all the fights that he should have lost, but he also managed to lose all those he should have won.

Quarry dipped in and out of retirement. He commentated for a bit and was good at it, but then attempted a comeback on another television network, and his bosses let him go. That was the kind of luck he made for himself. He eventually drifted out from the big lights in 1977, but then he kept coming back.

He needs help with everything in 1995, has to be coaxed into the most basic of things as if he is a small child. Forty-nine years old, but the brain is much older. *Like an eighty-year-old man*, one doctor says.

Quarry had more comebacks than Sinatra. He retired in 1975, 1977 and 1983. And then there was more fight, in 1992, against a guy whose name no one ever spells correctly, and that guy came in with a career of 3 wins, 4 losses and 1 draw. Quarry lost that one in his forty-seventh year.

Even by the low standards of boxing, it was a bad fight. There was Quarry, bigger and broader but not in a good way, losing over six to a fighter that would never win another one. And there he was afterwards, his teeth broken, just over the tipping point into that final, dark run.

'At first, all I could see is a big, 200-pound, six-foot gorilla, and it was hard for me to accept that he was an invalid,' his brother James tells the *Los Angeles Times*. 'Now I don't get upset with him. I do get a little frustrated when he walks off four or five times a day and we have to go find him. Sometimes we can't find him, and we have to call the police, and they bring him back.'

He goes on, 'He's spaced out most of the time. He hallucinates. He hears voices. He cries. He gets scared. He gets confused. He can't go outside because of the medication that he's on. It makes him real sensitive to the sun. He lives in a very, very small world.'[11]

There is a hope that Quarry, lost in the fog, is at some sort of peace. That the forgetting took away the bad memories and left him only in a warm glow. But that is probably futile. He probably knows that he is sick, that tomorrow he will be less than today.

La Habra, California, 2006. Eleven years later, they still talk about him in relation to Jerry. This is Mike, the light-heavyweight contender brother, a guy who lost his own world title fight and then carried on, edging further and further from the light.

The problem with Mike was that he could not punch. He was a beautiful boxer, skilled and fluid, but he stopped only sixteen opponents in sixty-three victories. His brother took out thirty-two of the fifty-three he beat.

And then there were the losses: thirteen for Mike, along with six draws; nine for Jerry, four even.

Jerry has been dead for seven years: pneumonia, heart attack, life support taken away. He made it, somehow, to fifty-three. And Mike is not far behind. He cannot walk any more. He is fifty-five.

These brothers loved to fight, usually with each other. Hard sparring day after day, week after week, the coaches and the corners pleading with them to stop. *There's no quit in a Quarry*, their father would tell them when they were young.

Mike's wife, Ellen, loves him, but she has already finished grieving. He has been gone for a while, left a shell of a man.

'I don't like boxing. I think it is stupid,' she tells the *Times*. 'I am sad at what my husband went through, sad at the many, many losses that occurred in his life because of boxing.'[12]

There is no simple equation to any of this, no formula where x number of punches to the head puts you at tipping point. No way yet of saying, 'OK, this is the most you can do.' You cannot calculate with certainty the amount of time that you can box for, or the number of fights, or the rounds of sparring that can be 'safely' undertaken.

Boxing is a game of smoke and mirrors, and so it is appropriate that much of what we know about the damage inflicted on brains is done in the shadows. Age is a factor because the older you get, the harder it is for the brain to recover, and the dimming of the reflexes means that punches are harder to avoid. So is style – if you take too many and take them badly, that stacks the odds. Length of career, too, for obvious reasons. And then there are the guys who move up in weight to take on those much stronger and more powerful than themselves.

And then there are genetics.

'The Quarry brothers are interesting,' said Dr Cantu. 'The two of them apparently whaled it out every day before they turned professional. And they both had fairly lengthy professional careers, had dementia, and then died young. That's a close gene pool. But there are also things that can make the symptoms worse that we don't have the ability to adequately test for. And it can be made worse by things such as hypertension, cardiovascular disease and physical inactivity. There is also alcoholic dementia.'

He went on, 'There are clearly other factors, because not everybody with the same exposure develops CTE. Some develop it with less exposure than others and there are those with high exposure who don't get it. But the greater the exposure, the greater the chance. So, there have to be other factors. The two factors that we can identify right now, in terms of the severity of CTE, are exposure and age. The second of those is that the longer you live, the greater chance that whatever CTE you have will get worse, because it's a progressive problem in most people.'

What else is there?

Gloves, because gloves worsen brain damage. As do helmets.

The purpose of the glove, since they were first introduced, was to protect the delicate bones of the hands. And heads are hard and angular, teeth are sharp, but wearing gloves gives a false sense of security, because if you are no longer in danger of hurting your hands, it is easy to aim everything directly at the head.

And put a man in a headguard, and you reduce his vision through the leather slit, so he loses those milliseconds in which to get out of the way of a punch. And the headguard will absorb his sweat as it flows out of him, and it will get heavier and swing with more force than before. The head also becomes a larger target.

There is not much that can be done. CTE is a one-way street, its impacts both irreversible and progressive.

'Most people with CTE,' said Dr Cantu, 'find it to be a progressive problem, so the therapies are kind of like kicking a can down the road. The symptoms are likely to come back and need more medication or therapy. We're not getting at the root cause of CTE and we're not getting at the underlying pathology. We're just treating the symptoms, which is what we do with a lot of illnesses.'

He can help, though.

'There are therapies,' he said. 'A person's cognitive symptoms can be helped with cognitive therapy. If they have vestibular balance issues or ocular issues, they can be helped with vestibular or ocular therapy. If there are emotional issues, they can be helped by counselling and psychiatric treatment. And if the therapies are not sufficient, there are many medications.'

He could help, but not heal. That was the best he could do. It was another one of those lessons that life teaches you. Sometimes – most of the time – there is no perfect answer.

Dr Cantu tapped his hand on his desk. He gestured to the pictures on his walls. 'These are some of the people who have come to me for help,' he said.

If it was all smoke and mirrors, was there ever a safe amount of boxing?

'In relation to CTE?' he said. 'Sure. The answer to that is "yes". If you were to take fewer than 3,000 or 4,000 blows, which is not very many. If you're a very skilled boxer and don't do much sparring and fight infrequently, you could go for two or three years and not receive much trauma to the head. But is there a safe amount of boxing, so that you're at *no* risk? No, because you can die from subdural haematomas.'

One day, a young man or woman may come into Dr Cantu's office and ask these same questions. Maybe they will be at the beginning of their careers and want some information. They may not yet have gone too far down that road. They will be being cautious.

They will ask, *Will I get CTE if I fight?*

And they will receive the same answers. *No, I cannot tell you definitively if you will develop CTE, but I can tell you your odds. I can advise you.*

'I would try to have them understand,' Cantu said, 'that taking repetitive trauma to the head is not a good thing. And if they're going to continue, to try and structure it in such a way that they're going to receive the fewest blows to the head. So that's a limited amount of sparring, staying in wonderful cardiovascular shape and not having their weight fluctuate. But, frankly, if they've got little power and they're not extremely scientifically skilled, I would encourage them to go into another trade.'

THE BRAIN BANK

Boston, Massachusetts, June 2023. The building was in the southeast of Boston, about half an hour on the public transportation from the main, beating heart of the city, beyond the university. After the tram stopped at the Heath Street station, and before it turned to go back the way it had come, it was another few minutes by foot up the hill.

It could not be seen immediately. It was at the back of a large, anonymous grey building that you have to go around the back of, in the place where deliveries arrive. And then you see it, only because they point it out to you. If you did not know exactly where it was, it would not exist. Or not *not* exist. Not exactly. It would be one of those sites that are dead spaces. An *un*space. The blind spots in the centre of your vision, so anonymous that they might not be there. The distant cousin at the wedding whose name no one could ever remember.

It was hard to know what to expect. A sign? A symbol? A memorial? Instead, it was generic and may well have been a factory, or a storage area, some hidden spot far away from prying eyes where a special key was needed to get in and there were no windows.

It was then that it could be seen, a small, brick building of one storey that sat behind the Veterans Administration hospital in

Boston. And there was no sign on the door, no indication that this was where they all go, where they are brought in the days after the lives they have supported have expired. It was there.

This was where the brains came in.

It is officially called the Understanding Neurologic Injury and Traumatic Encephalopathy (UNITE) Brain Bank, although most people use only the last two words. The Brain Bank. By 2023, it had spent fifteen years amassing the largest collection of brains post-mortem to examine the long-term effects of traumatic injury. It began when the Concussion Legacy Foundation (CLF) partnered with the US Department of Veterans Affairs and Boston University to create what was originally known as the VA-BU-CLF Brain Bank.

There, Dr Ann McKee met Chris Nowinski, co-founder of the CLF, then known as the Sports Legacy Institute. McKee had already examined the brain of one former boxer when Nowinski asked her if she would look at the brains of two former NFL players.

'That was my first exposure to CTE and football players,' McKee said in Boston. 'I found that both of them had been nine-year veterans of the NFL, and they had both been linebackers. And they had profound CTE changes. I'd really been looking at neurodegenerative disease up to that point, which affects an elderly population. So, it floored me that it was here in forty-five-year-old men.'

She went on, 'I was amazed to see this in the football players. And because I had been working with Alzheimer's disease and because I had set up the brain bank for that, along with the Framingham Heart Study Brain Bank, both here at the Veterans Administration, I set up this project to study the long-term consequences of brain trauma.'

McKee was not the on-call person to receive donations, though. That was Ray Nicks.

In June 2023, Nicks was in his early thirties. He was trim, his hair cut closely to his head, and he wore a neat, pressed shirt with no tie. He had a warm smile. 'I'm a *ray* of sunshine,' he said with a grin.

He had been with the Brain Bank for seven years. 'I'm originally from Canada,' he said. 'And in Canada, ice hockey is part of our religion. And I watched a bunch of my former teammates suffer with concussion issues. And then something made me decide that I wanted to be doing something more to help people. And doing this type of work was on top of my list.'

Nicks was the senior research fellow at the Brain Bank. His job was to receive and then manage the processing of the brains when they arrived. They collected, he said, somewhere between 250 and 300 brains a year.

'My phone,' he said, 'is my best friend and my worst nightmare, because it's 24-7, 365 days a year. If a brain comes, a brain comes.'

Nicks stood behind a long, steel table just inside the main door of the annex building. There was half of a brain in front of him. It looked like someone had densely packed a series of clear balloons with large, smooth pieces of tuna. The other half was elsewhere.

He picked it up. 'Lots of people feel squeamish looking at these.' He turned the brain in his hands and started pointing at the various parts – the amygdala, the hippocampus, the lobes. He put it back down. 'This is what we get.'

The phone would ring or the pager would chirp, Nicks said, and then the brains and the spinal cords – the Brain Bank collected both – were removed wherever the patient had died. The material was then transported on wet ice to Boston. It was better, he explained, than dry ice for preserving the samples.

'In an ideal world,' he said, 'we get the entire brain. When it comes to processing the brain, we'll hemisect it, with one half going into fixative and one half going into the freezers. We cut them in serial sections, and they all get individually bagged so we can go back and identify them later. Those are stored at minus eighty degrees. The other half sits in fixative for a few weeks before we go and process the case.'

'In most of pathology,' he said, 'between four and six blocks of tissue will be taken so that they can check for things. But here, we take somewhere between thirty-eight and forty-six, depending on the protocol. That means we have a much higher resolution on every case, because we have such a higher throughput of pieces of tissue. We're able to stain and check for more diseases, meaning we can come up with a more detailed diagnosis.'

The entire process is anonymised, Nicks said.

'The only thing we know,' he explained, 'is what study it belongs in, and that is because different studies have different protocols. From there, we do our entire analysis completely blinded to everything. We come up with a diagnosis, then the clinical team will do their clinical analysis through things like medical records. And then we'll all meet together to have something called "the consensus". That is when the clinical team goes in and presents everything that they found and says what they think the diagnosis should be using Traumatic Encephalopathy Syndrome (TES) criteria. Pathology presents what they found with the slides. And then they can see what it was.'

Nicks handed the half of a brain over to one of the other people in the lab then stepped outside. He began to wash his hands in a sink where the tap was operated by a lever you pushed with your knee. 'It's good protocol,' he said. 'It may seem a bit silly, but when we exit back into the clean room, we have to wash off in our sink. Even if we didn't handle anything that was soaking wet or dirty.'

He walked over to a separate room with expensive camera equipment inside. 'What we try to do is take encyclopaedia-grade photographs here,' he said. 'No matter what we are doing, whether it's a presentation, a speech at a conference or whatever, it's always nicer to have better photographs. And this way, if it does end up in court, you have these beautiful, detailed photographs. You don't want a lawyer to say, "Hey, this photograph is unprofessional. What other parts of your operation are unprofessional?"'

Nicks left the annex, walked over to the main hospital building and went up the stairs. He went into a lab room. 'This is the generic lab,' he said.

There were three scientists in the lab: Becky, Petra and Liz.

Becky sat at a bench with a piece of brain in front of her. She was preparing to slice it into sections. 'I just need to get a new blade,' she said, turning away.

'We would take a section of brain tissue', said Nicks, 'and get it embedded in paraffin wax. Becky is then able to cut it at ten microns, which is a fraction of the thickness of paper. From there, she's able to put it onto one of these slides. These are then dried out.'

Becky began to slice the tissue. It looked like particularly delicate filmstock, as wispy as butterfly wings. She placed the slices onto the slides, working fast but with great care.

'This is just a small piece of tissue. Then there's the staining, which is what Petra is doing. The tissue is exposed to a variety of different chemicals and techniques that have been around for hundreds of years. There's nothing new here; we're not splitting the atom.'

A neuropathologist looks at the finished slides. Beyond CTE, the Brain Bank looks for other, similar afflictions that may lie in the slides. Different accumulations of protein concentrations within the tissue or the presence of pathognomonic lesions may indicate other conditions.

'We do a composite collection of slides and stains', said Nicks, 'so we can look for a variety of diseases beyond just CTE. How CTE is defined is an abnormal accumulation of hyperphosphorylated tau protein, with pathognomonic lesion/lesions at the depths of sulci or perivascular. There is a pathognomonic lesion in these places because of the repeated exposure to traumatic brain injuries. If a person does not have the pathognomonic lesion, they do not have CTE.'

Then comes the 'consensus'. Nicks said that this stage comes after the neuropathologist comes up with a diagnosis based on the criteria for a number of diseases, including CTE, all done while non-cognisant of the clinical information.

Nicks said, 'They base their decision solely on what they see microscopically. At "consensus", the clinical team will present clinical information and the clinicians will try to determine whether they meet Traumatic Encephalopathy Syndrome. The pathology team will then present their findings and diagnosis. They would need to have the pathognomonic lesions necessary for CTE diagnosis. They may also meet diagnostic criteria for other diseases which are part of their diagnosis.'

When the tests are completed, the clinic reaches out to the families with the results. 'The one thing that separates us from others', said Nicks, 'is that at the end of the process, when the neuropathologist has the diagnosis, they don't just send out a piece of paper. They will sit down with the relatives, or do it over Zoom or over the telephone, and they'll go over the entire diagnosis and try to help them make sense of it. That's completely unique to our facility.'

This may not be the only meeting, though. Sometimes, there are additional conferences between the Brain Bank and the families. 'Usually,' said Nicks, 'the neuropathologists do a great job helping to counsel the family with the weight of the diagnosis. The response from families is variable, because it is impossible to predict how a family will react; however, the majority of families are thankful that we have gone to so much time and effort to help.'

PENDER

Boston, Massachusetts, US, May 1963. Paul Pender, middleweight champion of the world, felt that he was at the end of the road. He was the champion again after a close rematch, a narrow points decision following a stoppage loss. It had been as close as a man squeaking through a closing door, his shoulders nearly glancing the wood.

He had been unusually intelligent inside and out of the ring, able to not only analyse his trade like an academic, but to speak in their terms, too.

'Boxing,' he told a writer once,

should be manipulation, working out a puzzle, putting the pieces together into an end. That's the satisfying part of the whole thing – to plan, to analyze, to stay with a pattern until it's successful. When I'm in the ring, I don't think of hitting a person. No, it's not humanitarianism. It's just that hitting is only part of the objective. Blood and guts is not the purpose of fighting. But the fans, through the debasement of the sport and deterioration of the calibre of fighter, have been de-educated. The trend is swinging toward the brutes.[13]

He had been the most boxer of boxers, a fighter who stood and moved on his toes, his jab working away for him all the time, the right hand kept to the side of his head. He hooked when he could, but it was mainly jab jab jab. An upright European fighter, a craftsman, in a New England setting.

Hands with a tendency to break had led him to this style, and he went wholeheartedly with it. He believed, he told people, in 'manipulation, not that savage, vicious stuff'.

'Who needs', he would opine, 'this type of abuse?'

He had cycled in and out of boxing for years. Six bones broken in six bouts, one after the other, in four years, punctuated by a retirement and enlistment. But his hands still hurt, and when the military could no longer take him and his pain, he went back to fighting.

In 1956, he retired after that final break, the fragile bones in his hands giving way again. But then he gave it another go two years later after a doctor fixed his hands, and from 1958 he rode a wave that took him to a world championship.

He beat Sugar Ray Robinson, the greatest of the greats, then beat him again. He defended twice, lost, and then won the rematch.

Champion again, he waited a while for the next big-money fight, but when it became apparent that there was not one out there, he decided that the simplest answer was also the best: retire.

It was, he felt, a good time to get out. This was not a trade that rewarded people over the long term and those who did not leave the party early and with grace found that they did not have that option when the hour turned late.

1963 was a *gooooooooooood* time to retire.

Thirty-two years old; 40 wins, 20 knockouts; 6 losses, 2 draws.

Everything intact.

Healthy.

Still young.

Still strong.

No one doubted it was a good time to get out.

THE DOCTOR

Boston, Massachusetts, US, June 2023. Sixty years later, Pender was patient zero in the study of CTE.

Dr Ann McKee sat in her office on the twelfth floor of the main building at the Jamaica Plain VA Medical Center. Her desk was against the left wall of the room, a window looking out over Boston to its right. There was a shelving unit on the other side filled with books and certificates.

'He was the one,' said McKee. 'He fought Sugar Ray Robinson, and he was quite a celebrity in the New England area. But then he became demented in later life, with some unusual behaviours. It seemed to start in his fifties, but he was very, very impaired by the time he was in his sixties.'

Pender's family brought him to the Alzheimer's Center at the VA Hospital. He had reached the point where he could no longer hold down a job and his personality had changed – he was irritable, paranoid.

A later paper that McKee was lead author on described one fighter, probably Pender: retired by thirty-three, two-time world champion, fought forty-eight professional bouts.

He had become unbalanced in his late fifties, moving from happy and easy-going to paranoid and irritable. He withdrew from people and then started to forget who those around him were. He lashed out verbally at his wife, attempted to hit her. Suspected vertigo followed. A hospitalisation led to a neurological examination that found him disorientated with poor memory. He was inattentive, too. There were other impairments.[14]

Pender died in 2003 at the Veterans Administration Hospital in Bedford, Massachusetts, about twenty miles outside of Boston. A spokesperson for the centre told the New York Times that Pender had had Alzheimer's disease. His wife allowed McKee to look at his brain.

'The clinicians all thought it was Alzheimer's because he had retired so young,' McKee said. 'They thought it couldn't possibly be connected to the boxing because of the decades in between. But I did the post-mortem and I was floored when I saw his pathology, because it was the signature of CTE. I'd never seen anything like it. It was a tau pathology with this extremely unusual pattern. I'd seen thousands of brains by this point, but I'd never seen this pattern before then. Pender became my index case.'

She went on, 'He's the reason I'm interested in disease. And it was after that that I met Chris Nowinski.'

Pender is often lost in the shuffle in the dialogue around CTE. The story over the past fifteen years has centred around American football and the NFL, with hockey and the NHL following behind. But before the football players and the hockey players and the wrestlers and the soldiers, there was Pender. The first one to come out of the shadows. But then he was gone, dissipated like fog in the sun.

Boxing had started the conversation but wandered off before it could become part of it.

'I think,' McKee said, 'in the past century, we had some case reports of boxers and their pathology. There was the "The Aftermath of Boxing" in *Psychological Medicine*, by Corsellis *et al*, in 1973. And there was some interest in the 1990s. But boxing had become unpopular in the past century and people categorised it as something that did not affect people. There was little interest. It was still lucrative, with matches worth millions of dollars, but it had fallen away because people thought it was gory and messed up. People had accepted it was not good for your brain.'

She started out as a neurologist, before moving into neuropathology.

'That's not the usual path,' she said. 'It used to be quite common, but most pathologists now specialise in neuropathology. I was a clinician but the reason I became interested in this was because I had patients who I needed to understand. They were behaving oddly or having unusual cognitive issues. That was a mystery and looking at their brains after death answers that.'

McKee did not like boxing. She flinched at the thought of what fighters went through. 'I think it's just gruesome,' she said. 'When you see the injuries. The blood and the black eyes...'

She trailed off.

When she spoke again, she said, 'It was always obvious that there was head trauma in boxing. But I had no idea about football. That was a revelation.'

There had been a time when she was a big football fan, but not now.

'I'm from the middle of America,' she said. 'Wisconsin. The Green Bay Packers were my team. I grew up with the whole scene. My brothers played football. My dad played football. Our best friend was the high school football coach. I was steeped in it.'

She went on, 'I loved it, 100 per cent. I watched every game. I went to the high school football games. But I can't watch it now. I think they're all delusional. It's just a matter of time. You get someone like Tom Brady, who's revered in these parts, but his brain is no different than anyone else's.'

There was horror, too, at the thought of children in the boxing ring. She sighed and looked down at the idea of them with their frail frames and thin necks, hitting each other in the ring, being hit in return. Being hurt.

'I can't,' she said. 'I just can't. Not only do I not recommend it, but I think it's very misguided. A child's brain is probably more

vulnerable. Their necks are weaker, and they don't have the physical size or skills. They're set up for brain trauma. And the brains
don't finish developing until someone is twenty-five. It's a very, very
irresponsible decision by a parent to allow their kid into the ring.'

At the end of the day, McKee did not want to see boxing banned,
despite its costs.

'I do think there's freedom of choice,' she said. 'And banning it
is not a choice that I would want to make. I'd rather people were
more informed of the risk so they could decide, in a careful and
thoughtful manner, if it was worth it to them. You only get one
brain. It doesn't regrow. And it determines everything about you.
Your brain is you. It's everything that you would consider to be you.
And that is what you're risking.'

GHOSTS

Palmyra, Pennsylvania, June 2023. 'Dr Ann McKee? She's getting
my brain when I die!'

Alan Blyweiss hobbled to the car from the door of his home. He
moved like a man tiptoeing barefoot across a floor of broken glass,
a vape in one hand, an ice-cold can of vanilla coffee in the other.
There was a small black bag filled with medication over his shoulder. He sat in the back seat and pulled out the two cards he carried
with him.

*I intend to donate my brain to the VA-BU-CLF Brain Bank upon
my death*, read one. The other listed the symptoms of brain injury
that he could give to people if needed.

'I have good days and bad,' he said. 'But even the good days are
not good days.'

He was in pain all the time. Headaches. Huge swathes of him replaced in recent years. One new elbow, then another, his neck a lattice of screws and pins that made his upper-body movements stiff. A replacement for his chest cavity. Abdominal surgeries. Heart procedures. He needed a new hip and knee, too, but had been advised not to have it.

'I can't manage the anaesthetic with the CTE,' he said. 'It would take months to recover from it, my doctor tells me. That's if I recovered from it at all.'

This was all the outside stuff, the things that people could see. But there was also the insomnia, the forgetfulness, the once-frequent rages that had dissipated with the right medication. Paranoia. Parkinson's. Traces of schizophrenia.

'But I don't like people to see how bad I am,' he said. 'They don't need to see that.'

He was not allowed to drive any more. It was not clear if it had been his choice or another's. It had been a sound decision either way.

'One time, I was coming back from somewhere and saw a sign for the Catskills,' he said. 'And that's where I used to work as a sparring partner. So, I started driving off there, thinking that that was where I was supposed to be going. But then I got there and was lost, and the police eventually found me and called home. It was so late at night that I went to a hotel, slept there and came home the next day.'

That was not the last time, though. 'Another time, I woke up in the car in the middle of some lady's yard. And there were these little kids about ten feet away.' His face went blank. 'I had missed them by ten feet. *By ten feet.*'

He looked devastated at what could have been. He sucked on the vape. There was a marijuana smell. He used it for medical purposes.

'Have you seen this?' he said, pulling out a small dog's coat from his bag. It said, 'Medical Support Animal.' 'That's for Maui, my dog. He's there in case my heart stops beating. But I don't really need him for that now, since I'm doing better with the new medications.'

He has the heart of a twenty-year-old, he said. 'The problem is that my brain has got damage in one of the lobes so that it forgets sometimes that my heart is supposed to beat.' He tapped his chest. 'That's when the pacemaker kicks in.'

He was being driven around sixty miles to Shamokin, a small, industrial town in rural Pennsylvania. He and Shane Manney, the founding director at 5 Stones Fight Club in Annville, were looking to open a second gym in the small town. A local mill had heard of the gym's faith-based work and offered them a huge, open space in a former hardware store for just $400 a month.

Blyweiss settled into the back as Manney drove. He was both solidly built and frail, 6ft 2in. and 220lbs, but with plenty of mileage. He put his hand on Manney's shoulder.

'I'm going to sit here right and stretch out,' he said. 'Plenty of room.'

Manney laughed. He was used to Blyweiss's digs at his height.

Manney was 5ft 8in. and muscular, all dense and tight. He wore khaki trousers, running shoes and a black T-shirt, and he was bald with a beard. He had small eyes that watched everything intently but remained bright and avuncular. He lived frugally while he ran the 5 Stones Fight Club in the neighbouring town of Annville.

The lid of the can snapped, and Blyweiss took a long drink from the iced coffee. He fished out a small pill bottle from his bag and, without saying what it was, took out and swallowed a tablet then washed it down with some of his drink. The bag opened slightly, and a pack of Marlboro Lights could be seen at the top.

'I've given up pretty much everything,' he said, 'but these are the hardest. But I'm giving these up next week. I'm under orders from my daughter before her baby arrives.'

He had been born addicted, his biological mother a heroin addict. It seemed a lot of what would come later had been written for him *in utero*. It took six months in the hospital, getting clean, before he could even go home with his adopted parents.

His adopted mother hated him. His adopted maternal grand-mother, too. But he says it was not personal. 'They were mean, and they hated men. I'd look up to my mother with love, and she'd tell me, "You're not my son." And she would beat me. Her mother, too. They'd twist my balls when I was a child in the bath. There was so much scar tissue that the doctors thought a few years ago that I had cancer down there.'

His father was different. 'I loved that man. And he loved me. And when my mother died, he came to me and cried because of all the things that she'd done to me that he'd let happen. He loved her, you see, even though she didn't love anybody at all.'

Things boiled over, eventually. 'I took a knife and put it to her throat when I was thirteen, and I got arrested and sent away. And every time they tried to send me back, she wouldn't have me.'

Life was tough when he was young, growing up in Baltimore. 'I was the only white kid around,' he said, 'so the other kids called me "Ghost". They'd be like, "Hey, it's Ghost," or "It's my man, Ghost."'

He still gets called that today in some quarters. He went a few years ago to see former heavyweight contender Mitch 'Blood' Green, who had led the Black Spades street gang. While he was there, Blyweiss had guns pulled on him. It was Green who defused the situation, saying, 'Hey, it's Ghost, guys. He's one of the good ones.'

'I saw my first body when I was seven,' Blyweiss said. 'I was coming home one day and saw this guy on his knees in the street, some gang member in front of him.'

He shook his head, put his hands up. 'And then *bang*! He's on the floor. And the other guy's shot him. And I look at him and he says, "Ghost, I know where you live." And I took off. I told nobody, *ever*, what I'd seen.'

Blyweiss closed his eyes. He spoke about an amateur record of 88–12. 'My dad took me to the gym because I was being bullied. And I got bullied there for six months until they started respecting me. I ended up breaking my nose so often that my dad took me to a doctor who removed all the cartilage.'

He reached up and pushed his nose flat against his face with one finger. 'See?'

Manney pulled the car onto I-81. The fields of Pennsylvania flowed by. The speedometer began to touch seventy.

Manney drove for an hour. He and Blyweiss joked along the way. They spoke about some of the fighters in the gym, people they were trying to help guide through life.

'The problem isn't that he has a girl,' said Blyweiss, speaking about one of the members. 'And she's a good girl. The problem is that he's got her coming over to that house with the other guys and they don't want her there. It's supposed to be a place where they can concentrate. It's a fighter's home.'

They were travelling to sign the lease on the second premises in Shamokin. It was one of Blyweiss's daughters who had helped enable the deal.

'The mill guys', said Manney, 'were going to rent this space out for $3,000 a month, but then they heard about the work we were doing and wanted to get involved. They believe in what we do. So, they're letting us have it for just the taxes each month.'

Blyweiss and Manney met the latter's cousin Corey Parry in the car park of Clark's Feed Mill in Shamokin, before they all went in to sign the lease on the new space. They were met by Tessa, Bob and Will, who ran the mill, and went into a conference room in the basement, where they would sign the contracts.

'Is everything OK?' asked Tessa. 'Did you change anything?'

'Just some of the dates,' said Parry. 'Just to make everything the same.'

Tessa looked over the changes. 'That's all fine,' she said. 'When do you want to start?'

'As soon as we can.'

They talked over some of the details around the site, figuring out what security they would need and the few renovations and redevelopments that would be needed. The talk quickly moved on to the work that 5 Stones does in the community.

'That's something we really would like you to be involved with,' said Manney. 'If you want to be involved.'

Bob leaned forward and stroked his beard. 'Of course,' he said. 'We feel real good about this.'

'OK.'

'There's just one thing. When we have meetings like this, we'd like to start with a prayer.'

'Absolutely,' said Manney.

'And close with one, too.'

Manney nodded. 'Yes, sir.'

Blyweiss was largely silent during the meeting. He sat back in his chair, his legs stretched out in front of him. He occasionally closed his eyes.

'OK, I think we're all good. Shall we say a few words?' Everyone bowed their heads and closed their eyes. 'Thank you, Heavenly Father, for your blessing in this venture. May you bestow 5 Stones with your blessings and may we continue to be guided by your example. Amen.'

Everyone around the table said, 'Amen.'

Outside, Manney, Parry and Blyweiss reflected on the meeting. 'I think it went really well,' Manney said. 'The only thing was the prayer. I was going to suggest it, but I forgot and then it was too late. I'm glad they mentioned it, though. And we'll do that from now on.'

The team got in the car then drove to the new premises. It was already filled with exercise equipment, all of it donated. They went to look over some of the rooms and discussed what needed to be done. They planned to do all of it themselves. 'I can do a bit of everything,' said Parry. 'I'm a jack of all trades.'

Afterwards, they got back into the car and drove to Brewser's, a sports bar in Shamokin. They ordered lunch with ice teas, said grace when the food arrived.

Talk turned quickly to boxing. Teofimo Lopez had beaten Josh Taylor a few days earlier in New York to become the undisputed super-lightweight champion, then announced his retirement. Nobody thought it would stick.

'They always say that,' said Blyweiss. 'But they never do.'

He had been a professional boxer briefly. 'I had two fights', he said, 'and lost both of them. It was my fault. I got signed to a big promoter, who gave me $125,000. And I took that money and did everything I shouldn't have done with it. And that's why I lost. The second time, I broke my arm so bad that the bone was coming out of my elbow. After that, my promoter told me that he was going to make me wait out my contract, so my career was over.'

He took to the professional sparring circuit, working mostly for heavyweight champion Lennox Lewis. Training under Kevin Rooney, he sparred Mike Tyson in camp.

'The reason they used me', he said, 'is that I was small. I was like Evander Holyfield. I could imitate his size and style.'

That was the story for the next twenty years, as he cycled in and out of various camps with various champions. He travelled across Europe, part of the wandering circus that follows a heavyweight champion. He sparred them all.

'I'd be in there five or six days a week,' he said. 'Often doing more than ten rounds a day. That adds up. And I was there to be hit. When you're a sparring partner, there's no point in trying to look better than your boss. That's how you lose your job.'

He did not regret any of it. 'It gave me a good life. And it's still a good life.'

He made enough money, he says, from his career as a sparring partner to pay off the house. All in all, he reckoned he earned about

$3.5 million through the various camps that he worked in. But then he retired and the problems arrived. He ran his own boxing club for a while, but then he shut it down. He reckoned he had been on painkillers continually since he was a teenager, too. The body has a nasty habit of remembering everything you do to it.

Blyweiss was eventually declared to be disabled, unable to work. And then, one day, he found the 5 Stones gym in the local town of Annville.

Manney pulled the car around the back of the 5 Stones gym. There was a large, green area outside with some free weights and a tractor tyre with a large hammer. Blyweiss stayed outside in the sun to smoke a cigarette. Scott, a boxer in his mid-forties who worked from early in the morning to pour concrete, was skipping in one corner.

'I found it all here,' said Blyweiss, motioning to the gym. 'I was lost and started coming down here. Then one day, I walked in those doors and I heard a voice say, *You are home.* And there was nobody else here. That was God speaking to me.'

Some kids walked past. Blyweiss waved at them. They waved back, carried on walking. He walked over to the short wall at the end of the car park.

'Hey,' he said. 'You guys train?'

The kids stopped. 'No,' one of them said.

'You should.'

'Is this a fight gym?'

'It is.'

'Are you a fighter?'

'I was. I sparred Mike Tyson. I'm not doing great now, but I'll train you guys. Sort you out a free membership for a month if you want.'

'Maybe.'

'OK. Let's talk later.' The kids wandered off. Blyweiss took a drag on his cigarette. 'That's what I do now. That's my purpose,' he said. 'I'm here now to help people. I made my living, my claim to fame. Now, it's time to give back. That's what God has gotten me here to do.'

The kids had seemed uninterested, and maybe a little uneasy, at being approached and invited into a gym. But Blyweiss was trying. It was the new thing he was pouring his life into. He knew the damage boxing had done to him, and to others, but it was still the language he knew best.

A picture of Blyweiss, taken when he was younger, hung on the wall of the office. He had his hands up, his elbows apart. He had been fuller in the face and his hair was darker. Beyond that picture, in the small corridor past the office window, was a painting of David slaying Goliath.

The 5 Stones Fight Club has three main rooms: one for boxing, one filled with weight machines and one with a matted floor for grappling and jiu-jitsu. It also has some changing rooms, bathrooms and an office. There was a projector fixed to a beam above the ring pointed at a screen that took up one wall. A slew of chairs were lain against another wall and were used for church services at the gym.

It was hard to put a label on the 5 Stones. It was both fight gym and church, an insular place that opened freely its doors to others, where hurt and pain were met with love. They were careful to say that they did not proselytise but led by example. But it was hard to miss that everything done there was underpinned by faith.

'We're here to show everyone the right way,' said Manney, 'which is done in His Name. We not only have the gym, but we run missions in the Middle East, feeding people and building schools. We help combat child trafficking, too. And we're looking at opening other, new places. Maybe we'll even bring one to Europe.'

At the far end of the room reserved for boxing was a ring. A lone fighter stood at the side closest to the wall. He was a Cameroonian super-lightweight called Boris Nde, who had won four and lost two. One of his wins had been a technical knockout, but he had been stopped twice.

Blyweiss thought Nde had a good future. 'The two losses shouldn't mean anything,' he said. 'He got put in with two guys who were way, way heavier than he was. They usually weighed in at 155, and Boris is a 135 guy. That's where he'll be a world champion.'

Nde shrugged. 'I prefer 140,' he said, 'because that gives me some space to move in. It's hard to get down to '35.'

Blyweiss shook his head. 'No, you're a lightweight,' he said.

'Maybe.'

'Definitely.' Blyweiss turned. 'The problem is that his last manager wasn't looking after him. He knew Boris was fighting guys who weren't making the weight, but he still let him go in there. And when he got knocked out, he didn't care. He was off having a drink when Boris was unconscious. I'm going to look after him instead.'

There were some younger men training in the gym. Blyweiss went to each and gave pointers on where he felt they were going wrong. 'Most trainers,' he said, 'can teach them the basics of movement and how to punch, but I've got the experience to tell them how to put it all together.'

A middle-aged man came in with his son. The boy was short and heavy, but he smiled when he saw Blyweiss. It was his eighth time in the gym. Blyweiss asked if it was OK for him to be weighed. The father said it was OK if the boy was comfortable with it. Blyweiss and the boy went into the changing room then came out a few minutes later. The boy went over and started hitting a bag. Blyweiss went over to the father.

'I thought so,' said Blyweiss to the father. 'I guessed it within 2lbs. But that's OK. It's a good starting point for him.'

'Thank you, sir.'

'Why is he training?'

The man looked at his son. 'He needs his confidence building. He's playing football this year.'

'He's a nice kid.'

'Thank you, sir.'

Blyweiss looked over to the boy, who was throwing as many punches as he could at the punchbag. 'He's enjoying himself. That's good. He's determined, too. He's got good power and he doesn't give up. I like that.'

'Thank you, sir.'

Some other kids began to enter the gym. They stood around, waiting to be assigned a ride to a neighbouring gym. The plan was to meet at 4.15 p.m. at 5 Stones then leave and drive to the town of Lancaster.

A few were late. Blyweiss got on his phone and began to call around. 'OK, where are you? How long? Five minutes. OK.'

The two cars eventually left just after five o'clock. It took around thirty minutes to drive there.

Blyweiss sat in the back seat behind Matt, a local videographer who had made some promotional films about 5 Stones. Matt was in his early twenties, lived at home with his parents and was trying to make a living as a freelance photographer and filmmaker. He and Blyweiss discussed a documentary that they wanted to make about the latter's life.

'We've spoken to some people,' said Blyweiss, 'and there was one guy who did a film on one of our events, but we're not sure if we're going to go with him.'

The Jinji Boxing Club in Lancaster, Pennsylvania, is run by Fransonet 'Jinji' Martinez, who lost his left leg in a car accident weeks before his first professional fight. The same accident broke his right leg in nineteen places. He still managed one fight with a prosthetic before moving into training.

It was busy that night, with around twenty kids in the gym's main room. Another room, with heavy bags, was filled with fighters. It was hard to find space in which to stand.

A young boy from 5 Stones called Ricky got into the ring. He was about fourteen, his blond hair falling across his brow, and there was the wisp of a moustache forming on his upper lip. Blyweiss referred to him as his '401k'.

'The ability this kid has got is outstanding,' he said, a smile on his face. 'That's my pension plan right there.'

Ricky did not spar well that night, 'losing' to the other kid. 'He did so much better last time,' said Blyweiss, glumly.

The kids sparred hard. Blyweiss said he was cognisant of what they were doing. 'I'll always stop them if they're stunned,' he said. 'I'll get them to walk over to me if they get knocked down, and I'll stop it if it's too much for them. I'm also not in the habit of breaking people's dreams, but if they haven't got it, I'll tell them. There's no point in their getting hurt.'

Another young boy got in the ring. He wore a white T-shirt that quickly became speckled with blood. He seemed to take the rough end of it, too. After his sparring had finished, he sat on a bench and wiped at his face with his T-shirt.

'Bleeding, I don't mind,' said Blyweiss. 'That's part of boxing. But I'll not have someone get stunned and then have them carry on. That's not good.'

He still believed in sparring, although not as much as he had done. 'There's no point in sparring every day. You can learn just as much on the pads or on the heavy bag. A couple of rounds here and there, and a few more when you've got a fight coming up. But no more than that.'

Evan Hershey was the last to spar that night. The room went dark when he entered, all 6ft 7in. and 270lbs. He had a shaved head and spoke quietly and politely, seeming almost embarrassed by his size. He called everyone 'sir'.

Hershey was put in against a young fighter, around twenty, who weighed only 205lbs. The gym stopped to watch them spar for three rounds.

'That's the thing with the heavies,' said Blyweiss. 'Everyone likes to see them go.'

The noise became cacophonous, and the Jinji coaches shouted instructions to their fighter, while Blyweiss yelled to his. Others around the ring began to do the same. Blyweiss became frustrated and pulled at the ropes. His face became pink. 'Hey!' he yelled at no one in particular.

Afterwards, Hershey went and sat down on a bench. His skin was hot and pink, and his hands were wet when he took off the gloves, the fabric wraps drenched in sweat. He was breathing heavily and pushed his palm through the stubble of his head, then wiped the sweat on his T-shirt. He drank some water, then shook the front of his T-shirt to cool down.

He made space so Blyweiss could sit next to him. 'That was a good kid,' said Blyweiss of the boy from Jinji. 'I'm glad that you took your foot off the gas and didn't hurt him. We can use him for his speed.'

Blyweiss began to tell a story about Hershey. 'Last time I had him out, he was boxing this one kid. He was doing OK, but I told him before to watch out for my instructions. At some point, I saw where the other kid was open and I yelled at him to throw the overhand right. And he went, "Yes, sir!", threw it and knocked him out.' He laughed. 'That's the first time I've ever had a kid say, "Yes, sir!" then do as I told them *in the middle of a fight.*'

Blyweiss and his fighters left the gym quickly after the sparring. He got into the car again with Matt and was driven back to Palmyra. He reflected on the sparring.

'We've had better,' he said. 'And I was getting angry because of the noise. There were too many people shouting out and shouting over me. That's one of the things with the CTE that I find hard to deal with.'

It took about thirty minutes to drive back to where Blyweiss lived with his wife Chrissie, about ten miles from the gym. It was a large, quiet home at the end of a cul-de-sac.

The Blyweisses had married when they were in their twenties and started a family. But when he began to mess up, Chrissie divorced him. And then one day, his daughter wrote him a letter. *Daddy*, it read, *please come back to the family.*

So he did. And he and Chrissie then did what they always should have done: they got remarried and stayed that way. Fifteen years and counting.

It was nice to see them together, Blyweiss smiling each time he mentioned her name. Sometimes, he acted like a naughty schoolboy in the house in an effort to get a rise out of her. Marriage, it is often said, is finding someone you like and then trying your best to get their attention for the next forty years.

There was a prayer meeting that night, with around twelve people sat on chairs in the front room, many of them holding well-thumbed editions of the Bible. Four boxes of pizza lay next to a stack of paper plates.

It was an informal evening, the conversation moving in a circle around the room as each person spoke about what was going on in their lives that they felt they needed help with.

One couple had recently celebrated their twenty-fifth wedding anniversary. 'I'd like to thank God', the husband said, 'for his grace in allowing me to tolerate living with her all this time.'

The group laughed. The wife elbowed her husband. 'And may we all pray for the concussion he's soon going to get,' she said, laughing.

The stories continued until an alarm went. The group began to focus on the concluding prayer.

Blyweiss looked tired. He called a new guest the wrong name twice, apologising as soon as he realised.

Each member of the group laid out to the others what, in their life, they felt needed prayer. There were stories of illness and of estrangement, and the responses were a mix of reassurances of divine help and practical aid and advice.

Towards the end, the group joined together in prayer.

Blyweiss led: 'We thank you, Lord, for these blessings,' he said, his head bowed. 'And we ask for your help in the matters put forward to you. I'd like to ask, too, that the world learns more about brain damage and CTE and that, through your wisdom, this be granted.'

The meeting ended at eight o'clock, and people milled around outside. One of Blyweiss's children was there with her husband. They were expecting a baby in a few weeks.

Blyweiss hugged his daughter. 'It was her that brought us all back together,' he said. 'She's the one that wrote the letter.'

She took him to one side. 'I've got something for you, Dad,' she said, pulling something from her purse. It was a small, square photograph like a polaroid. A three-dimensional scan of her baby.

Blyweiss took the picture and looked at it. His face dropped and he raised a finger to his eye. He looked vulnerable for the first time that day, and he turned and left the room for a few minutes.

When he came back, he hugged his daughter for a second time.

'She takes me with her to all her scans,' he said. 'And I hold her hand. I can't believe I'm going to be a grandfather.'

Later, once everyone had gone, Blyweiss went outside to smoke a cigarette. He took a chair from the garage and sat on it in his driveway. 'My wife doesn't let me do this in the house,' he said, laughing. 'She's so good that I married her twice.'

He drew on his cigarette and looked out through the estate. It was a nice place and quiet, but he and Chrissie were thinking of moving somewhere near where he could have more support.

'My big worry', he confided, 'is that I'm going to become a grandfather, and that's when I'll go downhill. When they diagnosed me, they said there would be between seven and ten years before I got really bad. That was nine years ago. I'm never going to beat it, and it's going to take my life, but I'm doing my best to hold it back.'

He nodded then looked up. He closed his eyes as if in silent prayer, and his shoulders relaxed, the tightness disappearing out of and away from his back. The tension in his face dropped away, his skin smoothening in the cool air. Everything was still and the night was dimming. Darkness ahead.

CHAPTER FIVE

AFTER THE FIGHTS

LAID TO REST

Dundee, Scotland, October 2016. It rained in the morning and then fell away, the sky clearing in time for the funeral.

It had been two weeks since he had died. Three hundred people entered St Andrew's Cathedral in the centre of Dundee. Many wore T-shirts with 'Iron' Mike Towell printed on the back. They had come from the boxing club.

No one wore black; they wanted to celebrate him. And Towell had always hated red, so no one wore that, either. The hearse had floral tributes that read 'Daddy' and 'Iron Mike'. There were no other flowers. Collections were made to benefit the special baby care unit at Ninewells Hospital in Dundee, along with the neurology unit at the Queen Elizabeth University Hospital in Glasgow, where he had died. His birth and his life came together in a circle.

Jamie Wilson was at the funeral. 'It was my first proper one. With Mikey, I'd seen him a couple of times a week for the last eight months or so. I knew him, he was a good pal. We'd text every day. It's sad when you have those memories of him.'

Dale Evans was also there. People saw him, embraced him. They held no blame for him in their hearts.

The family saw Evans, loved him, adopted him as one of their own. They released a statement through the St Andrew's Boxing Club.

> It was a real comfort for us to have Mike's opponent Dale Evans at the funeral with us because our hearts go out to him. He has also been through so much and no fault will ever lie with him. This was just two boys boxing and doing what they loved best.

Towell's picture was on the order of service that was given out. His hair was still long, and he was smiling. He looked young, healthy. It looked like a photo captured without him posing, in the thickest and fullest part of his life, in that place that lies after growing up and before growing old.

Once the funeral was done with and the words said, they carried him back outside and placed his coffin in the car. Then they drove up through the centre of Dundee, out beyond the north of the city limits and laid him to rest in the peaceful earth beside his father.

Glasgow, Scotland, 2018–19. It was nearly two years before the Fatal Accident Inquiry began. The preliminary hearings took place over four days throughout September and October. Witnesses spoke before the inquiry over twelve days through November and December. Thirty-three people gave evidence.

There was little controversy. Most of the evidence was agreed upon. Some witnesses were found to be untrustworthy. Dale Evans did not give evidence. He was not asked to.

The final report was released in April 2019. It listed all the doctor visits, the hospital appointments attended and missed. There was paperwork, a trail running from start to finish.

There were criticisms. The inquiry said the boxing authorities were too reliant on the candour of those it regulated. There was too much leeway for someone to slip through.

The cause of Towell's death was head injury, the inquiry found. It said that it was not an accident.

The sheriff wrote: '[…] what occurred in the Radisson on 29 September 2016 cannot be described as accidental. In a situation in which persons intentionally strike each other, an injury such as that sustained by Mr Towell is neither without apparent cause nor unexpected.'

Dale Evans was not blamed. 'There was', the sheriff wrote, 'nothing untoward about his actings.' It concluded he was 'blameless'.

The inquiry outlined all the missed opportunities to prevent Towell's death: the non-disclosure of his seizures to the British Boxing Board of Control; the refusal to stop boxing on advice given by three doctors in 2013; the non-disclosure of an epilepsy diagnosis in 2013; the boxing regulators not using Towell's consent in 2014 and 2015 to contact his doctor; Towell's non-disclosure in 2016 about his hospital visits that September; and his refusal to follow Dr Skelly's advice in September 2016.

It found little fault with the doctors and the hospitals. It made recommendations for the boxing regulators.

It concluded that boxing was the centre of Mike Towell's life.

It said:

It was what he lived for. Regrettably, it appears that Mr Towell's love of boxing caused him to ignore the advice of doctors and not to accept the medical condition he had been diagnosed as suffering from. It is hard not to conclude that the very drive and commitment to boxing which Mr Towell demonstrated in his ascent to a final eliminator contest for the British welterweight championship in only his thirteenth professional fight is what led to his untimely death.

TO THE BONE

Berlin, Germany, July 2023. Trisha Sampson walked into Kilkenny's, an Irish pub beneath the tracks at Berlin's Hackescher Markt station. It had been a straight shot along the S7 from where she was staying with her daughter and her mother in the city's suburban district of Grunewald. The three of them were halfway through a family trip to the city.

She had not been in Berlin in nearly ten years.

It was a cool and damp morning at the tail end of what had been a disappointing summer, and the temperature had dipped back into the low twenties in recent weeks. Some bursts of rain in the few days before had surprised people here and there, and so it was still damp when she entered the bar nearly two hours before midday and saw her old friend.

They embraced. She had always done that, giving big and deep hugs to everyone when she entered the gym. And she still smiled a lot after all those years.

She sat down and ordered a drink. An S-Bahn carriage rumbled through the station above.

'It's so good to see you!' she said. She said this to everyone, and she always meant it. And because she meant it, no one ever felt she was playing them. She reached over and squeezed her old friend's hand.

She looked well. Different. Better in many ways. Her smiles had pushed back across her face, like ripples over water, and embedded themselves in the lines of her skin. There were some flecks of grey in her hair, seasoning on a life well lived.

She went by a different name now, but she would always, to her Berlin friends, be 'Trisha Sampson'. There was a ring on her finger, pushed down for permanence beyond the swollen knuckle, the legacy of a dislocation from an errant kick.

'I met my soulmate,' she said, with a grin. She smiled again. 'And I became a mom!' There were no longer any shadows in her eyes. *Look what happened to us*, she radiated. *Look at all the boring, great things we have become!*

Being back was different, exciting. Like running into an old lover or an old friend, the past was both common ground and a foreign country. She no longer recognised the city, nor could she find the places that she had once called 'hers' – *her* grocery store, *her* local *spatkauf*, *her* favourite bars, *her* favourite places to sit and meet friends. Even most of the buildings were now new or redeveloped, emptied of everything broken and worn that had once made them interesting.

The Berlin of 2023 was much different to the one that she had left. Money and people had been flowing into the city for years, and nobody could find a place to live now. The city had once been vibrant and interesting, but then all of that had been pushed and concentrated into one or two districts, and it was slowly being mopped out of the streets. It was a great time to be a property investor and a poor one to be anybody else.

But Sampson was happy to be back, even – *especially* – if it was just a visit.

She first came to Berlin in 2010, off the back of attending university in Switzerland. A friend was working in the city and managed to get her an interview as a teacher in an international school. Sampson would remain there for two years.

She had already been kickboxing in Canada, segueing into Muay Thai. That part of her story began when she went to study in Australia.

'I was looking for a gym at the university,' she said, 'and someone said there was this thing called Muay Thai that was the same. I called up the coach, who I'd never met before, and I said I'd done a few months of kickboxing, had really liked it and wanted to know about Muay Thai. Immediately, he had a thirty-minute conversation with me about it, saying it wasn't kickboxing. He was so passionate that I got excited listening to him, so I went to the gym and tried it out.'

She put her hands on the table in front of her, tapped her ring against the wood. Her eyes drifted, and she went into a part of herself that would always be in her twenties.

'The funny thing is,' she said, 'I still feel the same way, even now. Even though I'm forty-one and a mom, I still feel like I could do it with six months training. I'm pretty sure I could.'

She smiled thinly and shrugged her head. 'I *feel* that I could do it.'

It seemed hard for her to reconcile what she had been with what she had become, as though she found it difficult to see the joints and transitions connecting the two.

'The difference', she said, 'is that I no longer have to prove myself. Or, at least, I don't *feel* like I have to prove myself. It's simplistic to put it like this, but my dad left when I was five, and then I didn't have much contact with him growing up. And I wanted that. Every little girl does. So, yes, there was probably some part of me that was out there trying to prove I was good enough for something.'

She touched the top of her leg with her finger, as if pointing to something that could be easily seen. 'And then, when I was fifteen and sixteen, I had to get three screws in my hips. I had trouble walking all of a sudden. I had congenital hip dysplasia where the joint wasn't covering the ball. And the doctors told me after that surgery that I should do low-impact sport for the rest of my life because I might end up in a wheelchair otherwise. But I would have had nothing then, so I went off to climb the mountains.'

A memory surfaced and she smiled. 'I went to see that doctor when I started kickboxing, and he had the funniest look on his face, like he was secretly proud. He said, "From a doctor's perspective, you should absolutely not be doing this. You have three large screws in there and lots of scar tissue. But you're also one of my most successful patients. If I didn't know what you were doing, I'd tell you to keep doing it."'

A second drink arrived. 'You can tell I'm not in training, right?' she said, taking a sip. She laughed.

'Here's something I never understood,' she said. 'I don't know why I was so all-or-nothing. There was a Thai guy I knew when I was in Australia. His parents were poor farmers who sent him to a fight camp. The fighters slept outside in the rain every night and were only given meat with their rice when they started to win. They only got a bed inside if they kept winning. So he truly had to fight in order to live, and there are people in Thailand that still do it now for the same reason. People there don't get into this if they have other options. So I've never been able to square why I was so dedicated to it, coming from a relatively privileged country like Canada.'

She fell hard in love with Muay Thai. Each day for years, she would scrape herself out of bed at six o'clock and go to the gym. Two sessions a day, plus an hour of cardio that she would double whenever a fight was on the horizon.

It was never about the hitting, she said. 'I liked how I would go into myself. It was like meditating,' she said. 'I'd be in the ring and everything outside of it would fall away. I wouldn't be worried about work, or family, or life, or whatever else it was that I was supposed to be doing. It would be me and whoever the other person was. That was it. It was that focus.'

Dieting was equally disciplined. There was no solace in food, and she could not remember eating for pleasure as there was no margin for error, or fun, or just to kick back and relax after a hard week. Everything was weighed and calculated, engineered to fit together like building blocks for the day when there might have been a fight.

'It wasn't pleasant at all,' she said, 'but it was fuel to keep the body going. I stuck with leafy greens and broccoli. I thought like I didn't eat for taste any more, you know? I ate for performance. It was a chore, not a pleasure.'

She only managed four fights because her body conspired against her. When she trained full time, she tended to walk around at 165lbs, about thirty more than most female competitors. And there was nothing more she could carve off. She once went as low as 158lbs and crashed 14lbs the day before the fight. It was a weight that she knew she could never reach again.

There were some days when she thought that she would stop. She would say that she would quit, go away and find something else, but she always came back. She knew that she would come back because that's how it is when you have something that you love hard – no matter even if it's bad for you, or unrewarding, or returns to you nothing close to what you have given it. Because that is what love is.

One of the toughest things with coming back to Berlin was that a lot of her adopted, Muay Thai-centred family had scattered and left the city. Good things are defined by the fact that they do not last.

Her club in Berlin had been tightknit. Punch one, and you were liable to strike another standing by them. They trained together, fought together, ate and drank together. Some even lived together, people not just leading similar lives, but a quasi-family collectively living the same life.

She had been one of only two women. 'Guys tended to treat you one way or the other,' she said. 'There were some that did not want to train with you because they didn't want to hit a girl. I understood that, even if it was frustrating because training is training. You're supposed to leave whatever it is at the door and just go and train. But after a long-enough time, when they can see who you are, you get adopted as their little sister, and they get protective over you.' She nodded ruefully, laughed. 'Even when I was someone who didn't need that protection.'

A train rumbled in overhead. She looked up at the ceiling, and she paused. She seemed to be thinking of gone things. There was the low, metallic grind of the train pulling away.

Sampson listened, then she pointed to the wall of the bar. 'That one's going to Alexanderplatz,' she said.

She had some concerns over her brain. 'I've had two concussions, one in the gym and one when my bike slipped on black ice. I'm testing my spatial awareness.'

The first one had been in the gym. 'I got in with this other girl, and I said I wanted to go light, but they ignored me. And I knew, *knew*, when they started putting Vaseline on her that I should get out, but I didn't. And we started light, but things deteriorated. Afterwards, I was walking to the tram with the guys and my legs felt as if they were far in front of me and I was tumbling backwards, and I started to compensate, trying to stay upright. And then the guys took me to the hospital.'

The second one, back in Canada, was worse. 'That took months to recover, and I'm still not 100 per cent. There are some rides at the fairground that I cannot go on, because the movement throws my balance out. I'm hoping things will improve one day, but it's been nearly six years now.'

She had stopped, between the two concussions, fighting.

'I was in the gym one day and there was this one young guy who was chomping at the bit. He asked me if I wanted to spar, and I said I would if we went light. But then it escalated, and I was hitting him as hard as he was hitting me, and I didn't want to do it. I said to him a few times that we were going too hard, and eventually he turned and said, "Look, this isn't dance class." And that made me mad.'

Her nostrils flared, and she balled her hand into a tight fist. She splayed her fingers and pushed down until their tips went white. Her jaw tightened. Back in the day, no one would have said this to her and reasonably expected to survive. The unspoken rule was that if she had not taught this clown some respect, someone else would have, just on principle.

She drank. 'I could have said, "OK, asshole. You're right. Let's go hard." But I didn't. I took my gloves off and said to him, "If you can't do that, you don't have enough control and I'm not comfortable sparring with you." And I walked out. And that was the moment that I realised I was no longer that young, or hungry for a fight, or feisty.'

Time wears everything away. Sampson looked at her hands, thought about what it was they used to be able to do. At what they did. She said once in the gym, describing herself, 'I am a very loving person.'

'I never saw it as violent,' she said, in wonder and confusion. 'But how could it have been anything else? I had an MRI on my right shoulder recently and they said there was a fracture spur there. But I've never fractured it, as far as I know. My shins are damaged, too. The skin is completely stuck to them because of all the scar tissue. And that can only be from kicking. You look at these things and realise that none of us ever clocked the damage that we were doing to each other. And all those hits to the head that we absorbed. Sometimes, it's hard for me to look at Muay Thai now because of that, even though I can't stop loving it. So maybe, yes, it was kind of violent.'

A few hours had gone by. More moments ticked away. It was time to finish.

Did she miss the old days?

'Yes,' she said. 'And it was overall a positive thing. I really feel that. Obviously, there were negative parts to it too, but it made me feel strong.'

She was training recreationally again. 'But I have a hard boundary with it. I don't go near the sparring. Sometimes, the coaches will say to me, "Trish, it's cool. We'll go light." And I say, "No." I'm not getting back in there. I can't feel those things again. And I can't get hurt.'

She reached into her handbag and took out her phone, unlocked it and pressed and swiped until she got where she wanted to be.

'This is my daughter, Yvonne,' she said. 'She was my priority from the moment she was born. If I start getting competitive again, I'll go into that mindset of wanting to fight and of wanting to prove myself. And that's a selfish mindset. If I got hurt and did something to myself, even if it was my back or just something like my arm, I'd never be able to carry her on my shoulders again.'

Sampson stood up. She came over and hugged her old friend. It was big and deep, as always. A thing that had never changed. 'It was so good to meet,' she said, and she meant it.

She began to walk to the door. 'The funny thing is, I've got Yvonne doing martial arts now. Judo, although maybe she'll move on to jiu-jitsu or something else later on. But I've been teaching her things. I'll say to her, "What happens if someone tries to touch you or take you somewhere? They get bitten, right? They try something, and they get bitten right down to the bone."'

BONES GROW OLD

Here is the thing about boxing and how it seeps into your bones. Most people, before knowing anything about it, hate it. They hate it with a passion because they see its brutality and damage, and they think that the people who do it are themselves brutal and damaged. But then they get to see it a bit more and they learn a thing or two, and they come by degrees to love it. That is what happens when you understand more, when you can empathise with what is going on in the ring and can understand why it is being done, and when it has failed.

So, you love it. You have come to love it. And then you see what happens at the end, the damage it has inflicted, its brutality and its costs, and you begin to hate it once again. Because you look at everything that was young once when you were, too, and you see now how it is old and broken before its time.

The time in life when we are no longer what we were comes to us all, but it is particularly cruel to fighters. That change, when it comes to the average person, creeps in gently and secretly with quiet announcements of aches and stiffness in the morning. But with fighters, it is dramatic and becomes obvious over two or three fights.

Those around them will see it first with their trained eyes; the sparring sessions become more torrid as the reflexes dim, and the normal pains no longer fade away to nothing but remain in some diminished capacity.

The coaches will try to manage it, of course. They will put their fighter in with smaller, faster partners to try and stem the loss of speed. The sparring will be kept secret and behind closed doors. Match-ups become softer as they try to extend the run of final paydays.

But the slow erosion is inevitable and irreversible. It is one thing to fall out of shape and lose fitness, but to recover youth and vigour is the domain of some as-yet undiscovered country. To see a fighter go is to be reminded not only that life is finite, but that it is also ever moving away and unstoppable. Time is a cruel mistress.

It is the legs that go first, and the fighter will adjust their style to focus on technique. They will move slower as their legs turn heavy and wooden, clipping the ability they once had to fly. *I'm getting older and more economical with my work*, the fighter will say. *I'm more experienced.* But 'experience' is the label applied to things learned the hard way.

The reflexes go about the same time, and the punches that once missed by centimetres now sail past with only millimetres to spare. Eventually, they will not sail past at all, and enough of them will begin to land to test the adage that the chin is the last thing to go.

Others see it at this point, and it is cruel because the fighter is nearly naked and centred beneath bright lights when it happens. The world sees how little they have left, and the world knows, and the fighter and their people know, too. Everyone knows, even if they cannot all agree.

It is seldom over at this point. There's always a few more rings to fight in and a few more paydays for an aching body attached to a still-known name. The fighter may even convince themselves that the losses piling up are an aberration and the result of bad or lax training, and that it can all be fixed with a new team, or a new weight division, or a new regimen.

There was no time when Jermain Taylor had everything, but there was a point around 2005 when he seemed close.

That was a July night when he challenged Bernard Hopkins for the latter's undisputed middleweight title and, despite the opinions that it was too much and too soon for him, took the older champion to a split decision and defeated him.

Taylor was young and handsome, a bronze medallist at the 2000 Olympics, and he fought like a man on his way to becoming a megastar. He went into the ring with 23 wins, 0 losses and 17 knockouts. It was a slightly padded record, sure, and names like former WBA champion William Joppy were getting on while others like Daniel Edouard never achieved anything more of note than sharing a ring with the future champion.

But the important thing was that Taylor, with his twenty-six years of age, nice smile and 'aw shucks' demeanour, was going to be a star. He was going to be the next franchise, the one the public hooked their own stars to, with big fights in big arenas and stadiums; the one who crossed over from sports and into the mainstream. And from there? No one knew, but it all seemed open. Hollywood? TV? A comfortable retirement commentating on the next generation, smiling at the thought of what he would have done with them in his prime?

It was never going to be that good again. He won against Hopkins a second time, but it was a victory tarnished by what seemed to be a bad decision, and then he went along like a car slipping and sliding on a wet road, everyone praying that he would right himself, press down hard on the accelerator and pick up again on becoming the next Sugar Ray Leonard.

There was a draw after the second Hopkins fight against Ronald 'Winky' Wright, which would not be a shame on the way up, but Taylor *was* on top. Then he struggled against IBF 155lb champion Kassim Ouma, did the same against the IBF champion at welterweight and light-middleweight, Cory Spinks, and then he lost twice against Kelly Pavlik, who would also go on to burn out quickly, his own career slipping and sliding away from him after a beating from Hopkins.

Taylor had one win that looks worse and worse in hindsight, beating a shot Jeff Lacy on points at 168lbs, but then he started losing against the big names of the division, a defeat snatched out of victory against Carl Froch, knocked out in the final seconds of the twelfth round. And then... well, then there was Berlin.

Nottingham, UK, and Berlin, Germany, 2009. It is the first night in the Super Six World Boxing Classic, a tournament to decide on the world's best super-middleweight, and Carl Froch will win a split decision over Andre Dirrell. That is later. At that moment, the undercard for the UK event has finished and two screens, hanging from the rafters of the Nottingham Arena, are showing live the match in Berlin between Arthur Abraham and Jermain Taylor.

It is the twelfth and Taylor, the former middleweight world champion and the biggest US name in the tournament, is behind. He is fighting the former IBF middleweight champion Arthur Abraham in the latter's adopted home city. Taylor has always been a fighter who would never travel, but his career has been derailed by three losses in his last four fights, some of them brutal knockouts, and he is the visiting attraction, whether anyone elucidates it or not, a still-handsome man who has lost that 'aw shucks' charisma and is clinging to his name and his story.

Now, he is losing, behind by two, four and five points on each scorecard. He moves back and there are only a few seconds to go, but then Abraham lands a punch on Taylor's chin, which has been 'suspect' for a while, and Taylor goes back. He does not fall; but is rather propelled away and down like a man whose grip has been pried from the window ledge, and he lands flush on the ground, his head smacking against the hard wood of the ring. His arms rise in spasm, and he gasps like a man who has narrowly escaped drowning.

The arena in the UK winces. A collective gasp goes around. Someone in the press row utters beneath their breath: 'He'll never fight again.' It is painfully, brutally honest, and it is true. Taylor will never fight again.

Except he does. His brain bleeds that night, and it looks like he will not come back. He will withdraw from the tournament and wait a couple of years, but then he will come back. He is gone, though. 'Done' is another way to put it. He has five fights over the next three years, but they are best forgotten. He picks up the IBF middleweight title in his last fight, gives it up and then drifts into crime and madness.

In 2014, Taylor is arrested for shooting his cousin. He is arrested again in 2015 for threatening people, including a child, with a gun. He is given a mental health evaluation and sent to a treatment centre, where he is arrested again for assaulting a fellow patient and eventually pleads innocence by 'mental disease or defect'. In 2016, he pleads guilty to nine felony charges, six counts of aggravated assault, two counts of terroristic threatening and one count of second-degree battery. In 2018, he is arrested on suspicion of assaulting his girlfriend, putting a knife to her throat and threatening to kill her. Taylor claims to be 'indigent'. He says that he owes $400,000 to various people. He has to have public defenders. He goes to prison for a year.

It is the common story of a man who has fought for too long, the blows to the head eroding his impulse control. And Taylor was one of those who never stopped when he should have.

It would have been nearly impossible to stop him, anyway. Someone would always have given him a licence.

Imagine, the damage aside for one second, what it does to take a person's life and livelihood away from them. How it robs them of an identity they have forged.

Boxing may explain Taylor's actions, but it could never condone them. At the same time, his endgame in boxing is not an uncommon one and is as much as part of the narrative as the young contender and the mature champion.

The maxim is that the last thing that ever goes is a fighter's punch. But that is untrue. The last thing that a fighter ever has is their name, and that is often enough for one more beating, one more payday.

There are always calls for the old fighter to be stopped, but take away what a man does, and you take away some part of himself. It is why a shot fighter is always described as a 'ghost' of what they were. There is nothing left, a hollow where they used to be, holes everywhere that the younger fighters can walk and punch through.

They become, at a certain point, only their name. It is what carries them into large-but-diminishing paydays, the slide from the left side of the bracket to the right.

And as they grow older, as their vitality and their skills continue to ebb and fade, they take it on the road. The fighter who would never leave the US suddenly finds himself walking out first in front of a crowd in Montreal, or Berlin, or London. The visitor, the name, the visiting attraction.

And he looks out across the faces, the anonymous mass of people now turned on him, and the lines around his eyes wrinkle, and he thinks of everything he has become to them, and he thinks, *It's time to go. Time to go and remind them of what I used to be, of what they still think I am.*

Time to go.

NOSTALGIA

It is a great thrill to feel that all that separates you from the early Victorians is a series of punches on the nose. I wonder if Professor Toynbee is as intimately attuned to his sources. The Sweet Science is joined onto the past like a man's arm to his shoulder.

A. J. LIEBLING, *THE SWEET SCIENCE*, 1956

For something so immediate, boxing has a curious and symbiotic relationship with its own past. It is common for fighters in the flush of their careers to talk about their legacies, to opine not only of what they will leave behind, or of how they will be spoken of, but of how the generations following them will look back to make their comparisons.

The heavyweight boxing championship of the world, for much of the twentieth century, was the most coveted title in sports. The accolades of who is the best football or baseball player at any given time are subjective and continually revised, but the story of the toughest man on the planet was, for over 100 years, a strong, continual and almost unbroken thread.

It is this nostalgia that curls through and nourishes boxing like a vein. It is perhaps the most nostalgic of all sports. It is safer to grip the past tightly with one hand when you can only fumble for the future with the other. Recent years have seen MMA, spearheaded by the UFC, rise in popularity and skewer boxing in the sports landscape, even if much of this damage has been self-inflicted. You can see why the past appeals.

The *aficionados* will always say that the fighters of their youth were better. That they were faster, fitter and more powerful. They say that those today are lesser, despite their best efforts and intentions. The fighters of their youth were giants, grown men to wide-eyed boys. A champion was definitely a champion too, the *aficionados* remember, and being a champion was not determined by interpretation, guesswork or experience. You knew who a champion was because it was obvious. They were called 'the champion'. And there was an honesty about that. Everything was better because it was more honest, the thinking goes.

Nothing can be honest and true without clarity, and boxing has not had that for a long time. There have been too many fights masquerading as world title fights, too many champions fighting subpar challengers, too many big nights missed because of hangups over money, or prestige, or simply because one side did not want to fight the other. Geographical concentration has not helped – when was the last time a truly big fight pitched its tent outside of Las Vegas and headed to Chicago, or Houston, or Philadelphia? Unlike sports teams, there is no legacy in the sport – the Boston Red Sox in 2023 is the same team it was in 1973, even as time has shifted and changed its roster. Fighters go through their career, retire, come back and are eventually supplanted with new fighters. But there is no franchise, no hardcore fan base that stretches back for generations in the fight game. At best, you get the sons of fighters who follow their fathers into the ring and try to elicit some of that old *frisson*, some long-buried memories of what it meant two or three decades ago when someone of the same name who looked – if you squint your eyes tightly – much like the man now in front of you.

Nostalgia runs thick in the body collective, like the lingering memory of a first love. People always look back and think of how everything was better when they were young, of how *they* were better when they were young. It is always warming to think about when everything was in front of you rather than behind, and it is warming to feel that way again, even if it is only for twelve rounds.

MIKE TYSON AND ROY JONES JR. AT THE END OF THE DAY

Los Angeles, California, US, November 2020. Mike Tyson is in the ring again, and he looks *good*. Not good for a fighter, someone who is doing this for a living, someone with a destination, but good for a man of his age. If you look and trick your brain into thinking he is out of focus, it gives you license to squint a little and believe that he is young again. And if you do that, you can relax a little in your chest and breathe somewhat easier, because it means that *you* are a little younger, too, maybe even as young as you once were.

The first bell is about to go. Tyson has on his famous black shorts and his famous black boots. His gloves are black and red. He does not pace in his corner like he used to, like the caged lion about to strike. He steps from side to side.

Then the bell rings, and he comes out onto the white canvas. He touches gloves with Roy Jones Jr. They step away from each other, and Jones begins to move, trying to fly around the ring like he used to.

Jones, too, looks like he has always done, although he has neither rested nor retired from the ring. He is a working fighter in 2020, taking his trade and show from town to town. He has never completely lost his shape, but you can see how his body does not quite look like it used to, the same shape but thicker and wider, and everyone knows his knees are shot. And he is slower, the once-sculpted physique now seemingly layered with a thick trowelling of plaster.

Nostalgia drove hard the exhibition bout between Tyson and Jones.

It was an event that required you to ignore the evidence of your own eyes or, at least, to squint and look sideways long enough to pretend that it was some point in the '90s again. We all need to suspend our disbelief sometimes. You cannot be a realist if you do not believe in magic.

The 'fight' was never made out to be anything other than what it was, and the limitations of the two men were clear from the start. The gloves were heavier and the rounds shorter. Even the local athletics commission acknowledged that the event was to be nothing more than a 'hard spar'.

It was hard to feel much passion about it. Both men seemed to genuinely like each other. It was so genteel and so planned – so almost scripted – that it felt as if we were all in on the joke.

That Tyson and Jones were facing each other in a ring was a source of comfort, not unease. It was conceived to bring succour, because those watching wanted to believe that time could indeed flow backwards, if only for a night, and that the long-gone water could pull itself back to shore. They would pay their money to watch the fight not because they wanted to believe in it, but because they did not want to *not* believe in it.

And then there were some who watched it, who would have gone ringside, so they could make it a part of their story. 'Hey,' they would say, generations from now to their grandkids, 'have I told you about when I watched Mike Tyson fight live? And Roy Jones Jr.? When they fought each other, and *I* was there?'

They were both old. Tyson was fifty-four and Jones was fifty-one. That was not just old. That was *old*.

And they were both gone, albeit in different ways. Tyson had last fought in 2005, losing against Kevin McBride, pulling out after the sixth round, his mind catching up with his body in the knowledge that there was nothing left and he was barren as a fighter. McBride pushed Tyson, leaned on him and made him quit. He had eight fights after that night, and he lost six of them.

Jones was still active, although he had strayed and skidded until he was far from the bright lights. His relevance had dimmed and faded from 2004, when he had been knocked out twice, brutally by Antonio Tarver in the second round and then chillingly and sadly by Glen Johnson, five months later, in the ninth. He had hung around the scene since then, reluctant, unwilling or unable to go, and so he travelled the world as a visiting attraction. These were places where people were glad to see what was left of him, to watch whatever body was still attached to the name. There are not many places left to go in boxing after the places that Jones would visit – Boise, Biloxi, New York, Pensacola, Sydney, Las Vegas, Moscow, Atlanta, Lodz, Riga, Krasnodar, Concord, Mashantucket, Phoenix, Wilmington.

Tyson had also done the 'visiting attraction' tours in his later years, booking fights in Europe against second-rate opposition. He was seen in Manchester, Glasgow and Copenhagen, knocking out unknowns in front of huge crowds. And then he went back to the US and fought Lennox Lewis in Memphis and was knocked out in eight. He went back to the same ring a little later and beat a disinterested Clifford Etienne in forty-nine seconds, then lost in Louisville, while injured, to a Danny Williams who never performed better again. And then he finished up, on a stool, against McBride in Washington DC.

New York, US, 2003. Mike Tyson applies for bankruptcy, saying that he has earned around $400 million over the course of his career but ended up over $20 million in debt. He sues his former promoter Don King for $100 million the same year, before settling for $14 million, all of which he puts towards debts totalling $38.4 million.

Pensacola, Florida, US, 2014. The US's Internal Revenue Service brings liens against Roy Jones Jr. for $3.5 million in unpaid taxes. Jones, in his mid-forties, works out a five-year deal to repay his debts, much of it seemingly predicated on his willingness to continue fighting. A year later, a Russian promoter begins to pay off the tax debt by writing a $1 million personal cheque. He says that Jones has lost his money in failed business ventures, real estate and a recording studio.

They had suffered financially in the years since their careers had stopped being relevant. Money was a factor, and it was rumoured that Tyson had entailed Jones in the venture to give the latter a needed payday.

The numbers ended up being vague and were never confirmed, but it was believed that Tyson was guaranteed $10 million for the exhibition, with Jones getting anywhere between $1 million and $3 million after the pay-per-view revenues had been accounted for.

Youngstown, Ohio, US, 2006. It is a circus without a tent. Mike Tyson, retired, is walking to the ring, wearing black shoes, black shorts and a white T-shirt. He is doing the *Mike Tyson World Tour*, a series of paid exhibitions.

Corey 'T-Rex' Sanders, a middling heavyweight with a heavy, drooping gut, one fully working eye and a black headguard, is opposite. Sanders has 23 wins, 15 inside, and 11 losses. Tyson has already been introduced as a 'softer, gentler, kinder' version of himself.

The signs are not good. 'Why would anybody buy a heavyweight exhibition?' the commentators have said before Tyson has even entered the arena. 'The fact of the matter is that Mike Tyson is that popular. You really don't want to miss it when he gets in the ring, even though it's an exhibition.'

Sanders is on the floor within a minute. He gets up and Tyson moves away, holding back his punches, tapping at Sanders.

'Corey is not putting any pressure on him,' say the commentators, embarrassment rising in their voices. 'Remember that this is a forty-year-old Mike Tyson. It's an exhibition and not for real.'

'Some of the best fights I ever saw were in the gym,' says the other announcer.

The crowd begins to chant. *Bullshit! Bullshit! Bullshit!*

The commentators begin to laugh at the haplessness of the event. There is not much else they can do because they know that people have eyes.

Between rounds, the referee comes over and says that the crowd do not know any better. But the problem is that they do. They have seen the Tyson of old. This is what they expect and have paid to see.

The commentators keep using the word 'sparring' to remind the people at home that this is what they are watching.

Towards the end, Tyson catches Sanders again. The knees of Sanders buckle. Tyson takes him in his arms and pulls him up so he does not fall. The commentators laugh.

It is the last exhibition fight that Tyson undertakes for nearly fifteen years. The *Mike Tyson World Tour* does one stop, one show, and is quietly abandoned.

They have been once-in-a-generation fighters, sublime in their younger years. Not merely good but great, in ways that went beyond hyperbole. And those times for each man had overlapped and co-incided in places. Tyson had become the youngest heavyweight champion in the world at twenty by knocking out Trevor Berbick in two rounds. He had been awesome, considered the greatest and most destructive fighter of his – or any – age. His fights were all fireworks and noise, knockouts and knockdowns. For the longest period, it seemed – and it would turn out to be true – that his most potent enemy would be himself.

He had been a maelstrom, a spinning and revolving cloud of chaos that seemed poised always to turn the destruction from outwards to inwards. He took on the ugliness he thought was inside him by painting it on the features and forms of other men, men often scared of who – or what – they were in the ring with. He had come from the meanest streets and seemed to take out every injustice he felt against him on the world.

Jones, meanwhile, was quicksilver, shooting from the 1988 Olympics to be the best undefeated and undefeatable fighter on the planet. He lacked the intimidation of Tyson and the brawn of his violence, but he struck everyone with awe. His hands and feet were not just faster than his opponents, but *miles* faster. He was an alien force, the likes of which had never been seen anywhere, never mind in a boxing ring, who had come to earth to fight. He was all speed and angles and flaws, the last of which he was too fast for anyone to exploit. Nobody touched Roy Jones Jr., the greatest fighting machine on the planet, literally or metaphorically, until they did.

The endings came for each of them eventually, and they were surprises both times. Invincibility is like virginity; once it has gone, it does not come back. The first defeat sets the myth aside and offers a blueprint for future foes.

Tyson lost his invincibility in Tokyo. It had been fading with close calls and blows from others that stunned, but James 'Buster' Douglas took it upon himself to fight the ten best rounds of his life. He had an answer that night that he never had again. To best

Tyson, all you had to do was walk into his fire, push him back and punch him around. The rest would take care of itself.

Jones's invulnerability took longer to be snapped. He lost once on a disqualification that he avenged five months later with a first-round knockout and, when it seemed he was bored, he went up to the heavyweight division and picked up a minor title.

But the bad nights began to come. He squeaked past Antonio Tarver, a middling champion who would become his nemesis, and then he went back and got himself knocked out in the second round. Old-timers said that the move up to heavyweight and then back down, nearly 25lbs in weight, had killed him. Jones, some observed later, looked as if the shift had drawn and drained something out of him.

Los Angeles, California, US, November 2020. The empty arena looks strange, like a fight in an abandoned car park that someone has tried to legitimise with lights and screens.

There has been noise in the build-up about the health of both men. The thinking, the science, is that severe, acute injury is more common and a bigger risk as a fighter gets older. Especially a fighter after the age of thirty. But Tyson and Jones are in their fifties, and Jones has been knocked out badly by Tarver and Johnson at first, then by Danny Green in Australia, and Dennis Lebedev and Enzo Maccarinelli in Russia.

'Men in their fifties,' writes Thomas Hauser, 'shouldn't be punching each other in the head.'[15]

But there is a gross, pious hypocrisy in those words, even if they are meant well. No old man in a just world would ever fight another for the entertainment of others. Jones has had seventy-five professional fights, Tyson fifty-eight. And they have boxed as amateurs, have spent decades sparring week-on-week in gyms against other men who were trained to hurt. The damage has been done. But it is this fight, this glorified sparring, that is problematic. It is *this* that should not happen? This is where the line has to be drawn? After all those miles on the clock?

The fight is harder than people thought it would be. Some of the landed punches make the watching crowd wince. Tyson and Jones gasp when they throw. They clinch a lot.

After the fight is finished, they come together in the centre of the ring.

A sweating Mike Tyson and Roy Jones Jr. stand next to each other. They are out of breath. The 'fight' has been ruled a draw. 'I'm good with that,' says Tyson. 'I'm good with a draw. I entertained the crowd. The crowd was happy with it.'

Jones says he is not happy with the result. 'I wear drawers,' he says. 'I don't do draws.' He says that they might have to do it again. He makes a point to say hello to his Russian friends.

Milwaukee, Wisconsin, April 2023. It is the first day of the month and – no joke – Roy Jones Jr., fifty-four years old and counting, is fighting again, only this time it is against someone who has never had a professional boxing fight. Anthony Pettis, aged thirty-six, is new to boxing after a career in MMA. Jones, who came shirtless to the ring, looks chunky, the muscles in his body finally giving way to fat. After eight tepid rounds, in which Jones barely moves, the fight is declared a victory for Pettis by majority decision.

Jones speaks after the fight. 'For me, I like to come in and entertain the fans,' he says. 'My job is to come in and make sure that the fans get what they paid for, and I'm all good with that. I think it was a good fight. He did a great job and fought a very smart fight. I think I educated him and taught him a lot in this fight.'

He talks about a rematch that no one wants. The once-unbeatable fighter has now lost ten fights.

THE MORAL QUESTION

There is no good, safe way to enjoy boxing, not if you are a good person. The costs are too high, and the price extracted is too much.

Boxing, someone once wrote, used to be about opportunity: the granting of a chance to leave behind impoverishment and move up a social class or two. But now, they wrote, it is the *opposite*: boxing is what you do when you have nothing else.

Even that argument misses some vital points. Boxing and fighting will always exist because people want it to exist. Boys want to fight in order to become men. Their fathers want that, too. Perhaps it is just that simple. *Men just fight, that's all.*

Death happens, sometimes rarely and sometimes frequently, in all sports. As the writer Hugh McIlvanney pointed out, boxing was once left trailing by motor sports in the ratio of fatalities to the numbers participating. Climbers die, too, in great numbers. It is motive and not statistics, said McIlvanney, that call pugilism into question.

We know more than we ever did about the brain and sports, and what we know is not pleasant. Many NFL players have developed CTE, as have hockey players and wrestlers. There is even an argument that heading the ball in soccer has led to permanent mental disability for players of yesteryear.

In 1984, the British Medical Association called for boxing to be banned. Its position in 1995 remained the same.

For years, those cries would rise again whenever there was a serious injury or fatality in the ring. When Michael Watson was injured fighting Chris Eubank in 1991, as when Gerald McClellan was injured in 1995 against Nigel Benn, the same noises went up. But, today, those demands have lost their volume. The current attitude seems to be that it is a problem that should be managed, not abolished.

A wise man once pointed out that humans, for millennia, were concerned only with their day-to-day survival. Life was a series of attempts at surviving, at making it through one day and into the next. Food, shelter, heat, water. Survival. But now, the wise man says, we have everything we need, but our mindset has not changed; we cannot plan for the future.

And that is the problem. Is it right that young men and boys can make the choice to fight when we do not know for sure the outcome of this decision? Every future is murky, but none more so than fighting for a living. Success is not guaranteed, but neither is disability. How does someone budget for a future when the price is unknown?

There are still pockets of people who call for boxing to be banned, who say, rightly, that one set of people should not hit another in the head for the enjoyment of spectators. And they are right, but they are also wrong. If there is to be a ban on boxing, should there not also be a ban on all sports that damage the brain? Do we say goodbye to football, rugby, karate, or even soccer? Where do we draw such lines?

Any ban would cause more problems than it would solve. Fighters, deprived of their livelihoods, would travel abroad to find work instead, exposing themselves to the lax medical standards and regulations of other nations. Any ban would result, within six months, in a raft of boxers plying their trade in eastern European backwaters such as Latvia, where the only entrance requirements are two hands and a heartbeat, and even those are negotiable.

What is left, then, is to manage it like a chronic condition, pushing for stringent medicals and monitoring, being brave and principled enough to know when to throw in the towel on a career. The existence of boxing relies on the deep morality and decency of those undertaking it.

And of what boxing gives? It gives a lot. The gym in Runcorn sits in a town that no one wants to acknowledge, and it is managed by a group of men dedicated to providing something better to the children there. But no one who has never worn a glove wants to put their full strength behind it. 'We do a lot here,' said O'Sullivan one day as he coached two of the older kids on their exams to become trainers. 'It'd be nice if they acknowledged it. There's a lot we do.'

There is. Every child who comes through and goes on to something better, even if it is not boxing, is not a tragedy. And sometimes that is the best thing you can hope for – that something does not become a tragedy. For every boy who learns not by trial and error, but in places where the stakes are lower, and goes on to stability and adulthood and decency, is that not a victory in itself?

These are quiet men who run these gyms, who give freely of themselves. To paraphrase James Baldwin, they are inarticulate in the way people are when more has happened to them than they know how to express. They have seen things that they cannot name, and they know the answers even if they cannot articulate the questions. They run the gyms and the clubs not because they love the sport, but because they love the boys. They do what they can through them in the language they know best.

Most of the time, you can only take the best that is on offer. There is a lesson there.

CHAPTER SIX

MEMORY IS TIME

AFTER

There is an old jewellers in the centre of Dundee, just along the main high street, and about 400 yards from Caird Hall, where Mike Towell fought his sixth professional fight.

The premises, named Robertson & Watt, has stood on the site since 1841. The firm changed hands following the Second World War and was, in 2023, still run by the same family.

Perhaps the most interesting part of the jewellers' front is a large metal model of a building just above the entrance, to the left. It is a model of the original Dundee Town House, completed in 1734, partially burned in 1773. From then onwards, it went through a slew of uses until it was torn down in the 1930s and became lost to time.

But the original model remains, placed above the entrance to Robertson & Watt. And embossed on its side, there is a saying that anyone walking past reads: *Memory is Time*.

The ripples from Mike Towell's death spread amongst his family and friends. No one remained unscathed.

Chloe Ross is still the public face of the family, but she has pulled away in recent years. She did not want to be interviewed for this book, but she still sent her best wishes for its completion. Even though she said she had been burned too many times by the media, she still let it be known around Dundee that she did not object to others speaking about her former partner. Every person who spoke of her spoke of what a wonderful person and a good mother she is. There are no bad words about her in this book; none exist.

Dale Evans's career lasted for two more fights. He returned less than a year later to outpoint journeyman Kevin McCauley over four rounds in Swansea. It was the second time the pair had fought. Evans told everyone he could that he was fighting in the name of Mike Towell.

'The dream of Mike', he said to *Boxing Wales*, 'was to win the British title, the same as mine. I've kept in contact with the family, we speak now and again. It's always going to be with me and with it being on my shorts, it feels like Mike's with me. It's going to be on my shorts for the rest of my boxing days.'[16]

The months after were hard, and he barely left the house. He found it difficult to talk about.

Evans spoke about the weight of the guilt he carried eighteen months later. He tried to minimise his own pain. He told Donald McRae of *The Guardian*, 'Sometimes, sitting in silence, I'd break into tears. It will stay with me forever. I came home from that fight and Mike didn't. Mike had a girlfriend, Chloe [Ross], who is mum to his young boy. There's no way I should dare think it's hard for me.'[17]

Word was passed down to Evans about the writing of this book, but there was understandably no response. He was no longer willing to expose that part of himself.

He got a British title fight in August 2017 against Bradley Skeete but lost on points. He wore the name 'Iron Mike' embroidered on his shorts. It was his last fight. He knew he had nothing left. 'I once had that nastiness in the ring,' he told Donald McRae. 'It's gone now.'

He announced his retirement at the beginning of 2018. He said he had been offered a big fight. Some thought it was for a European title. He turned it down.

'After some time out and questioning if I would fight again,' he wrote on Facebook, 'a big fight was offered. As always I jumped at it. But the spark, the hunger and determination wasn't there. Just worry and fear, I'll openly admit. So that's why I've made the decision I have.'

He still travelled up to Dundee each year on the anniversary. He sat with Towell's family and raised a drink to him. There seemed a genuine bond between them all. They had built something from the weight of their dead.

And no one blamed him, then or now.

LAST WORDS

Death of a Boxer was a long time in gestation and a relatively short period in the actual process of writing. The original aim was to write boxing's *Into the Wild*, to give the sport its own cautionary but educational tale of a young man and his quest for manhood.

It was in the early days, shortly after the idea was given oxygen and light, that the publisher said that while Towell's story was an interesting one, more needed to be said.

'This is a foreign country to many,' they said, 'and the readers need a guide. Make it about larger, universal themes.'

So I went on the road, where much of this was put together, travelling from one country to another, with only a suitcase and a hope that somehow, some way, it would coalesce into something else, something bigger.

In the final days, I sat with a writer friend and explained all the travelling. I had just gotten back from Poland, which had itself followed a trip across three US cities, and was about to head to Cardiff, then London, for the final stages. I had already been to Dundee, Madrid and Göppingen.

'And these people let you speak to them?' my friend asked.

'No,' I answered. 'They speak to me.'

'They must be really nice.'

'They are.'

'All of them?'

'It's a common thing.'

One thing I discovered along the way is that most people do not want to talk; instead, they want to be listened to.

And it is true that *Death of a Boxer* would not exist without any of them. I was welcomed into gyms, homes and lives. I sat with people in their most vulnerable places and they told me of the most vulnerable parts of their lives. They placed great trust in me. I dearly hope I have not betrayed that.

The narrative of Mike Towell's life and death has been that he ignored the warnings until he ran out of road to travel. But it is not that simple. I do not know whether the epilepsy was enough to preclude him from boxing, whether it was a cause of his death. Correlation does not equal causation. His death may have been coincidental to the seizures. It is likely that we will never know for sure.

But what I do know is that he was loved, dearly. And by many. Every word spoken of Towell by those who knew him was delivered with a smile. If a man's life is measured by the love held for him in others after he has gone, Towell died a rich man.

I have never known greater love, after family, than that between fighters. And, even then, the lines are often blurred.

This is the story of *Death of a Boxer*. There is no more to write.

When I set out to write this, someone asked me what the story was about. Well, these are all love stories.

So this is my love story, my valediction, to the fighters and those around them. I offer this up. And I ask for nothing in return.

Pete Carvill
Berlin, September 2023

APPENDIX

A GUIDE TO BOXING

Most know the parameters of boxing: two combatants, dressed only in trunks and boots, enter a square ring and use their gloved hands to fight one another until one is declared to have won on points or by some sort of stoppage.

That rudimentary foreknowledge is a good place to start, but the complexity quickly runs much deeper. There are a lot of smoke and mirrors for something that takes place exclusively under bright lights. Other factors including, but not limited to, balance, reflexes, movement, speed, stamina, pacing, adaptability, planning, preparation, technique, style and – yes – genetics play roles that ebb and recede in importance. You can study boxing for a lifetime and believe that you have a tight grasp of its complexities, only to learn the following day something new that scuppers a belief that you once held firm.

The fundamental first lesson is that it is all about balance, both in the literal and figurative senses. You attack with one hand while protecting yourself with the other, use your back foot to go forwards and your front foot to go backwards. Old-timers say that everything starts with the right stance, that the hands can do nothing unless the feet are properly in alignment. That, itself, is an act of balance. Another is that as one man wins, another loses.

There are rules throughout when you talk about technique. *Keep this here, hold that there, move like this.* Some of the complexity comes from the myriad rules and how they act and interact with each other.

The rest of it comes from the fact that there is an exception to every rule, that some fighter somewhere and somewhen was successful by *not* following the common and accepted wisdom. The fact that there are exceptions to every rule is a rule in itself.

STANCE

Most boxers, being right-handed, lead with their left foot. To approximate this, stand with your feet a shoulder width apart and take a step back with your right foot. Position your weight and sink so that about two-thirds of it is on your back leg, then twist five-to-ten degrees to your right so that your left foot, knee and shoulder are in alignment. Raise your hands, clenched into fists, to your cheekbones. Keep your elbows tight against your ribs. This is the stance. Do everything in the opposite direction if you are left-handed.

It is more than likely that you will modify this as you unearth your style. Fighters who are short for their weight division will widen the gap between their feet to make themselves even lower for their opponent. Taller fighters will do the opposite and bring their feet closer together to strain out every advantage of their height. Graceful boxers who move and glide will favour their back leg when they settle to punch, while those with no reverse gear and a penchant for hooks will reverse the proportions of their weight in order to favour their forward leg.

MOVEMENT

To move forwards, push down first on your right leg and then step forwards the length of one of your feet so that the back of your ankle rests where the end of your toe was. But do not go too far as you will overextend, leave yourself off-balance and be vulnerable to shots. Likewise, moving your back foot first when going forwards will also leave you unstable, as your feet will be too close together.

It is the opposite when moving back, but the movement follows the same principle. Push on your front foot and move first your back leg.

The same philosophy applies when moving to either side. To go left, push off from your right foot. To go right, push off from your left. And crossing your feet will also rob you of balance.

PUNCHES

There are five-and-a-half punches in boxing: the jab, the cross, the hook, the uppercut and the overhand right. The half-punch is known as the 'bolo punch' and is thrown only by the preternaturally gifted (and the Cubans). Everything that follows is written from the perspective of an orthodox fighter:

1. The jab, thrown with the left hand, is the lightest and most versatile of the punches. It is both range finder and defence, and it

can be thrown swiftly, in a series of rapid blows, slowly, singly, with power and without. It can be used when going forwards or when going backwards. But rarely is a fighter seriously hurt or stopped with a jab, and a fighter who can do so to their opponent is truly a competitor of great wonder. The most important thing with the jab is to remember to throw it in a straight line, raising your shoulder to protect your chin and bringing it back quickly. When thrown, the opposite hand – your right – should be positioned to protect the opposite side of your face. Like all punches, a fighter should not 'load up', meaning that they should throw the jab with the fingers loose inside the glove, tightening at the last possible second in order to generate the most power.

2. The cross is thrown with the right hand, its power generated from the twisting of the body. This is a blunt and powerful punch. It also carries, arguably, the biggest payload. However, it can be countered by every other punch, meaning that it should only be used sparingly and with great care and precision. When a fighter comes out throwing right hands, something has gone wrong and they are looking to end a fight early. A good cross is built not just from the turn of the body and hips but is buttressed also by the rotation of the shoulder and the clenching of the fingers in the millisecond before impact.

3. Hooks can be thrown with either hand, although ones coming from the back are broadly less successful because of the greater distance travelled. This punch begins by a slight twisting of the body in the opposite direction to coil energy. Those throwing the punch then rotate to their right, bringing their fist over – fingers, again, loose until the penultimate millisecond – in as straight a

line as they can, the elbow and fist at the same height. An imbalance on landing will dull the hook's power. And, if you keep your arm straight and miss a good hook, you can still catch your opponent with the elbow that follows. But that is a move that is *technically* illegal if you *mean* to do it.

4. Uppercuts are thrown upwards, either on the outside to the body or on the inside to the head. These punches are much more complex than they may at first seem. It is hard to throw a good uppercut well. Throwing a left uppercut begins by dipping your knees a degree to the left, twisting your body in the same direction and then pushing off and rotating up and to the right, the inside of your glove facing your chest.

5. The overhand right is used against taller opponents who leave their jabs extended. These involve going low and trying to throw your right as if you are finishing the bowling of a cricket ball, the fulcrum of which is the top of your opponent's arm. Thrown successfully, the overhand right will come into contact with your opponent's chin, accelerating from the impact of your inner elbow on their arm. This type of punch is high risk and high reward, given that it is easily deflated by your opponent stepping back and leaving you unbalanced, off-guard and open.

6. The bolo punch is a hybrid made famous by the Cuban welterweight Kid Gavilan in the 1940s, and it comes from the movement of cutting through sugar cane with a machete. It lies somewhere between an uppercut and a hook, and the fighter who throws it needs to be extremely fast and athletic and their opponent slow and staid. It is a blow that only once-in-a-generation fighters or Cubans from eight decades ago use. And while

it is flashy and impressive, it carries little power and can be used only sparingly. Its main purpose is to embarrass and humiliate an inferior foe.

STYLE

There is an old maxim that styles make fights. Two fighters may be the best in the world at what they do, but how they fight can make any bout between them mix like oil and water. A match between two counterpunchers who prefer to go backwards will likely be terrible. The same can be said of any fight between an orthodox fighter and a southpaw.

Case in point: the long-awaited meeting of Manny Pacquiao and Floyd Mayweather Jr. in 2015 was always going to be a damp squib. Pacquiao was a southpaw who liked to go forwards while throwing hundreds of punches in each round, while Mayweather was an orthodox fighter who countered from his back foot, did not punch with any authority and eschewed risk and danger for measured and clinical points decisions. Conversely, the week following that bout saw Saul 'Canelo' Alvarez and James Kirkland meet in a fight that anyone with a knowledge of styles knew would be what is known as a 'barnburner'. And it was.

A long-enough time spent studying boxers and their styles will eventually put you in a position where you can recognise a 'trade fight', the meeting of two combatants in which their dispositions and styles of fighting guarantee a good match, regardless of their standings within the division. The light-welterweights Arturo Gatti and Micky Ward faced off in 2002. The pair had a combined record of 71 wins and 16 losses, with 55 stoppages. Neither was the best in the division, but they were best matched in fighting each other. Other great style match-ups over the years include the three fights between Muhammad Ali and Joe Frazier, particularly their third, brutal fight in Manila in 1975; the two fights between Alexis Arguello and Aaron Pryor in 1982 and 1983; and the domestic clash between Jamie Moore and Ryan Rhodes in 2009.

Styles are complex at the macro level, each fighter adding or discarding varying elements. Some will prefer to fight tall, relying on a high guard and movement while others crouch low and come forwards, forsaking jabs for uppercuts and hooks. There are those who prefer to fight at the length of an arm, while others prefer their work done up close. There are preferences, too, for whether to move sideways, or to stay 'in the pocket', or to move backwards and try to counter and check punches. When training a fighter, the key is to recognise their style, add to it, strengthen it and try to iron out some of its weaknesses.

WEIGHT

Boxing matches are fought in weight classes, of which too many exist today. They are:

- minimum weight (105lbs)
- junior flyweight (108lbs)
- flyweight (112lbs)
- junior bantamweight (115lbs)
- bantamweight (118lbs)

- junior featherweight (122lbs)
- featherweight (126lbs)
- junior lightweight (130lbs)
- lightweight (135lbs)
- junior welterweight (140lbs)
- welterweight (147lbs)
- light-middleweight (154lbs)
- middleweight (160lbs)
- super-middleweight (168lbs)
- light-heavyweight (175lbs)
- cruiserweight (200lbs)
- bridgerweight (220–224lbs)
- heavyweight (no limit)
- super-heavyweight (amateur side only)

The names of the divisions have variants, such as light-middle-weight being known in some quarters as 'super-welterweight', but the brackets remain the same. The term 'catchweight' is used when it is agreed that a bout is to be contested somewhere between the accepted limits, such as when two fighters meet at 165lbs. The most recent addition is the bridgerweight division, in which there has yet to be a fighter or fight of note.

Weight divisions proliferate on the argument that it is beneficial for the fighters. But the real purpose is to create more 'title' fights and extract more of the resulting sanctioning fees. Fights are also easier to sell to the general and unknowing public if they can be advertised as a 'world title' fight, regardless of the quality of the participants or their match-up.

The existence of weight divisions means that fighters have to meet their target weight as part of the arranged bout. Coming in over the agreed amount leads to sanctions like fines, the cancellation of a bout or even, in extreme cases, the forfeiture of titles.

The weigh-in happens the day before the fight, although earlier check weigh-ins, in which the fighter must be within a certain range of the target weight, sometimes happen. These occur in the month before a fight.

Fighters often find weight-making to be the most gruelling part of their lives. It involves weeks of restricted eating and severe dehydration in its end stages. Diuretics have been known to have been used in the past. In the moments after the target weight has been reached and verified, the fighter will begin gaining back as much weight as they can. Gaining 10–20lbs in the time before the fight is common.

THE GLOVES AND THE WRAPPING OF THE HANDS

The hands of a boxer are the tools of their trade, and the measures of wrapping them in gauze and tape, and then covering them with gloves, are taken to protect those tools. There is no protection there for the head.

Boxing gloves come in different sizes, but 8oz gloves are used for fighters in the welterweight division and below, with 10oz gloves used in every division above. The different brands behind gloves are said to have different qualities – Reyes gloves, for example, are made in Mexico and with their tighter stitching and compressed padding are considered to be 'puncher's gloves', meaning that they maximise a fighter's power. A more defensive boxer will opt for

Grant gloves, as they are wider and bigger than other brands, even as the softer padding robs the boxer of firepower.

All gloves used in the professional ranks in the modern era have thumb attachments, a piece of material that affixes the thumb to the rest of the glove. This is to prevent an errant thumb going into the eye of an opponent.

Laces are still apparent on professional-grade gloves and once tied before a bout will be wrapped in tape. However, normal training gloves use Velcro to close the wrist opening.

Beneath the glove is the tape and gauze used to wrap a professional's hands. The current rules in Nevada state that thirty yards of bandage, maximum two inches wide, along with a maximum of ten yards of surgeon's tape can be used on each hand. Every coach has their own unique way of wrapping hands, one that they will adapt to each of their fighters.

CHAMPIONSHIPS AND SANCTIONING BODIES

There are four main sanctioning bodies for world title fights. These are, in no order of importance, the World Boxing Council (WBC), the World Boxing Association (WBA), the International Boxing Federation (IBF), and the World Boxing Organization (WBO). There is also a proliferation of lower-tier bodies such as the International Boxing Organization (IBO) and the World Boxing Union (WBU). The purpose of all of them is to extract money and hope from the public and the fighters. The only limitation on starting your own sanctioning body is if you are too creatively stunted to name your organisation from the following words: 'world', 'international', 'global', 'council', 'association', 'federation', 'union', 'organization' and 'boxing'. A drinking game that *aficionados* could play would be to write down these words on cards, shuffle them and see if you can randomly draw out the name of a new sanctioning body, with losers drinking a shot.

The various sanctioning bodies exist to not only glean money and hope from the sport, but to provide a modicum of organisation. What this often means is that two fighters can carry belts in the same division, be considered the best in their ranks and spend years avoiding fighting each other by defending only against their mandatory challengers, i.e., whoever has been political enough to be managed into the top slot amongst contenders.

Perhaps the best advice is to generally hold all titles in contempt and look instead at the quality of the match-up and how well the styles of the participants may gel. To paraphrase Hauser, the best bouts come from two fighters competing not for the championship of the world, but for the championship of *each other*.[18]

THE RULES

Here are some rules, although the boxing world has many different permutations of them. But it is good to start with the basics:

1. Bouts are fought between the bell that begins the round and the bell that finishes it. Throwing a punch after the bell rings to signify the break between rounds is a foul. Regardless, a fighter should protect themselves at all times.

2. Punches have to be with the knuckle part of the glove and be thrown to the body or the head. Slapping with the inside or the

outside of the glove are fouls. So is 'lacing', which is when a fighter rubs the laces or the tape of their glove over the face of their opponent. Kicks are not allowed.

3. You cannot hold and hit your opponent. Likewise, you can be penalised for excessive clinching.

4. Spitting out the gumshield intentionally is a foul. Some fighters do this in order to buy extra time after a knockdown. It is also often the sign of a fighter who has given up.

5. Fights are only stopped on cuts or an injury if either is so bad that the boxer cannot continue. A cut *above* the eye, for example, is way more likely to end a match than one *below* it, as the former guarantees a downward flow of blood that may inhibit vision. Fighters will try to fight on with a cut rather than take a loss. They have also been known to fight on through broken jaws and hands. Adrenaline explains much of this. But it is not that fighters do not feel pain, but rather that they have been conditioned to not care about it.

6. A white towel thrown in does not automatically stop the fight, although it should. Some referees will throw a white towel out. The ringside doctor can always stop a fight on medical grounds.

7. Counts are given when a fighter is knocked to the canvas or is left with the ropes supporting them. A referee may start a count in both cases. If the fighter is judged unable to continue, the fight will be stopped.

8. Fights stopped on medical grounds (a cut or other injury) will be recorded as a technical knockout, unless the injury resulted from a foul. The final result will then be determined on whether the foul was intentional, usually as a no-contest or by going to the cards.

SCORING

Scoring is done on the ten-point-must system, in which the winner of a round is awarded ten points and their opponent a lower number. For rounds with no knockdowns or points deducted for fouling, this would be nine. A fighter suffering a knockdown in a round would lose that round 10–8. A second knockdown would make the round 10–7. A third knockdown in the same round automatically ends a fight in places that have the three-knockdown rule; otherwise, the round would be scored 10–6. Points are taken for fouls only after a number of warnings, although an egregious foul can end the fight immediately.

Fights end with a points decision, a stoppage, a draw, a disqualification, or a no-contest:

1. In places where three judges score the fights, fighters can win by unanimous decision, split decision or majority decision. The first is when all three judges score for one fighter, the second is when two judges score for one fighter and the third scores for their opponent, and the third is when two judges score in favour of one fighter while the third scores the bout a draw. Draws can also be split, with the third judge scoring the bout equal with the other two split on the two fighters, or majority, when two of the judges score a bout to be even.

2. A stoppage is either a 'knockout' or a 'technical knockout'. The first is when the fighter remains on the canvas for the whole count, and the second is when the fighter is still on their feet but is judged unable to continue or is not intelligently defending themselves.

3. Disqualifications are uncommon and it takes a lot for a fight to end this way. For example, Mike Tyson was not disqualified in 1997 for biting Evander Holyfield, but for *repeatedly* doing it.

4. A no-contest occurs when a fight is stopped at an early point due to an accidental injury, usually within the first three or four rounds. A fighter who later fails the drug tests may also have a victory declared to be a no-contest, although this will come weeks and possibly even months after the fact.

REFERENCES

CHAPTER TWO

1   Sheriffdom of Glasgow and Strathkelvin at Glasgow, 'Determination by Sheriff Principal C D Turnbull Under the Inquiries into Fatal Accidents and Sudden Deaths etc (SCOTLAND) Act 2016 into the Death of Michael Towell', 2018

2   'Oleksandr Usyk beats Daniel Dubois: Briton wants "justice" after low blow "lie"', BBC Sport, 2023, available at https://www.bbc.co.uk/sport/boxing/66631986

CHAPTER FOUR

3   Harry L. Parker, 'Traumatic Encephalopathy ("Punch Drunk") of Professional Pugilists', *Journal of Neurology and Psychopathology* (1934), vol. 15, no. 57, pp. 20–28

4   Joe Hall, Brad Utterstrom, 'The Death of Douglas Dedge', *Sherdog*, 2007, available at https://www.sherdog.com/news/articles/The-Death-of-Douglas-Dedge-10270

5   Abhinav R. Changa, Robert A. Vietrogoski and Peter W. Carmel, 'Dr Harrison Martland and the history of punch drunk syndrome', *Brain* (2018), vol. 141, no. 1, pp. 318–21

6   Harry L. Parker, 'Traumatic Encephalopathy ('Punch Drunk') of Professional Pugilists', *Journal of Neurology and Psychopathology* (1934), vol. 15, no. 57, pp. 20–28

7   Jason Shurley, Jan S. Todd, 'Boxing Lessons: An Historical Review of Chronic Head Trauma in Boxing and Football', *Kinesiology Review* (2012), vol. 1, no. 3, pp. 170–84

8   Robert H. Boyle, 'Too Many Punches, Too Little Concern', *Sports Illustrated*, 1983, pp. 44–67

9   Ann C. McKee, Thor D. Stein, Bertrand R. Huber *et al.*, 'Chronic traumatic encephalopathy (CTE): criteria for neuropathological diagnosis and relationship to repetitive head impacts', *Acta Neuropathol* (2023), vol. 145, no. 4, pp. 371–94

10 Ann C. McKee, Robert C. Cantu, Christopher J. Nowinski *et al.*, 'Chronic traumatic encephalopathy in athletes: progressive tauopathy after repetitive head injury', *Journal of Neuropathology & Experimental Neurology* (2009), vol. 68, no. 7, pp. 709–35

11 Steve Wilstein, 'There Is Still No Quit in Jerry Quarry: Ex-Boxer Has the Brain of an 80-Year-Old; "If He Lives Another 10 Years He'll Be Lucky"', *Los Angeles Times*, 1995, available at https://www.latimes.com/archives/la-xpm-1995-10-29-sp-62464-story.html

12 Bill Dwyre, 'A Fight to the End', *Los Angeles Times*, 2006, available at https://www.latimes.com/archives/la-xpm-2006-jun-15-sp-dwyre15-story.html#:~:text=%E2%80%9CI%20am%20sad%20at%20what,always%20punching%2C%E2%80%9D%20she%20says.

13 Gilbert Rogin, 'Like a Real Champion', *Sports Illustrated*, 1961, available at https://vault.si.com/vault/1961/01/23/like-a-real-champion

14 Ann C. McKee, Robert C. Cantu, Christopher J. Nowinski *et al.*, 'Chronic traumatic encephalopathy in athletes: progressive tauopathy after repetitive head injury', *Journal of Neuropathology & Experimental Neurology* (2009), vol. 68, no. 7, pp. 709–35

CHAPTER FIVE

15 Thomas Hauser, 'The Tyson-Jones Exhibition in Perspective', *Boxing Scene*, 2020, available at https://www.boxingscene.com/tyson-jones-exhibition-perspective--153649

CHAPTER SIX

16 Dewi Powell, 'Dale Evans Returns to the Ring and Pays Tribute to Mike Towell', *Boxing Wales*, 2017, available at https://boxingwales.com/posts/dale-evals-return-mike-towell/

17 Donald McRae, 'Boxer Dale Evans: "Sometimes I break into tears. It will stay with me forever"', *The Guardian*, 2018, available at https://www.theguardian.com/sport/2018/mar/27/boxer-dale-evans-boxing-title-fight-mike-towell-glasgow#:~:text=%E2%80%9CIt's%20not%20often%20I%20cry,fight%20and%20Mike%20didn't.

APPENDIX

18 'Thriller in Manila', directed by John Dower, performances by Joe Frazier and Muhammad Ali, Darlow Smithson Productions, 2008